A TRAILS BOOKS GUIDE

PADDLING ILLINOIS

64 GREAT TRIPS BY CANOE AND KAYAK

MIKE SVOB

Trails Books
Madison, Wisconsin

A Note of Caution

The reader is advised that paddling sports can be dangerous. This guidebook is not a substitute for proper training, experience, and common sense. The users of this guidebook assume full responsibility for their own safety. Weather, water conditions, and individual abilities must be considered before undertaking any of the trips in this guide.

Library of Congress Catalog Card Number: 2007928283
ISBN: 978-1-934553-00-8

Editor: Stan Stoga
Photographs: Mike Svob
Maps: Mapping Specialists Limited
Cover Design: Kathie Campbell
Cover Photo: Michael Shedlock

Printed in the United States of America
12 11 10 09 08 07   7 6 5 4 3

Trails Books, a division of Big Earth Publishing
923 Williamson Street • Madison, WI 53703
(800) 258-5830 • www.trailsbooks.com

CONTENTS

ACKNOWLEDGMENTS

The best thing about writing a paddling guidebook is meeting a wide array of interesting people and renewing friendships with long-time paddling partners. Paddling the rivers and streams of Illinois for this book has been a wonderful experience, but the "people part" has been especially enriching for me. I can't begin to thank everyone who has assisted me along the way, but I'd be remiss if I didn't mention some of my principal helpers.

First of all, I'm grateful to my wife, Donna, for her patience and for her willingness to serve as a sounding board for ideas. Thanks, too, to the many fellow paddlers who accompanied me on many of the trips in this book, especially Ken and Marie Bohnen, Cliff Counsell, Bob and Val Deichman, Dan Faust, Gary Heinz, Bob Kane, Bill Koenig, Rob Lewis, Art Mayfield, Ed Nelson, Kim Parsons, Craig Reidner, Don Schueman, and John and Marilyn Ziegler. I'm also indebted to many paddling friends from the Mackinaw Canoe Club with whom I've spent hundreds of happy hours on Illinois streams over the last 30 years, particularly Larry and Cindy Noble, Roger and Loretta Fandel, Karl Dion, George Burrier, Jim and Alice Deck, Ron Thompson, Lou and Lois Pronga, Tim and Lynnette White, Wally and Jeannie Morse, and Steve and Lisa Vodisek. Members of other Illinois paddling clubs and organizations who have been especially helpful to me over the past year are Steve Simpson, Joe Hunt, Sigrid Pilgrim, Sandon Bate, and Rich Buerger. Ralph Frese, long-time advocate for Illinois canoeing, provided his usual good advice. The assistance of such DNR personnel as Gary Clark, Ed Hoffman, and John Stuckel has been invaluable, and Gary Mechanic (coordinator of the Illinois Paddling Council's Access Project) has helped me work through the intricacies of the access issue. And, of course, I'm grateful for my relationship with the very capable and encouraging folks at Trails Media Group: Stan Stoga, Patty Mayers, Anita Matcha, and Judy Ettenhofer.

Thanks also to the following "locals" for spending time with me and providing a wealth of useful information: Ken Haas of Elizabeth and Fritz Fuchs of Galena (Apple); Tudi Smith of the Murphysboro Shawnee National Forest Ranger Station, Gene Crawshaw of Murphysboro, and the staff of Shawnee Trails Outfitters in Carbondale (Big Muddy); Jim Waycuilis of the DNR office at Belknap, John Henderson of Cache Core Canoes, and Liz Jones of the Cypress Creek Refuge office at Ullin (Cache); Wayne Hermansen of Willow Springs (Des Plaines); Max Jones of Canoe Limited (Embarras); Bill Bickett of Ayers Landing and the staff of Mountain Tops in St. Charles (Fox); Mark Moran of Galena and Daryl Watson of the Galena-Jo Daviess County Historical Society (Galena); Steve Moser of the Hennepin Canal Parkway staff (Hennepin); Jill Jackson and Bob Schwiesow of the I&M Canal State Trail staff (I&M Canal); Ken Howell and Bill Osborne of Watseka (Iroquois). Also, Jim Reed of Reed's Canoe Trips (Kankakee); Paul Tripp of Shelbyville (Kaskaskia); Steve Hakes of Rockford and Kathy Grimes of Belvidere (Kishwaukee); Rick Killian of Streator and Bob Lyons and Hank Kibilka of the La Salle area (Little Vermilion); Jack Emery of Carmi (Little Wabash); Steve Crabb of Golconda and Walt Zyznieuski of Springfield (Lusk Creek); Diane Rudin of the Nature Conservancy office in Eureka and Dan Thames of Mackinaw (Mackinaw); Rich Melchans, Kickapoo State Park ranger (Middle Fork). Also, Robert Lee and Chuck Dominic of Streator (North Vermilion); Stan Hayes and Bruce Lizer of Pecatonica (Pecatonica); Kerrie Bolhous of Oregon, Vicki Carlson of Dixon, and Bruno Catalina of Grand Detour (Rock); Stan Sisk of Equality, Bob Brown of Saline Landing, Willie Wilson of Harrisburg, and Jim Balsitis (Saline); Marilyn Black of Clinton (Salt Creek of the Sangamon); Steve Lane and Gary Welker of Danville and Jim Smith of Homer (Salt Fork); and Gerald Makinen of the Sugar Shores Camping Resort (Sugar).

A big thank-you also to the many local chambers of commerce, city offices, forest preserve districts, national forest offices, and county and city park personnel for their help. There are, indeed, a lot of people and groups throughout the state who care about preserving the remaining wild places in Illinois; they deserve everyone's gratitude.

Let Us Hear From You!

We welcome your suggestions and comments on this book. If there are other rivers or streams that you would like to see included in the next edition, please let us know. If you find any errors in the text or maps, we would appreciate hearing about them so that we can make corrections. Send the information, along with your name and address, to:

PADDLING ILLINOIS
Trails Books
923 Williamson Street
Madison, WI 53703
books@bigearthpublishing.com

INTRODUCTION

Contrary to the experience of travelers who hurry through on interstate highways, there's much more to Illinois than cornfields and boring flatland. This large state is amazingly varied in terrain. Yes, it includes a great deal of flat farmland, but it also offers rolling hills, dense forest, tallgrass prairie, rugged cliffs, swampy bayous, and picturesque rivers and creeks. Many of Illinois's most attractive locales can be viewed by motorists, bicyclists, or hikers, but the most intimate perspective of all is enjoyed by canoeists and kayakers. There is no better way to experience the excitement and diversity of the state's geology, wildlife, and scenery.

Most of the state's topography was shaped by several waves of glaciation that swept down from the north long ago. In fact, glaciers covered almost 90 percent of Illinois's surface at one time or another, sparing only the seven southernmost counties, a small area in the west, and the northwestern corner—the most rugged parts of the state. By the time the last glacier retreated about 10,000 years ago, the surface had been covered by rocky material, sand, and rich silt. The most recent glacier—the Wisconsinan—covered only the northeast quarter of the state, leaving behind a series of concentric ridges (end moraines) that are still prominent in the landscape. Much of Illinois was the drainageway for the receding glaciers; vast quantities of meltwater helped create the 33,000 miles of rivers and streams that today flow in and around the state. No mere textbook exercise, glaciation and its effects shaped the watersheds of Illinois and are often in evidence to canoeists as they paddle between moraines, under silt-laden cutbanks, past sheer cliffs, and through wetlands.

Another effect of Illinois's size, central location, and glacial heritage is a rich diversity of flora and fauna. Extending 400 miles from north to south (i.e., from the latitude of Massachusetts to that of Virginia), the state is home to an astonishing range of plant and animal species. The profusion of oak, maple, hickory, ash, pine, cedar, and other trees of the northern and eastern forest-biology zones is not surprising, but many first-time visitors to southern Illinois are taken aback at the "exotic" bald cypress and tupelo gum trees that abound there in Louisiana-like swamps and bottomland forest. Bankside wildflowers are one of the biggest enticements of canoeing in Illinois, including not only such common beauties as hepatica, bluebells, and trillium, but also such rarities as the bird's-eye primrose. Most of the state's animal species are difficult to spot, but paddling trips are usually enlivened by sightings of great blue herons, ducks, Canada geese, owls, hawks, deer, muskrats, turtles, frogs, snakes, and many other creatures, including numerous songbirds and occasional eagles.

Nowhere have rivers figured more prominently in shaping history than in Illinois. For thousands of years, Native Americans used the rivers of the state for travel, transport, and trade, and established villages at many riverside locations—including famous sites at Cahokia,

Rock Island, and Utica. European presence in Illinois began in 1673 when Marquette and Joliet, after paddling down the Fox, Wisconsin, and Mississippi Rivers, returned to Lake Michigan via the Illinois, Des Plaines, and Chicago Rivers. For 175 years afterward, the "Chicago Portage" was a major route from the eastern United States to the Mississippi Valley and beyond. Later, the great explorer La Salle paddled the St. Joseph and Kankakee Rivers to get to the Illinois Country. Other historically significant Illinois rivers include the Galena, a major steamboat stream during the heyday of lead mining; the Rock, memorialized by Chief Black Hawk; and the Sangamon, on which Abraham Lincoln himself floated canoes and other watercraft. Three major rivers—the Ohio, Mississippi, and Illinois—are too big and commercial to be considered good canoeing streams, but all three were historically vital in the exploration and development of America.

WHICH WATERWAYS ARE INCLUDED

The principal aim of this guidebook is to provide a wide selection of day trips throughout the state, not to present an all-inclusive compendium of paddleable waterways. With a couple of exceptions, only stretches that usually have enough water to paddle for a significant portion of the paddling season are included. (Please remember, however, that this factor is highly dependent upon the amount and frequency of precipitation in a given season.) Scenic value is another criterion for determining which sections to include. Many of the prettiest places in Illinois are to be seen along the rivers and streams described here. For an occasional change of pace, there is something to be said for city paddling—such as the unique urban vistas of the Chicago River—but in this book the emphasis is upon quiet, natural places.

Safety, too, is an important consideration; thus, there are only four trips requiring portages of dams. Such portages are not only time-consuming and sometimes difficult, but often dangerous as well. Wide, currentless, and often windy lakes and impoundments are not included—only moving water (although it's *barely* moving in a few sections, notably the Illinois and Michigan Canal and the Hennepin Canal).

Although some dyed-in-the-wool paddlers with a high inconvenience threshold don't mind brush and logjams, most canoeists regard them with annoyance and dread. Consequently, I have described only sections where paddlers are not likely to encounter total blockages. This sometimes means eliminating the narrow (but often attractive) upper reaches of such rivers as the Iroquois, Mackinaw, and Big Muddy, where such logjams are common. Convenient and safe accesses are another criterion for inclusion, but these are scarce on a few of the state's best canoeing rivers (e.g., the Spoon and the Salt Fork of the South Vermilion).

Illinois is almost surrounded by big rivers—the Mississippi, Ohio, and Wabash—and bisected diagonally

Riverside cliffs on the Apple River

by the Illinois. All of these are occasionally canoed, but their width, volume, current, windiness, and barge traffic make them unattractive and dangerous for most paddlers. Thus, they are not among the rivers described in this book.

Illinois is almost exclusively a quietwater state, but there are several good whitewater rivers and creeks. In order to present the whole spectrum of paddling opportunities, I've included a couple of these—both of which present very real dangers. Finally, I would like to be able to say that I've excluded all streams that have some degree of pollution. Indeed, many of the rivers and streams in this book have been given fairly high marks by the Environmental Protection Agency, but some (such as the Chicago River and Salt Creek in Cook County) you won't want to swim in.

This book presents thirty-three paddling rivers and streams in Illinois, typically recommending one, two, or three of the best and most accessible sections. A total of sixty-four sections are mapped and described in detail. No waterway is covered in its entirety, but many trip descriptions include supplemental vignettes (labeled "Other Trips") that briefly point to other paddleable stretches. Actually, there are few rivers and creeks in Illinois that are suitable for paddling along their entire length. Dams, logjams, artificial straightening (channelization), and intensive commercial boat traffic make many river stretches unattractive for canoeists. However, adventurous paddlers who are willing to do their homework and take proper precautions will find there are many other opportunities for pleasant and safe paddling in Illinois.

Many other streams that are not described and mapped in this book are canoeable, at least part of the year. I have paddled many of these myself and have been

told about others by canoeing and kayaking friends. Generally, these represent typical creek paddling: small, winding, intimate, often obstructed, sometimes riffly streams that have enough water for canoeing only in the spring or after sustained rainfall. Among these streams are Rooks Creek near Pontiac, Carroll Creek near Mt. Carroll, Bay Creek near Bell Smith Springs, Kyte Creek near Rochelle, Kilbuck Creek near Rockford, Kickapoo Creek upstream from Pottstown, Mud Creek near Morton, Kickapoo Creek near Lincoln, Sugar Creek near Springfield, Covel Creek near Grand Ridge, the Little Vermilion River near Georgetown, and many others. Most are not included in this book because of the narrow window of paddleability, private property considerations, safety factors, and other reasons.

Many of these out-of-the-way, seldom-paddled streams are described in detail in a recently published book by Bob C. Tyler, *Canoeing Adventures in Northern Illinois: Apple River to Zuma Creek* (iUniverse, 2004).

INTENDED AUDIENCE

Illinois presents a surprising variety of canoeing and kayaking opportunities, including intimate streams, wide and powerful rivers, isolated creeks, urban waterways, man-made canals, rivers that flow past awesome rock formations, and even some exciting whitewater. All of these are represented here. Obviously, such variety means there are plenty of places for paddlers of all interests and skill levels to go. Consequently, this book is intended for beginner, experienced/intermediate, and advanced/expert paddlers alike. Trip descriptions of individual sections provide an indication of which skill level is appropriate. In addition, a chart in Appendix 1 provides a convenient listing of sections by skill level.

Most of all, *Paddling Illinois* is meant for people who love nature, scenic beauty, and solitude. Most of the state's original wild places have disappeared in the face of urbanization, road building, and agricultural development, but many beautiful places remain. It is hoped that canoeists and kayakers who experience these precious locations firsthand will aid in the effort to protect them.

WHAT'S IN THE BOOK

Each of the book's day trips is described in two parts: (1) a map that shows roads, put-ins and take-outs, mileage, and other significant information and (2) a detailed narrative. After a general summary, each description covers camping opportunities, shuttle routes, canoe rentals and shuttle services (when available), average gradient, water levels, and accesses. Then the paddler is led systematically down the river or stream. There is a suggested length for each trip, but in most cases it is easy to make the trip shorter or longer by using alternate accesses (which are indicated in the narrative and on the map). No attempt is made to estimate paddling time because this is dependent on such variables as skill level, weather conditions, speed of current, type of boat, etc. Generally, 2 to 3 miles an hour is a good rule of thumb for making a rough estimate of time on the river.

Maps

The maps in this guidebook are designed to provide all the essential information that boaters need to get to the designated stretch and paddle down it safely and enjoyably. Maps are kept as simple and uncluttered as possible, although some are necessarily more detailed than others—especially those in the urban northeast portion of the state. All roads are not included—only those that are relevant to paddlers (for running shuttles and other purposes). Because of the small scale of the maps, all river bends cannot be shown. Eight important components and their symbols are indicated in the key to each map: accesses, mile-markers, railroads, rapids, cities or villages, campgrounds, public land, and nearby bicycle routes.

Cities and villages are shaded to the full extent of official corporate limits, as shown on Illinois Department of Transportation county maps. In several Chicago-area maps, however, where city shading would occupy all or most of the space, cities are indicated by descriptive labels.

Mile-markers provide a convenient means of estimating trip length and determining how long you can expect to be on the water. Calculating mileage for a river or stream is not an exact science; we have done our best to be as accurate as possible. Incidentally, local people are often excellent sources of information on nearby streams, but you generally cannot count on them to provide an accurate estimate of river miles on a stretch. They are usually on the high side. Canoe rental firms are fairly dependable in this respect, however.

Unlike such nearby states as Wisconsin and Kentucky, Illinois has little whitewater. There are lots of exhilarating riffles and Class I rapids, however, and even a few Class IIs and IIIs. These are mentioned in the trip narratives, but only the significant rapids (i.e., Class II or higher) are marked on the maps with hash marks. For the criteria used to classify the difficulty of rapids, see the later section "Paddling Safely."

Paddlers can determine where they are at any given time by observing such features as creek mouths, bridges, bends, prominent islands, etc., and comparing these with the map. A compass is helpful, too.

If additional maps are desired, several of the following publications are recommended:

Perhaps the most useful single resource is the *Illinois Atlas and Gazetteer* (published by the DeLorme Mapping Company and available in bookstores), which provides eighty-one quadrangular maps of the state. DeLorme is especially helpful in locating back roads, state parks, campgrounds, etc. Serious paddlers always have a well-worn DeLorme tucked away somewhere in their vehicles.

For detailed information on elevations, contours, wetlands, etc., consult the topographical maps available from the U.S. Geological Survey in various scales. Overall, the 7.5-minute maps are most detailed and useful. To obtain free indexes and catalogs and to order maps, contact USGS Information Services, Box 25286, Denver, CO 80225.

The Illinois Department of Transportation publishes a detailed highway map of each of the state's counties, in two scales: 1/2 inch per mile and 1 inch per mile. These inexpensive maps show all state and county roads but no city streets, and are thus more useful for the less-populated parts of the state (i.e., outside the Chicago area). To order copies, contact the Illinois Department of Transportation, Map Sales (Room 121), 2300 South Dirksen Parkway, Springfield, IL 62764.

Although public land represents only about 5 percent of the total area of Illinois (compared with 19 percent in neighboring Wisconsin), many rivers and streams do pass through county forest preserves, city and county parks and conservation areas, national forest, state parks, and private conservation areas and nature preserves. Maps designating these areas are available upon request from the appropriate agency or organization (e.g., the forest preserve districts of Cook, Kane, Du Page, Will, Lake, Boone, McHenry, and Winnebago Counties; the Illinois Department of Natural Resources; the U.S. Forest Service; and the Nature Conservancy).

Quite handy for paddlers in the Greater Chicago area is the *Chicagoland 6-County Atlas*, which shows all roads and streets in the area of the Des Plaines, Chicago, Du Page, and upper Fox rivers and Salt and Nippersink creeks.

For streams that pass through urban areas (e.g., the Fox River through St. Charles, and the Rock River through Dixon), city maps are helpful. These are available at local and area chambers of commerce.

To determine land-ownership along any stream in Illinois, consult the *Land Atlas and Plat Book* for the appropriate county. These may be found at most county courthouses and libraries, or may be ordered from Rockford Map Publishers, in Rockford IL (www.rockford map.com). Plat books are particularly valuable when you are trying to determine whether shoreline land is privately or publicly owned, and when you want to identify landowners for the purpose of seeking permission to gain access to a stream.

A word on map orientation in the book: All trip descriptions are written from the perspective of canoeists and kayakers paddling down the stream, and the accompanying maps reflect this orientation. Thus, if a landmark is described as being on "river-right" or "downstream-right," the boater will see it on the right bank as he or she paddles by. Similarly, if a trip description calls for an *"upstream-left"* take-out near a bridge, the landing will be found on the left bank before the paddler gets to the bridge; a *"downstream-right"* take-out will be found on the right after the paddler has passed under the bridge. Such descriptions are especially important for accesses, which are often difficult to spot from water level. Thus, put-ins and take-outs are usually described in terms of being (1) upstream or downstream from a bridge, dam, or other location, and (2) on the right or left bank.

Biking Trails

Because canoeists often combine paddling and bicycling trips, biking trails that are located near recommended stretches are shown on the maps. Illinois has many excellent off-road bike trails that parallel or cross the Des Plaines River, Fox River, Du Page River, Kankakee River, Pecatonica River, Chicago River, Rock River, Middle Fork of the South Vermilion River, Hennepin Canal, Illinois and Michigan Canal, Salt Creek of the Des Plaines River, and other waterways. These trails are often used by hikers as well. A number of excellent books describe such trails, and contain a wealth of information relating to the rivers and streams in *Paddling Illinois:*

Jim Hochgesang. *Hiking and Biking in Cook County, Hiking and Biking in Lake County, Hiking and Biking in Du Page County, Hiking and Biking the I & M Canal, Hiking and Biking the Fox River Valley.* Lake Forest, Ill: Roots & Wings, 1994–1998.

Always dishes to do!

Bicycle Trails of Illinois. Libertyville, Ill: American Bike Trails, 1996.
Ray Hoven, *Hiking & Biking Lake County, Illinois.* Amer Bike Trails, 2004.
Walter and George Zyznieuski. *Illinois Hiking & Backpacking Trails* and *Guide to Mountain Bike Trails in Illinois.* Carbondale: Southern Illinois University Press, 1993 and 1998.
Susan Post. *Hiking Illinois.* Champaign, Ill.: Human Kinetics, 1997.

Camping

Both public and private campgrounds that are located on or near a given stretch of water are mentioned in the narrative and shown on the map. Illinois has a first-rate system of well-maintained state parks with attractive and inexpensive campgrounds. Some of the rivers and streams of Illinois lend themselves to multiday canoe-camping trips because of conveniently located riverside campgrounds. For canoe-camping trips, think twice about leaving your shuttle vehicle(s) in remote, isolated locations. Usually it's no problem, but occasionally cars are vandalized under such circumstances.

Shuttle Routes

The easiest and most obvious shuttle route from the put-in to the take-out is described for each trip. In a few instances this is not the shortest possible way to go; feel free to change the recommended route if you like. Of course, the recommended route also will have to be altered if you modify the trip by using different accesses.

Beginning boaters often ask about the best way to shuttle people, boats, gear, and vehicles between the put-in and take-out. At times, shuttling can get quite complicated, but usually it's a rather simple process. Paddlers generally meet at the put-in at a designated time, drop off their boats and gear (along with at least one person to look after the equipment), then drive to the take-out to leave most of the cars. Crowding into as few vehicles as possible, the entourage heads back to the put-in, where they park the shuttle vehicle(s), climb into the boats, and paddle off. At the end of the canoe trip, most of the paddlers load up their vehicles and head for home, but someone must drive the shuttle driver(s) back to the put-in to retrieve the vehicle(s) left there. Variations are possible. For example, the above process is occasionally reversed to save time at the beginning of the trip. Or if one or more boaters in a group wish to paddle only part of a trip, their car(s) can be dropped off at an intermediate access point so they can take out there. Finally, boaters with only one vehicle can double their exercise by using a bike shuttle. Drop your boat and gear off at the put-in; drive to the take-out and drop off your car; bicycle back to the put-in and secure the bike; paddle down the stream, then load up your boat and gear; drive back to the put-in and pick up your bike.

Canoe Rental and Shuttle Service

Whenever there is a known provider of canoe rentals and shuttle service, that information is included. Some outfitters provide shuttles only for customers who rent canoes, but others will shuttle canoeists' boats and vehicles for a fee. Incidentally, these service providers are often an excellent source of water level information.

Gradient

Riffles and rapids are most common on rivers and streams with a relatively high gradient (i.e., the rate of descent, expressed in feet per mile). As a general rule, a gradient of 5 to 9.9 feet per mile indicates the likelihood of riffles and rapids, while a gradient of 10 feet or more is a predictor of demanding whitewater. Gradient is a nonfactor on most Illinois waterways, but nine stretches included in this book have a drop of 5 feet or more: Apple River 1 (8.3 feet), Big Bureau Creek (5.5 feet), Du Page River 1 (5 feet), Du Page River 2 (5.3 feet), Little Vermilion River 1 (7.7 feet), Little Vermilion River 2 (14.7 feet), Lusk Creek (8.6 feet), Middle Fork of the South Vermilion River (5 feet), and North Vermilion River 3 (6.7 feet). Several others are in the 3.5- to 4.9-foot range and thus are often riffly: Kishwaukee River 1 (4.2 feet), Mazon River (4.7 feet), North Vermilion River 2 (4.3 feet), and Salt Fork of the South Vermilion River 2 (3.5 feet).

Water Levels

Water level is one of the most important pieces of information that you need to have before going paddling. Ideally, the water will be flowing at a safe, pleasant level. But if it's too low, you can be in for a miserable time, dragging your boat through shallows. If it's too high, your life can be in peril. EVERY RIVER AND STREAM IN THIS BOOK IS DANGEROUS WHEN HIGH, ESPECIALLY IN THE SPRING. If you drive to the put-in for a day of paddling and discover that the water is high, turn around and go home.

The best source of current water level information is the United States Geological Survey Web site that presents "real-time water data." At this Internet location you can obtain recent readings (i.e., within the last twenty-four hours) from 197 active gauges located on rivers, creeks, canals, lakes, and reservoirs throughout Illinois. This data may be accessed at http://waterdata.usgs .gov/il/nwis/current/?type=flow. Other Web sites provide the same information plus additional data (http:// il.water.usgs.gov/nwis-w/IL, for instance, also has precipitation data). Paddlers are urged to become familiar with the USGS data; by clicking on various options, you can obtain a wealth of information that will enhance the enjoyment and safety of your trips. Whenever an active gauge is located on or near a given section, this book indicates the station number of the gauge in the trip description.

The significance of the data is not immediately clear. The current reading for each station is presented in terms of (1) a water level number (e.g., "Stage: feet above datum") that is based on an arbitrary gauge and (2) streamflow expressed in cubic feet per second (cfs). By themselves, these figures do not tell you whether the stream is low, medium, or high, unless you have paddled it many times before and can make a correlation. Fortunately, you can obtain graphed historical data from the USGS for the previous week, month, or other period of time, thus giving you a good idea of how high and low a given stream gets and what the current gauge reading means. Note that the gauging stations are not always advantageously located for judging how canoeable a given section is, so you may have to make a water level estimate on the basis of a gauge located some distance away. Paddlers also should be aware that not all of the gauges they see on rivers and streams are currently active.

In addition, paddlers seeking general information on water levels often telephone canoe rental businesses, campgrounds, forest preserve districts, and state, county, and city parks that are located on or near a given stream. You will find that some sources of water level information are more reliable than others, for a variety of reasons. The methods of judging water conditions as a criterion for canoeability are somewhat inconsistent, varying from place to place and person to person. Gauge readings are arbitrary and localized, and terms such as *low* and *high* tend to be subjective and to have different meanings for paddlers of different skill levels. Nevertheless, when you have been informed by a local source that a river is low, medium, or high, you are wise to take heed. Ultimately, you are responsible for deciding whether or not to paddle. For some indicators of high water, see the later section "Paddling Safely."

"No, east on 2400N would be better."

One of the excellent canoe landings funded jointly by the DNR and a local community (at Streator on the North Vermilion)

In general, canoeing conditions are best through June. Typically, water levels start to go down in July, and by August many Illinois rivers can be too shallow to canoe. Even in the ordinary dry months of late summer and fall, however, heavy rainfall can quickly restore low rivers to paddleability.

Accesses

Put-ins and take-outs range from attractive and convenient park landings, to easily missed clearings on the riverbank, to extremely difficult accesses requiring physical fitness and great caution. Paddling in Illinois often requires a high tolerance for muddy accesses, especially in the springtime and after rainfall. Always check out the put-in and take-out carefully before beginning a trip: if either access appears to be too difficult or messy for you, you can always select another section or do something else with your day. When in doubt about being able to spot an inconspicuous take-out (especially when something ominous lies downstream), it's a good idea to hang a bright bandanna or piece of surveyor's tape from a branch at the landing. Most of the accesses in this book are public landings, or private ones that are commonly used by the public with permission. Whenever in doubt, be sure to ask permission from landowners.

Trip Descriptions

After these preliminaries, the trip description itself provides a verbal road map of the river section, conveying a lot of information that is not on the map. Except for a few rivers that are normally paddled in the springtime, the descriptions are based on normal summertime flows, that is, neither low nor high. Places where it is appropriate to scout and, perhaps, portage are pointed out, together with historical sites (such as old mills), pleasant lunch spots, nature preserves, alternate accesses, scenic highlights, etc.

Other Trips

Usually, when the river upstream or downstream from the described section is not included elsewhere in the book, a brief paragraph summarizes other paddleable stretches, if there are any.

Good Reading

When an outstanding publication is available to provide further information on a given river or stream, that fact is often noted. In addition, a short list of highly recommended publications is provided in Appendix 2, with a list of paddling-related Web sites in Appendix 3.

Fishing Opportunities

Drawing upon a variety of sources—mainly direct observations of what fishermen are catching, conversations with anglers and DNR fisheries personnel, and material gleaned from published works—I have mentioned the fish that are commonly found in various streams. Not all of the stretches included here are great producers of fish, of course, but some are quite popular with fishermen.

Several useful publications are available from the DNR:

Illinois Fishing Guide. A 64-page booklet that describes the fish found in the state's lakes, rivers, and streams, and lists many accesses.
Illinois Fishing Information. An annual booklet that summarizes state fishing regulations and lists places to fish, including many rivers.
Fishing the Rock. A 16-page booklet that describes fishing opportunities on the Rock River, including detailed maps showing access areas.
Fox River Access Areas & Fishing Guide. A 28-page booklet.
Fishing the Kankakee & the Iroquois. A 16-page guide.

Also recommended are the following:
Art Reid. *Fishing Southern Illinois.* Carbondale: Southern Illinois University Press, 1986.
John W. Nelson. *Chicago Area Paddling & Fishing Pages.* <www.chicagopaddling.com>

Historical Background

Most rivers and streams in Illinois are deeply steeped in historical significance. Some of that history is briefly recounted in the trip descriptions and in occasional sidebars.

The old locks on the Hennepin Canal are popular with fishermen.

RIVER READING AND MANEUVERS

Many of the trips described in this guidebook normally are placid and suitable for beginners. But most sections involve situations that require at least a modicum of ability to "read" the water and to maneuver a boat. Moreover, even the peaceful stretches occasionally present obstructions and other hazards for the unwary paddler. Thus, for both enjoyment and safety, all paddlers should master the basic principles of river dynamics and boat handling. Moving-water technique is much more complex than lake paddling.

In addition to knowing about equipment (boats, paddles, life jackets, boat flotation for whitewater, throw-ropes, etc.), canoeists and kayakers should learn the fundamentals of river current. These include current differentials, downstream and upstream Vs and waves, and the effects of obstacles, such as eddies, trees and limbs, "holes," horizon lines, ledges and falls, and "rock gardens."

In order to maneuver a boat in moving water, boaters need to become familiar with six basic paddling strokes: forward and back, draw and pry, sweep and brace. These allow paddlers to move forward efficiently, to stop movement downstream or even go backward, to turn, to move the boat sideways, and to prevent it from capsizing. By combining these strokes with the ability to read the water, paddlers can execute such river moves as sideslips, eddy turns, peel-outs, and ferries, all of which are essential if you wish to paddle whitewater.

Confidence and skill in river reading and maneuvering are essential for safe paddling. An added bonus, however, is the spirit of playfulness that such skill makes possible. It is fun to "run" a river, certainly, but it is pure joy to be able to slow things down and play on the river in a leisurely fashion.

Since this is a guidebook, not a manual on canoeing and kayaking, detailed information on river reading and maneuvering must be found elsewhere. Of course, the best source of such information is a paddling class or clinic. Fortunately, many such opportunities are available in Illinois; for a listing, see Appendix 4. Other excellent sources are the instructional books and videotapes that introduce the basics of paddlesports; for a selection, see Appendix 5. Still another way for novice paddlers to learn about the basics is to accompany safety-oriented, experienced boaters on nonthreatening trips. Watch, ask questions, follow the example of accomplished boaters, and don't be reluctant to walk your boat around situations that don't feel right. For a list of paddling clubs and organizations in Illinois, see Appendix 6.

PADDLING SAFELY

Canoeists and kayakers paddle for many reasons, including relaxation, communion with nature, excitement, fellowship, and self-development. But whatever their intent, all paddlers should have one overriding consideration at all times: safety for themselves and their companions. Knowledge, skill, and good judgment are essential to having a good, safe time on the water, unmarred by damaged equipment, injuries, or perhaps worse. To that end, the following eight potential hazards warrant special emphasis. All are encountered somewhere on the trips described in this book, and all demand extra care.

1. High Water

During the spring and after downpours, all of the rivers and creeks in this book can become dangerously high, a situation that causes fast current, huge waves, powerful eddies, and sometimes big holes. High water requires skillful boat control and quick decisions, takes away slow, shallow recovery areas, and increases the odds that you will encounter fallen trees and floating debris. Add the likelihood of cold water, and you have a high-hazard situation. No one has any business being on the water when it is in flood. In general, inexperienced and

The historic Baltic Mill on the Kishwaukee at Belvidere

Icicles on the Mazon: springtime paddling requires extra caution.

unskilled boaters should limit themselves to low-to-medium water levels. If in doubt, don't go.

Telltale signs that a river is dangerously high are water flowing through the trees or shrubs; fast, turbulent, muddy, sometimes "boiling" current; water close to the bottom of bridges; and floating debris.

2. Cold

Usually, after springtime thaw, most Illinois rivers and creeks flow forcefully, and boaters enthusiastically take their equipment out of winter storage. Unfortunately, the early weeks of the paddling season are prime times for hypothermia, a potential killer. Water temperature below sixty degrees is dangerous; immersion can quickly take away your strength and even your will. Wear a wet suit or dry suit and layered synthetic fabric whenever the air or water temperature is low. Unless you are skilled, properly equipped and clothed, and accompanied by other skilled paddlers, you should not venture out under such conditions.

3. Strainers

Fallen trees and limbs are potentially lethal on all of the rivers and creeks of Illinois and always should be

avoided. Small streams like Lusk Creek and the upper reaches of larger rivers (e.g., the Des Plaines and Mackinaw) are especially prone to such "strainers"—so-called because water rushes through them, trapping boats and boaters. Be especially watchful for strainers on the outside of bends, in constrictions, and under bridges. Trees often fall into the water as a result of bank erosion or storms, sometimes in unexpected and awkward places. If you're lucky, a passage of open water allows you to paddle by (often through a very narrow opening). If the blockage is complete, however, don't take any chances; pull over to the shoreline well upstream and portage around the obstruction. Occasionally, such portages are unpleasant and difficult, especially when the banks are steep or muddy. Always take strainers seriously; they are the commonest hazard you will encounter on Illinois streams. Incidentally, the terms *strainer, snag,* and *deadfall* essentially mean the same thing.

A sure sign of high water: insufficient bridge clearance (State Line Road bridge on the Kankakee)

A related hazard that is occasionally encountered in Illinois is wire and fencing strung over the water from bank to bank. Usually you can squeeze under it somewhere, but sometimes it must be raised with a paddle or portaged. Obviously, you can quickly get in trouble if the water is fast and you don't see the wire in time. An electrical charge running through the wire adds another unpleasant factor.

4. Broaching

In general, you must keep your boat parallel to the current, particularly in rapids or in other situations where there are obstacles in the water. Otherwise, you are at risk of pinning the boat sideways on an obstruction (a "broach"). The force of moving water is awesome, and can quickly "wrap" your craft, with you in it! Potentially catastrophic though a broach is, you can usually avert disaster by staying calm and aggressively leaning the boat *toward* the obstruction so the onrushing water won't flip

Downed tree ahead!—the greatest danger on Illinois streams

Try to stay upstream from your boat when you dump (Wildcat Rapids on the North Vermilion).

the boat and fill it. (Remember: leaning upstream, away from the obstruction, is the worst thing you can do.) Maintaining the downstream lean, you can often work your boat off the obstruction by "scrunching" it forward or backward a few inches at a time, then continuing on downstream. Sometimes if the situation allows, you can step out onto an obstruction, free the boat, and climb back in. Fellow paddlers can be of assistance, too. Broaching is especially dangerous when bridge piers and old pilings are involved; stay clear of such obstacles, and keep your boat parallel to the current.

5. Capsizing

All boaters "dump" sooner or later. For properly equipped paddlers on a warm day in calm, unobstructed water, it's no big deal. But coming out of your boat when the water is swift, cold, obstructed, or turbulent is a different matter. If you capsize in quietwater situations, stay with your boat if possible (upstream from it), and work your way toward the shore or a shallow spot, staying clear of any brush and other obstructions. Fellow boaters can help. In a capsize situation, the first concern should always be the safety of the paddlers involved; retrieving equipment is a secondary consideration. It's always a good idea to take along extra clothing in a drybag just in case. ALWAYS WEAR A PERSONAL FLOTATION DEVICE (PFD) OR LIFE JACKET. Most canoe and kayak fatalities involve people who aren't wearing one!

In whitewater, try to stay upstream from your boat (so it won't crush you against a rock), lie flat on your back with your feet pointed downstream, and back-paddle to slow yourself down as you head toward shore. Do not try to stand up until you're in very shallow, slow water; otherwise, you're in danger of trapping your foot in a crevice, a not-uncommon cause of drowning. In the hands of someone who knows how to use it, a throw-rope can be used in rescuing capsized boaters.

6. Dams

Because of the danger posed by dams, together with the monotonous paddling upstream from them, this book includes only a few dam portages. Dams are dangerous in many ways and should be given a wide berth, particularly so-called low-head dams (low, uniform structures that may appear innocuous but are often fatal because of the recirculating current downstream, which can pull you into danger and keep you there). Some dams in Illinois are notorious killers (e.g., at Bernadotte on the Spoon River, at Danville on the South Vermilion River, and at Riverside/Lyons on the Des Plaines River). If you put in below a dam, be sure to launch your boat as far downstream as possible to assure that you don't get pulled into the turbulence. If you choose to paddle on an impoundment, take out as far upstream from the dam as possible. Inexperienced boaters often underestimate the

life-threatening danger of dams. The best practice for all boaters is to go nowhere near them.

7. Holes

When swift water flows over a dam, rock, or ledge, it sometimes creates a downstream depression into which the surrounding water rushes turbulently, creating a "hole" (also known as a "hydraulic" or "reversal"). The recirculating current in particularly strong holes, which are called "keepers" or "stoppers," holds onto a boat and traps swimmers. Small, weak holes can easily be run (and even played in by skilled boaters), but large, "sticky" ones

Low-head dams are notorious killers (Yorkville dam on the Fox).

should be carefully avoided, by portaging if necessary. In addition to the deadly hydraulics found just downstream from many Illinois dams, holes develop at various locations on the whitewater sections of the Vermilion and Little Vermilion Rivers.

8. Rapids

Illinois has only two whitewater rivers—the North Vermilion (downstream from Lowell) and the Little Vermilion (upstream from La Salle). Both can be quite dangerous (especially the latter), not only because of difficult rapids, drops, and holes but also because of lowhead dams that must be portaged. Exciting but brief and less intimidating rapids are found on a few other streams

A dangerous recirculating hole at the Oregon dam on the Rock

such as the Des Plaines River (between Isle a la Cache and Lockport), Lusk Creek, and the upper Apple River.

Much more common are riffles—fast, wavy, relatively unobstructed water that is usually safe and easy to run. Experienced paddlers will enjoy the many riffly sections on the Du Page River, Galena River, Kankakee River (downstream from the city of Kankakee), Mazon River, Middle and South Forks of the South Vermilion River, Big Bureau Creek, Kishwaukee River (upstream from Cherry Valley), and North Vermilion River (between Streator and Sandy Ford). As noted earlier, the gradient of a stream is usually a helpful predictor of riffles and rapids.

Standing waves (or "haystacks") are often formed when water rushes through a constriction, over submerged rocks or shallows, or into slower water, sometimes accompanied by a drop. Waves can mark the deepest, most unobstructed channel for paddlers to follow, but in high-water conditions they can be large enough to "stall out" a canoe and swamp it. Often they can be skirted along one side or the other to avoid the biggest ones. Big waves are often found on the North Vermilion River in the "narrows" downstream from the cement factory, on the Des Plaines River downstream from Isle a la

Cache, and on the Du Page River downstream from Interstate 80.

For seasoned whitewater paddlers, rapids are beautiful and exhilarating—a wonderful complement to the much more plentiful quietwater that is the norm in Illinois. Remember, however, that rapids pose dangers, especially for the inexperienced and unskilled. Even veteran paddlers sometimes run into trouble when they fail to scout, attempt rapids that exceed their skill level, paddle when the water is too high, or simply "have a bad day."

Turbulent water is infinitely varied, ranging in difficulty from easy, relatively unobstructed riffles and waves to extremely violent water that threatens the lives of all boaters, including experts. In order to provide a consistent method of comparing rapids worldwide, the International Scale of River Difficulty was devised to categorize rapids, using six classes from "easy" to "extreme." The following is a brief adaptation of this scale, and is the rating system used in this book. Please note that whenever the water is high and/or cold, rapids are usually considered at least one class higher.

Class I: Fast water with some waves and obstructions but easily negotiated; requiring little maneuvering and involving slight risk; suitable for paddlers with some moving-water experience. Class I rapids are one step up from riffles. Most rapids in Illinois are Class Is.

Class II: Fast water with awkwardly located rocks, ledges, sizable waves, and other river features requiring considerable river-reading ability and maneuvering skills; broaching a possibility; suitable for trained and experienced (intermediate) whitewater paddlers. At lower water levels, Wildcat Rapids on North Vermilion River 3 is a solid Class II.

Class III: Very difficult rapids with large, often irregular waves, "pushy" current, big drops of 3 feet or more, difficult-to-determine routes, holes, and other features requiring complex maneuvers and precise boat control; often involving negative consequences in case of a dump, including difficult rescue; suitable only for advanced whitewater paddlers. At medium-to-high water levels, Wildcat Rapids becomes a III. Canyon Rapids on Little Vermilion 2 is a III at normal levels.

Class IV: Intense, powerful, turbulent, sometimes unpredictable and dangerous rapids involving large, often unavoidable holes and big waves; necessitating fast "must-do" maneuvers under pressure; consequences of capsize often nasty; rescue quite difficult; suitable only for highly skilled paddlers with much whitewater experience. Canyon Rapids at high water levels is a very hazardous IV.

Class V: Long, obstructed, violent, and extremely dangerous rapids, with such features as big drops, constricted routes, undercut shorelines and rocks, broaching situations, and "keeper" holes; grave danger to life and limb; little chance of rescue; suitable only for teams of experts under optimal conditions of weather, water level, etc.

Class VI: Super difficult, unpredictable, and dangerous; all of the above criteria carried to an extreme; injury or death likely; suitable only for suicidal fools.

There are no Class Vs and VIs in Illinois. You'd have to go to West Virginia, California, Washington, or other whitewater states in order to find examples.

An Important Reminder

Whenever in doubt about what lies ahead, especially when you suspect a hazard of some kind, do not hesitate to get out and scout. (Incidentally, be careful when scouting. Slippery rocks and other shoreline hazards can be just as injurious as dangers on the water.) If scouting reveals something that you're not sure you can handle, portage. Never let false pride, peer pressure, or daredevilry push you into situations that exceed your skill and experience level. Always wear a suitable PFD, and don't paddle alone.

THE ISSUE OF PUBLIC ACCESS

Whenever the car in front of you is equipped with boat racks and slows conspicuously at every bridge, you can assume that you're following an avid canoeist. For such paddlers, the sight of an unfamiliar stream with sufficient water to float a canoe or kayak sparks the desire to return as soon as possible to try out this newly discovered opportunity. Who knows what excitement and scenic joy lie around the first bend downstream! Surely the only significant considerations are water level and ease of access, right?

Unfortunately, it's not that simple. Nowhere in the whole country is it that simple, as a matter of fact. Wherever you paddle, you must take into consideration the legal rights of landowners, whether it's in California, Tennessee, Illinois, or anywhere else. In Illinois, however, boaters must be especially careful, for two basic reasons: (1) most of the land through which the state's rivers and creeks flow is private property and (2) existing state law makes relatively little provision for recreational boating.

Basically, the question of which bodies of water in Illinois may be paddled by the public is answered (although somewhat ambiguously) in two places: (1) the Rivers, Lakes, and Streams Act (Chapter 615 of the Illinois Compiled Statutes), and (2) a number of important judicial decisions that have addressed matters of waterway use. First passed in 1911, the Rivers, Lakes, and Streams Act has been changed occasionally over the years—the definition of "public waters" has been refined somewhat, for example. But the basic situation remains the same for recreational boaters. The act specifies that the DNR has "jurisdiction and supervision over all the rivers and lakes of the State of Illinois, wherein the State of Illinois or the people of the State have any rights or interests, and shall make a list by counties of all the waters of Illinois, showing the waters, both navigable and non-navigable." A list of "public waters" (forty-eight

natural and ten artificial waterways) has been developed and is published in the Illinois Administrative Code. Because of its obvious importance to the access issue, the list is included in its entirety in Appendix 7 of this book.

Estimates of the total number of stream miles in Illinois vary, but the most commonly cited figure is 33,000. The list of public bodies of water, however, comprises only about 2,500 stream miles—eight percent of the total. Actually, the percentage is considerably lower when the waterways that are unattractive to most paddlers are discounted (e.g., the Mississippi, Ohio, and Illinois Rivers), together with some that don't even exist anymore. In all fairness, it is necessary to point out that the percentage could never approach 100 percent

The best-known rapids in Illinois: the Wildcat on the North Vermilion

because thousands of stream miles represent tiny creeks that are seldom paddleable by even the most ardent canoeists and kayakers. Nevertheless, the "official" list of public streams is a short one—indeed, one of the shortest in the nation—and does not include hundreds of miles of rivers and creeks that have been enjoyably paddled for many years.

The criterion for inclusion in the list is that the waterways "were navigable in their natural condition or were improved for navigation and opened to public use." The term *navigable* can be quite confusing, especially because various states interpret it in many different ways. Some states, such as Wisconsin, define it in a very broad and liberal fashion that opens up large numbers of waterways to recreational use, while other states are much more restrictive. Illinois is in the latter group, consistently interpreting *navigable* within a trade-and-commerce context. Thus, according to the Rivers, Lakes, and Streams Act, public bodies of water are "all open public lakes and streams capable of being navigated for commercial uses and purposes."

It has been pointed out repeatedly by many observers that the current definition and list of public waters are narrow and antiquated (essentially going back to the 1800s when Illinois was surveyed and settled), and that they fail to make provision for the recreational potential of numerous "nonnavigable" streams in the state, many of which have long supported commercially viable canoe-rental businesses. To confuse the situation further, the Army Corps of Engineers has its own list of "navigable" streams, which includes eight rivers and creeks that aren't on the Illinois DNR list, notably the Mackinaw, Embarras, Middle Fork of the South Vermilion, and South Vermilion rivers. Currently, the only streams recognized by the DNR as public bodies of water are those enumerated in the Administrative Code.

The upshot of all this is twofold. First, recreational canoeists and kayakers may legally paddle on all of the officially recognized public lakes and streams. Twenty-seven of the sixty-four mapped and described day trips in this book are on the DNR list: the Big Muddy River; Des Plaines River 3; Fox River 1, 2, and 3; Galena River 2; Hennepin Canal 1, 2, and 3; Illinois and Michigan Canal 1 and 2; Iroquois River 1 and 2; Kankakee River 1, 2, and 3; Little Wabash River; Pecatonica River 1, 2, and 3; Rock River 1 and 2; Saline River; Sangamon River 2 and 3; Spoon River 3; and the Sugar River. However, the fact that you can paddle on these waterways does *not* mean that you can access private property on the banks.

Secondly, the right of the public to paddle most streams not on the list of public bodies of water is less clear. In Illinois, the banks and streambed to the center of the stream are the property of riparian (streambank) landowners. Thus, property holders who own land on both sides also own the whole streambed. Consequently, wires and fencing strung across a stream to enclose cattle are not uncommon. Many unlisted streams have long been paddled heavily by the public (e.g., the Mackinaw River downstream from Congerville and the Kaskaskia River downstream from Shelbyville) with little or no objection from riparian landowners. On the other hand, some of the listed streams and many unlisted ones are rarely if ever paddled for a variety of reasons, including inadequate water levels, excessive brushiness, unattractive channelization, inaccessibility, and objections from landowners. Streams in this rarely-or-never-paddled group are typically quite small and are unlikely to generate interest in the paddling community.

A number of streams that are not on the DNR's list of public bodies of water are nevertheless canoer friendly because they pass wholly or partly through county forest preserves, national forest, or DNR land. For such waterways, the term *public use streams* is sometimes used. Examples are the North Branch of the Chicago River

upstream from Whelan Pool, the Des Plaines River upstream from the Hoffman Dam at Riverside/Lyons, the Kishwaukee River downstream from Cherry Valley, Lusk Creek, the Middle Fork of the South Vermilion River, Salt Creek between Graue Mill and the Des Plaines River, and the Cache River swamp trail. Moreover, canoe or raft rental businesses operate on a number of excellent paddling streams that are not on the DNR list: the Cache River, Du Page River, Embarras River, middle Kaskaskia River, Mackinaw River, Middle Fork of the South Vermilion River, Nippersink Creek, and the North Vermilion River. The Middle Fork is a special case, of course, because it's a state-managed component of the National Wild and Scenic River system; paddling is not only allowed but encouraged.

Obviously, then, it would be oversimplified and inaccurate to categorize all of Illinois's streams as either "public bodies of water" (thus, open to paddlers), or private, nonnavigable rivers and creeks that are off-limits to the public without landowner permission. Almost all of the stream sections described and mapped in this book are frequently canoed and kayaked, although technically the majority are not on the public-bodies-of-water listing. None are likely to result in unpleasantness with landowners, as long as boaters are respectful of private property; this includes asking owner permission whenever it is recommended in the trip descriptions (e.g., on Apple River 1) and whenever you're unsure about put-ins, take-outs, lunch stops, etc. When in doubt, ask. When told "no," don't argue and make a big deal out of it. There is nothing to be gained by making a scene, even when you don't understand or agree with the nonapproval. And there's always time to sort out the legalities later.

"Unfair" though it might seem to some canoeists, a private landowner with property on both sides of a "nonnavigable" stream can, under the current interpretation of Illinois water laws, say "no" to boaters who want to paddle over his streambed. In practice, few property owners do so; many, in fact, welcome paddlers who are unobtrusive and appreciative. Boaters who are oblivious to the rights of private landowners should not be surprised, however, if a complaint is lodged with the local sheriff or DNR enforcement officer. Fortunately, this doesn't happen very often. The bottom line is that you're not likely to have a problem if you always put yourself in the place of the landowner.

In recent years, there has been some progress toward increasing public boating opportunities on Illinois streams. In 1999, for example, a detailed Northeastern Illinois Regional Water Trails Plan was completed. Sponsored by the DNR and developed by the Northeastern Illinois Planning Commission, the Openlands Project, and the Illinois Paddling Council, this exciting plan presents a coordinated system of canoeing and kayaking trails on ten waterways in Cook, Du Page, Kane, Lake, McHenry, and Will Counties. The same process is planned for "other streams near major metro areas and high quality recreational-use rivers."

The DNR's Boat Access Area and Development Program is available to local governments to acquire and develop public accesses, resulting already in a number of excellent landings (e.g., on the North Vermilion River at Streator and on the Kishwaukee River at Belvidere). To encourage private landowners to increase access, the state legislature has enacted a Recreational Use Statute that diminishes owner liability for accidents incurred by paddlers and other recreational users if the owner doesn't charge for use of his property. In response to the 1998 recommendations of the Third Conservation Congress, the DNR indicated that, although passage of a new water resources act is unlikely at the present time, the agency will move toward improving access and augmenting the stream miles available for public recreational use: "To improve public access, DNR will (1) begin planning to develop and promote water trails on the public waters of the state, and (2) identify where the purchase of easements along private streams could lead to additional water trail development." Indeed, the overall climate is improving for Illinois paddlers—slowly, to be sure, but in a decidedly positive direction. The paddling community has everything to gain by becoming actively and cooperatively involved in the process.

If you'd like to delve further into this complicated and often confusing topic, the following sources are recommended:

> R. E. Beck, K.W. Harrington, W. P. Hardy, and T. D. Feather. *Assessment of Illinois Water Quantity Law.* Springfield: Illinois DNR, Office of Water Resources, 1996.
> Gary R. Clark and Ed Hoffman. "Water Law and Recreational Access: Some Questions, Answers, and Considerations." Springfield: 1998, unpublished paper.
> Margit Livingston, "Public Recreational Rights in Illinois Rivers and Streams," *DePaul Law Review* (1980): 353–81.

Paddlers who experience access problems are urged to contact Gary Mechanic, coordinator of the Illinois Paddling Council Access Project (<accessproject@chicago paddling.com> or 4905 N. Hamlin, Chicago, IL 60625).

WHAT TO BRING ON A CANOE TRIP

As an aid to beginning paddlers, here's a basic checklist of things to bring along on canoeing and kayaking trips. All the items listed are not necessary on every trip, of course, and you may wish to bring other things not listed here. It's a good idea to develop and use a checklist of your own. Even experienced paddlers forget important items occasionally (to their chagrin and embarrassment).

A good PFD.

An extra paddle.

Clothing appropriate for the weather, including rain gear and an adequate hat and shoes. Dress warmly; you can always shed a layer of clothing, if necessary.

A bailer (made from a bleach bottle) and a sponge to keep your boat dry.

A plastic water bottle with plenty of drinking water.

A waterproof bag or box for extra clothing, lunch, wallet, camera, and everything else you want to keep dry.

Car keys (in a secure place). Not having these at the take-out is quite awkward!

Basic first aid materials.

Sunscreen.

Insect repellent.

Short lengths of cord for tying gear to thwarts.

For whitewater: an air bag tied into the boat to keep your boat afloat in case of a capsize, and a paddling helmet to protect your head from rocks.

For overnight canoe trips: basic camping equipment and supplies.

PADDLING RESPONSIBLY

Along with the enjoyment of paddling the waterways of Illinois come certain responsibilities for all of us:

Rain gear can make all the difference on a drizzly day.

1. Be considerate of other paddlers when you're on the water. If you're with a group, keep other members of the group in sight at all times, and don't go off on your own. On most trips, the first boat and last boat ("lead" and "sweep") are paddled by experienced boaters; always stay behind the lead boat and in front of the last boat. Follow the instructions of designated trip leaders when you go on trips sponsored by canoe clubs.

2. Help preserve the environment by leaving no litter, especially when you stop for lunch. When you find trash left by others, it's always a good idea to remove

Paddle with a club and meet a lot of nice people.

foot on private land, and express your gratitude. Please keep the noise level down, and stay away from cattle. Giving cattle a wide berth is a matter of common courtesy toward the owner, of course, but it's also a prudent way to avoid being trampled.

4. For obvious reasons, it's not a good idea to take alcohol on canoe trips.

5. If you plan to fish, be sure to obtain an Illinois license and abide by the regulations. See the annual *Illinois Fishing Guide* published by the DNR.

6. Illinois residents must also register and title their canoes and kayaks. See "Watercraft Registration" at the DNR Web site <http://dnr.state.il.us>.

7. Because radios and other noise generators detract from the get-away-from-it-all benefit of paddling, they are generally considered taboo on canoe trips.

8. If your dog is well behaved and under control, it's okay to bring it along. Otherwise, for everyone's sake (including the dog's), leave it home.

9. Be responsible for your own safety and well-being. This includes paddling only on streams that match your skill level, being properly equipped, staying with your group, knowing how to swim, wearing your PFD and weather-appropriate clothing, following your trip leader's instructions, kneeling in rough water (to stabilize your boat by lowering the center of gravity), installing extra flotation in your boat if you're going to paddle whitewater, mastering the essentials of boat control, turning your bow into the wake created by powerboats, and staying away from strainers and other obstructions. Failing to follow basic principles of safe paddling not only puts you in harm's way but also may put fellow boaters in the position of endangering themselves to rescue you. Poison ivy is another factor to consider when paddling in Illinois. It's almost universal in the state, so stay clear of it during put-ins, take-outs, lunch stops, and portages.

10. Don't allow yourself to be goaded into paddling situations that exceed your ability or confidence level. Canoeing and kayaking skill develops with experience in steady increments.

11. Canoeing club members should contribute to the group by volunteering to lead a trip, write the newsletter, keep track of memberships, or participate in other activities according to their interests and abilities.

12. When parking vehicles at the put-in or take-out, don't block access for motorists, farmers, property owners, or other boaters. Keep your parked vehicles away from driveways, lanes to farm fields, and accesses to motorboat ramps, and don't park along shoulders with part of your vehicle on the road.

some (or all) of it in a bag and dispose of it later in an appropriate place. Build fires only where you know it's permissible to do so (e.g., in riverside parks that provide fire rings).

3. All of the waterways of Illinois have at least some private property on their shoreline. Always put yourself in the place of the landowner and respect his or her rights. Ask permission before stepping

AN IMPORTANT CAUTION
FOR ALL PADDLERS

All rivers and streams are constantly subject to change. A section that is completely open today, for instance, may develop a big logjam next week as the result of a storm. An excellent access may disappear because of erosion or change of land ownership, no-trespassing signs may appear, or a new canoe landing is made available by a governmental entity. Bridges can be built or washed out, riffles or rapids sometimes appear where there were none before, and dams become more dangerous or are occasionally removed. Last week, perhaps, you ran a Class II drop with no problem, but this week your scouting of the drop reveals a potentially lethal limb at the bottom. In short, paddlers must always be aware that river sections are quite changeable in many ways—some good, some bad. The descriptions in this book represent the most recent condition of the thirty-three rivers and streams when the author last paddled them. Please always bear in mind the changeability factor. Whenever you become aware of a significant alteration (like those listed above), we at Trails Books would appreciate hearing about it (see the address on page vi).

APPLE RIVER 1
Townsend Road to Elizabeth–Scales Mound Road (11.7 Miles)

Although the Apple River is "on the bubble" in terms of the basic criteria for including rivers and streams in this book, its great beauty and unique setting call out for inclusion. Typically, its small watershed and relatively steep gradient make it suitable for paddling only in the early springtime and after sustained rainfall. After rainstorms, however, the river rises quickly and becomes quite dangerous. Add to these water level qualifications the caution that **you must seek permission from landowners along the river before paddling this section**, much of which flows through private pastureland and farm fields. Failure to do so may result in your being arrested for trespassing!

These caveats notwithstanding, the upper Apple may be the most beautiful stretch of river anywhere in the state. Never very wide (20–40 feet), it winds intimately back and forth through the rough, unglaciated terrain of northwestern Illinois, often skirting magnificent cliffs of limestone, dolomite, and shale. The clear water flows delightfully through innumerable riffles and often requires maneuvering between rocks and around tight bends—thus, it's not suitable for beginning paddlers.

Camping is plentiful in the area. The most attractive is at Apple River Canyon State Park, north of Stockton. A few miles farther east is Lake Le-Aqua-Na State Park, just north of Lena. Private campgrounds are found north of Galena (Palace Campground), north of Savanna (Lakewood Resort), and south of Lena near Highway 20 (KOA). Also see Apple River 2.

The **shuttle route** (5.9 miles) for the prettiest part of the river, a short trip from Townsend Road to Grebner Road, goes west on Townsend Road, north on Scout Camp Road, west on Schapville Road, and south on Salem Road to Grebner Road. For a longer trip to Elizabeth–Scales Mound Road, the shuttle route (12 miles) continues past the Grebner Road bridge to Apple River Road, west on Highway 20, and north on Elizabeth–Scales Mound Road. Always drive carefully in the area because there are many hills, blind curves, and narrow shoulders. Watch out for passing cars when unloading and loading boats.

The **gradient** is one of the steepest in Illinois: 8.3 feet per mile for the entire stretch. Most of the gradient is in the first 6 miles (i.e., to Grebner Road), which has a pitch of 13.3 feet per mile; the rest of the trip is only 3.5 feet per mile.

Water levels can be estimated by checking the one gauge on the river (station #05419000 downstream at Han-over) on the USGS Web site listed in the introduction.

Put in downstream-left at the Townsend Road bridge, where there is very little room along the shoulder to park cars. Townsend Road is the farthest upstream point to put in; boats are not allowed in the main unit of Apple River Canyon State Park upstream. Riffles begin immediately after the bridge; you can determine from these whether there's enough water to paddle. Deadfall is usually infrequent and easy to get around, but be on guard.

In the first right turn, there's a magnificent rock cliff on the left, about 50 feet high, with beautiful mosses and ferns growing on it. The water is pooled here, in an enchantingly peaceful setting—the first of many on this trip. After a small island and creek mouth, the river swings left past an attractive home on the right bank where there's a small rock dam in the right channel of an island, forming a drop of about 18 inches. Riffles, cliffs, and low stone formations continue all the way to the Scout Camp Road bridge. After the bridge, more breathtaking cliffs begin—sometimes towering 100 feet and topped with yews. Then, after a left turn, the setting becomes increasingly agricultural, with cultivated fields, rolling pastureland, a few farm buildings, and wire occasionally strung across the river to enclose cattle. Squeeze under the wire at its highest point; do not disturb it any more than you have to.

The best riffles of the trip, with a pleasant little ledge, precede the charming old truss bridge at Apple River Road, which can be accessed upstream-left. After the bridge, riffles continue, but the cliffs and stone formations almost disappear. The setting is completely open before and after the next bridge, and farm buildings appear. A succession of calm pools and enjoyable riffles takes you to the new Salem Road bridge, followed immediately by the old metal truss bridge at Grebner Road. There's a decent place to take out upstream-left at Grebner Road; park along the road southeast of the picturesque old bridge, toward Apple River Road. At this point, you have experienced the best that the Apple River has to offer.

In the sharp bends downstream from Grebner Road, sheer silt cutbanks appear for the first time, often honeycombed with swallow nests. The setting is generally more open than before, with fields, occasional farm buildings, brief wooded areas, and high, steep banks that tend to forestall a clear view of the surrounding area. Indeed, the river after Grebner Road is of a very different character than the upstream portion—and much less attractive.

After passing under two more bridges at Goose Hollow Road and Georgetown Road, **take out** at the Elizabeth–Scales Mound Road bridge, upstream-left (having secured permission in advance from the nearby homeowner). This isn't an easy access.

One of the many beautiful cliffs on the Apple

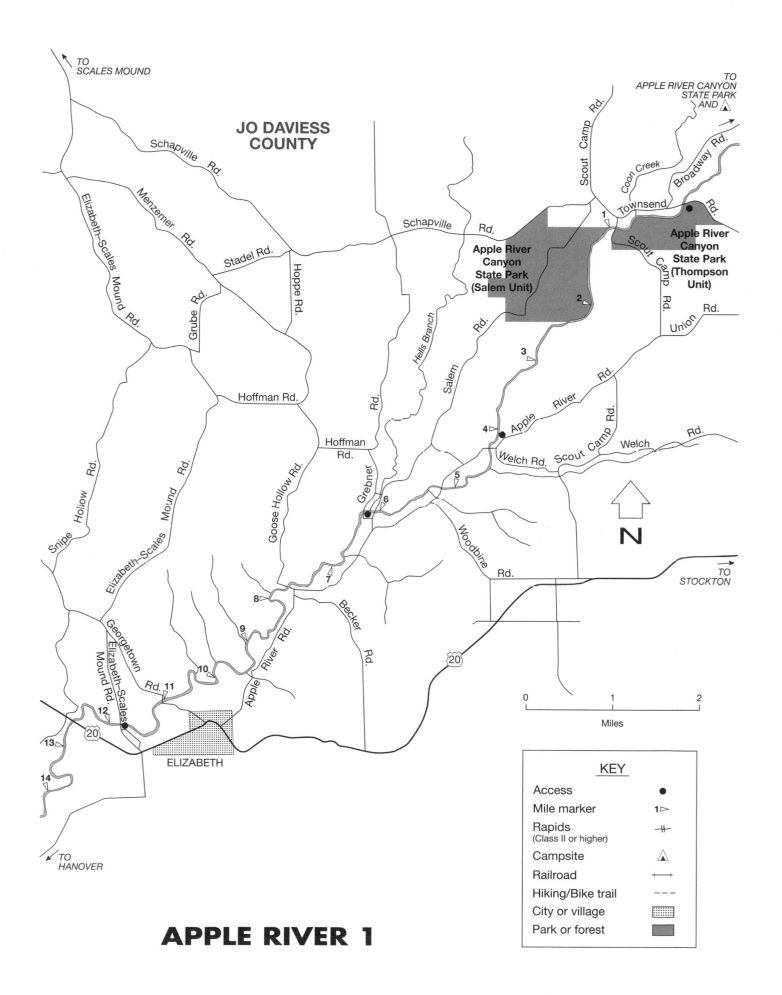

APPLE RIVER 1

APPLE RIVER 2

Hanover to Whitten Road (9 Miles)

"Mallard Capital of the World"

Back in 1827 when the first white settlers arrived at the site of modern-day Hanover by paddling up from the Mississippi River, they encountered big rapids. Within a year, a dam had been built to provide power for a sawmill and gristmill. Named after a town of the same name in New Hampshire, Hanover is a pleasant little town that calls itself the "Mallard Capital of the World." A local firm hatches and raises over 200,000 mallards a year for hunting clubs, research, and other purposes; its farm is seen along Highway 84 on the shuttle route.

For natural beauty, this lower section of the Apple River doesn't compare with the stretch below Townsend Road, but it certainly provides a pleasant three- to four-hour paddling trip and has the advantage of easy accessibility. Although Highway 84 twice touches the river, there is almost no development. Banks are usually rather steep and covered with vegetation. Consistently narrow here (40–50 feet), the river flows through woodland and past occasional cultivated fields and forested hillsides. At lower water levels, there are several enjoyable riffles over rocky shelves.

Public **campgrounds** are located a few miles west of Hanover at Blanding (near Lock and Dam 12 on the Mississippi River) and a few miles south at Mississippi Palisades State Park near Savanna. A visit to Palisades Park is highly recommended, even if you aren't camping. The cliffs that front the Mississippi River are quite impressive, and a network of trails enables visitors to explore the beautiful bluffs and ravines. Drive south from the Whitten Road take-out to Savanna and you'll see some of the cliffs alongside Highway 84. For other campgrounds, see Apple River 1.

The **shuttle route** is short and simple (4.2 miles). From the put-in in Hanover, take Fulton Street to Highway 84 (Washington Street), then drive south to Whitten Road. There is a gravelly pull-off area alongside Highway 84 at the Whitten Road bridge (upstream-left)—large enough to accommodate several cars.

The **gradient** is subdued, compared with Apple River 1, averaging less than 2 feet per mile.

For **water level,** see Apple River 1.

Put in along Fulton Street in Hanover, several hundred yards downstream-right from the dam. The curved dam has a sheer drop of 8 feet and is dangerous. Opposite the cemetery there's a grassy area where you can unload boats and carry them down a gentle slope to the

bank. The river can also be accessed from the Siebe Corporation property, downstream-left from the dam. Ask permission at the office, then carry boats across the grassy lawn to the river.

When the water level is neither too high nor too low, a series of standing waves develops for about a hundred yards below the dam. Be careful at the put-in not to turn sideways and be swamped by the waves. The banks are fairly steep from the beginning, averaging about 12 feet in height. After a short straightaway, the river heads abruptly right, then quickly twists left. The small layered stone outcropping in this left turn is the only rock seen on the trip. Only 30 feet wide at this point, the river develops riffles at lower levels. A long left arc follows in a pretty, tree-lined setting, and the streambed widens to about 40 feet.

After a 25-foot-high, clay-and-sand bank on the right, the river goes into a long right bend, in the midst of which a suspended pipeline crosses overhead. A series of bends and short straightaways follow, with occasional cornfields. Some deadfall is encountered here and there, but usually it's easy to get around. The farther you get from the dam, the more the current slows.

As the river twists and turns, a high wooded ridge approaches the right bank—the most attractive part of the trip so far.

Immediately after several small buildings (the first since the put-in), the bridge on Crazy Hollow Road appears. Then the river heads toward Highway 84, going through several loops before swinging to the right alongside the road and a high wooded ridge. Thereafter, the river goes through several big curves in which it loops back upon itself, widening somewhat and passing by attractive wooded hillsides.

A farmhouse and barn are seen high up on the right bank in the approach to Whitten Road—the first buildings in a long time. A big left bend ends at Highway 84 and the adjoining ridge. Then a sharp right turn brings the Whitten Road bridge into view. **Take out** upstream-left on the bank (often muddy) and carry up to the nearby gravel-and-dirt parking area alongside Highway 84.

Other trips: The Apple River from Elizabeth–Scales Mound Road to Hanover is similar to the second half of Apple River 1: high, steep banks, with few riffles, no rock outcroppings, and frequent farm fields. If you wish to paddle it, you must take out before the dam at Hanover. Highway 20 is a poor access. The suggested take-out is at the point where the Apple River flows alongside Elizabeth-Hanover Road north of Hanover. Ask permission at the nearby farmhouse. There are no good take-outs for the short stretch between Whitten Road and the Mississippi River.

When you paddle the Apple, don't miss the restored fort at Elizabeth, scene of a battle during the Black Hawk War.

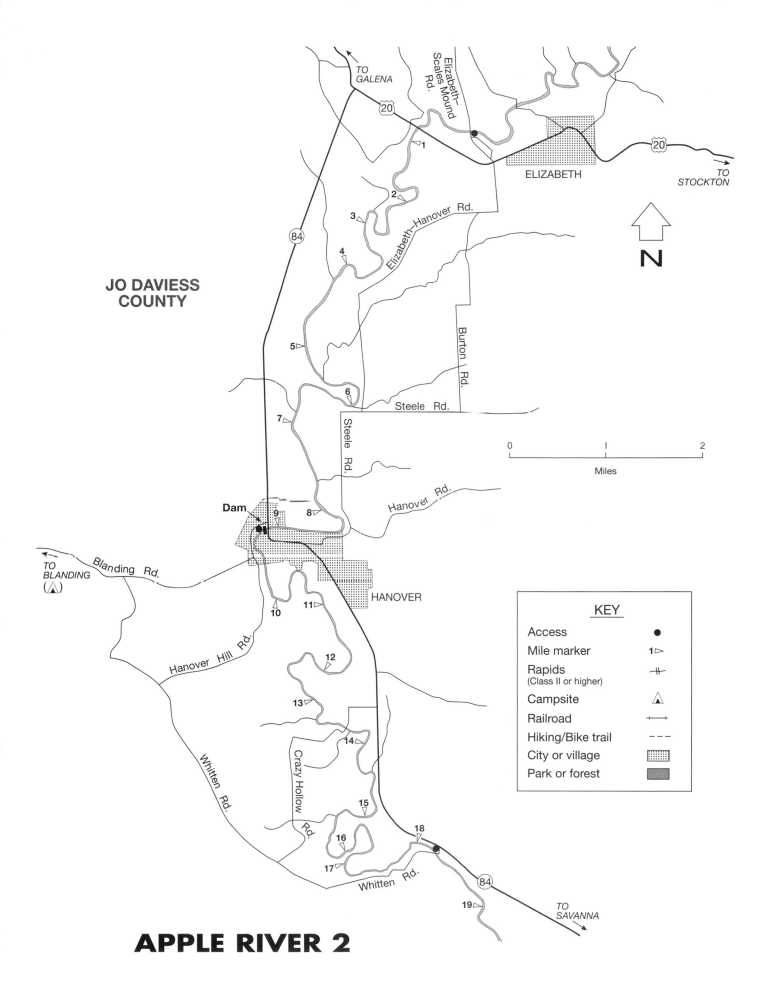

APPLE RIVER 2

BIG BUREAU CREEK
Red Covered Bridge at Princeton to Tiskilwa (12.6 Miles)

A delightful, twisting stream with countless riffles, Big Bureau Creek features a series of imposing cliffs formed as the creek veers into high wooded bluffs. Unlike the stone cliffs on the Apple, North Vermilion, and Rock rivers, these are composed primarily of sand, clay, and gravel but are dramatic nevertheless. Big Bureau Creek is a clean, intimate stream with numerous gravel bars for relaxation—or lunch stops. Deadfall is seldom a problem, but there are narrow spots and constrictions that require maneuvering; thus, only boaters with some experience should paddle this section. The banks are mostly forested, with occasional open fields and only a few houses.

By some accounts, the creek takes its name from a Frenchman—Pierre de Beuro or Bureau—who married the daughter of a Potawatomi chief, was very successful in the area as a fur trader, and eventually was killed by other, envious traders.

Public **camping** is available to the west at Johnson Sauk Trail State Park between Annawan and Kewanee, at several locations along the nearby Hennepin Canal (see the three Hennepin Canal descriptions elsewhere in this book), at Lake DePue Park southeast of Princeton, and at Starved Rock State Park to the east near Utica.

The **shuttle route** is 8.7 miles. From the put-in at the red covered bridge, go south on Highway 26 to

The Red Covered Bridge at Princeton

Princeton; continue south through town on Main Street, which becomes Tiskilwa Road. Immediately after crossing the canal bridge, turn right on 1150N. There's room for a few cars at the take-out bridge.

The **gradient** of 5.5 feet per mile produces one exhilarating riffle after another.

For **water levels**, check the gauge near Princeton (station #05556500) on the USGS Web site listed in the introduction.

Put in at the historic red covered bridge north of Princeton. Built in 1863, this landmark is still open to vehicular traffic and is a popular spot with photographers. For many years, a very dangerous corrugated metal dam has been located just downstream from the bridge. Recently it was cut to a lower level, but it is still there and remains a serious hazard. Thus, putting in downstream-right from the bridge and the dam site is the best and safest option; however, you should secure the landowner's permission before putting in here.

Starting out only about 35 feet wide, Big Bureau Creek winds around over a sand-and-gravel bottom past a wooded shoreline. After several turns and a short straightaway, the creek bends right into the first of many high cliffs, 80–100 feet tall and surmounted by trees. An island follows the second cliff; watch out for deadfall in both channels. Three more cliffs precede the first bridge at 1800N, followed by another in an abrupt oxbow. In the following right bend, the streambed gets wider and slower, with fields on both sides. You may encounter wire strung across the creek in this area; duck under the highest part. Woods start again within view of the Interstate 80 bridge.

Before the next bridge at 1600N the creek establishes a pool-riffle-pool rhythm. After Epperson Run enters on the left, there's a right bend where deadfall tends to collect; be careful here. Shortly thereafter there's a good access downstream-right at the Highway 6/34 bridge. After the bridge, numerous gravel bars and riffles continue, and the creek runs narrow and deep along Lover's Lane Road. Dramatic cliffs are found in the wild-looking area that follows, and the riffles become more frequent.

After an abrupt right turn, the creek quickly bends left past a long expanse of huge cliffs. These, in turn, are followed by the site of the old aqueduct that once carried the Hennepin Canal over the creek. The aqueduct was swept away by floodwaters years ago, and a siphon now runs under the creek to carry water from the eastern side of the canal to the western side. Part of the old towpath bridge can still be seen. An irregular 18-inch dam has been built of concrete chunks to protect the siphon, and it's difficult to make a clean run of this rough structure. You can easily get out just above it and portage. After a couple of bends, the bridge at 1150N is a good place to **take out** (upstream-left).

Other trips: The creek is also pleasant to paddle upstream from this stretch. Canoeists put in at 2200N or 2525E (ask permission) and take out at the small park upstream-right from the red covered bridge.

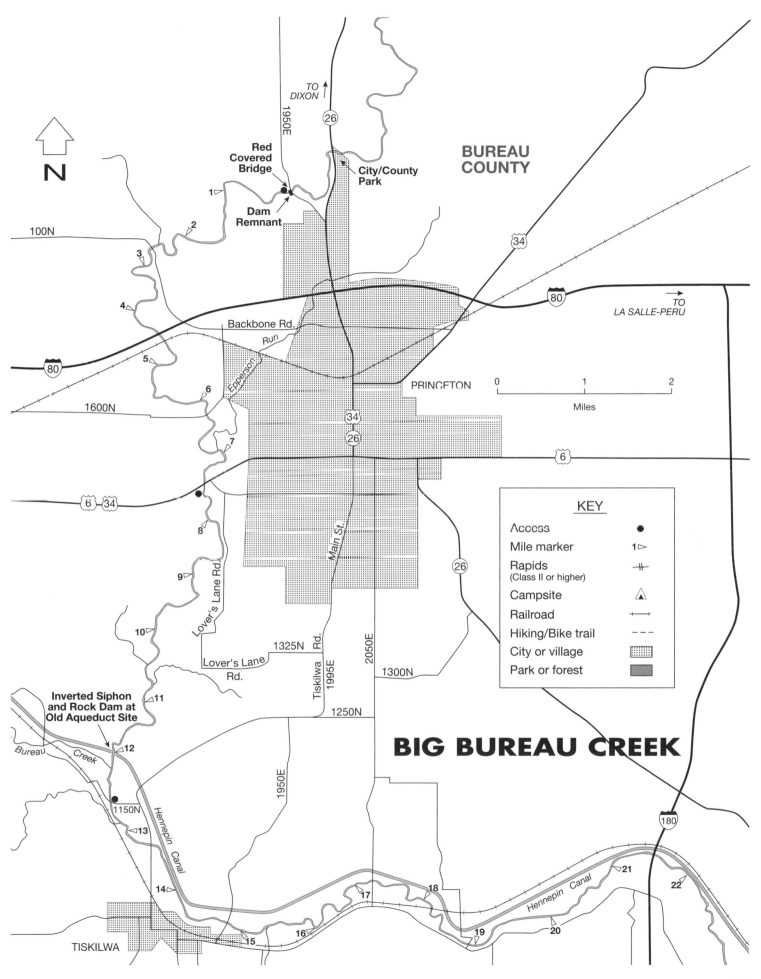

N

TO
DIXON

26

BUREAU
COUNTY

34

Red
Covered
Bridge

City/County
Park

80

TO
LA SALLE-PERU

1

2

100N

Dam
Remnant

3

4

Backbone Rd.

Run

Epperson

PRINCETON

5

80

6

1600N

0   1   2

Miles

7

34

26

34

26

6

KEY

Access ●

Mile marker 1▷

Rapids
(Class II or higher)

Campsite ▲

Railroad

Hiking/Bike trail

City or village

Park or forest

6 34

8

Main St.

9

Lover's Lane Rd.

10

1325N

Tiskilwa Rd.

2050E

26

Lover's Lane
Rd.

1995E

1300N

11

**Inverted Siphon
and Rock Dam at
Old Aqueduct Site**

1250N

1950E

Bureau

Creek

12

BIG BUREAU CREEK

1150N

Hennepin Canal

13

180

14

21

22

Hennepin Canal

17

18

20

TISKILWA

15

16

19

BIG MUDDY RIVER
Turkey Bayou to Rattlesnake Ferry (8 Miles)

Appropriately named (the French called it the *Aux Vases,* after the word for "mud" or "slime"), the Big Muddy is not one of Illinois's most beautiful rivers. Upstream from Murphysboro, it is often subject to logjams. Downstream from Murphysboro—the section once designated the "Big Muddy Canoe Trail"—the river is wide enough to make logjams unlikely, but much of this stretch flows through relatively open agricultural area, with steep, muddy banks punctuated by trees killed in the great flood of 1993.

Not surprisingly, the most attractive part of the river flows through the Shawnee National Forest, where a couple of excellent boat landings are provided. The trip described here exposes paddlers to the best that the river has to offer: convenient ramps at the put-in and take-out; several Ozark-like wooded bluffs along the shoreline, with a few stone outcroppings peeking through the trees; wild, undeveloped surroundings; and the likelihood of spotting such wildlife as egrets, herons, turkey vultures, turtles, and deer. A variety of fish are caught here, including channel cat, bullheads, crappie, largemouth, and sunfish. Copperheads, cottonmouths, and rattlesnakes are also fairly common, so you must be careful where you step.

Excellent public **camping** is available at Turkey Bayou Campground near the put-in; at Lake Murphysboro State Park and Johnson Creek Recreation Area west of Murphysboro; at the community of Grand Tower, near the boat landing on the Mississippi River; and at the beautiful and ecologically rich LaRue-Pine Hills Natural Area about 20 miles south of Murphysboro.

The **shuttle route** is quick and easy (9.5 miles). From the boat ramp at the east end of Oakwood Bottoms Road head west to Highway 3. Drive south to Howardton Road, which heads east and ends at the Rattlesnake Ferry Landing (good parking). If you have enough time, you will undoubtedly enjoy a drive on Levee Road, where you get a close-up view of the Greentree Reservoir in the Oakwood Bottoms, with its hardwood forest and teeming wildlife. Incidentally, the shuttle on Highway 3 takes you past a large and interesting fish-farm operation.

The **gradient** is negligible (less than a foot per mile).

For **water levels,** check the Murphysboro gauge (station #05599500) on the USGS Web site listed in the introduction.

Put in at the boat ramp at the east end of Oakwood Bottoms Road, just south of the Turkey Bayou Campground. A short paddle upstream will take you to the small creek that formed Little Grand Canyon, where huge, rocky bluffs tower over the river. (You can also drive to the canyon and experience the rugged terrain and beautiful views from 3.6 miles of hiking trails.)

Downstream from the **put-in** the river begins with a wide, heavily wooded straightaway, then bends right. The banks are high, steep, and muddy, and will remain that way most of the trip, making shoreline stops unpleasant if not impossible. Dead trees are mixed in with live ones wherever the flood of 1993 reached them. Farther into the right bend, a huge wooded bluff appears on the left a couple hundred yards from the river, with an attractive stone face about halfway up. After a brief open area, the river heads left, widening by 50–100 feet, and a creek enters on the right. A set of power lines crosses overhead in the long left bend, then another set where a high bluff forces the river to turn sharply to the right. Not far downstream is a rock outcropping and some big boulders on the left shore, providing momentary relief from muddy banks. After a straightaway, the river turns right again, away from the bluffs. Then a big left loop carries the river back toward the bluffs. Except for the landing and power lines, there is no sign of human activity.

One more time, the river hugs the bluffs on the left after a right turn. After swinging away from the bluffs again, the river makes a final right turn. More willow trees begin to appear, and the banks are much lower (but still muddy). Just downstream from another set of power lines, the Rattlesnake Ferry **take-out**, an excellent gravel landing, appears on the right. (Be forewarned, however: high water often leaves deep mud on both landings.)

Other trips: (1) Although there isn't much to recommend it, a trip from Murphysboro to Oakwood Bottoms Road is another option. To get to the excellent boat landing at Riverside Park, turn south off Highway 149 in Murphysboro onto 20th Street; proceed south and turn right on Commercial Avenue; then turn left just before the park gates and continue to the boat-launch parking lot. Most of this stretch flows through a relatively open agricultural area, but the trip ends on a high note as you pass the Little Grand Canyon. (2) The Highway 3 bridge is sometimes used as a take-out for trips starting at Oakwood Bottoms Road or Rattlesnake Ferry. The Illinois Department of Transportation owns land on both sides of the bridge, but this is not a convenient access. If you're considering this section, you should first drive Levee Road from Highway 3 to Howardton Road; from this vantage point you can see the lowland setting through which the river flows, with low mud banks and lots of dead trees in the water.

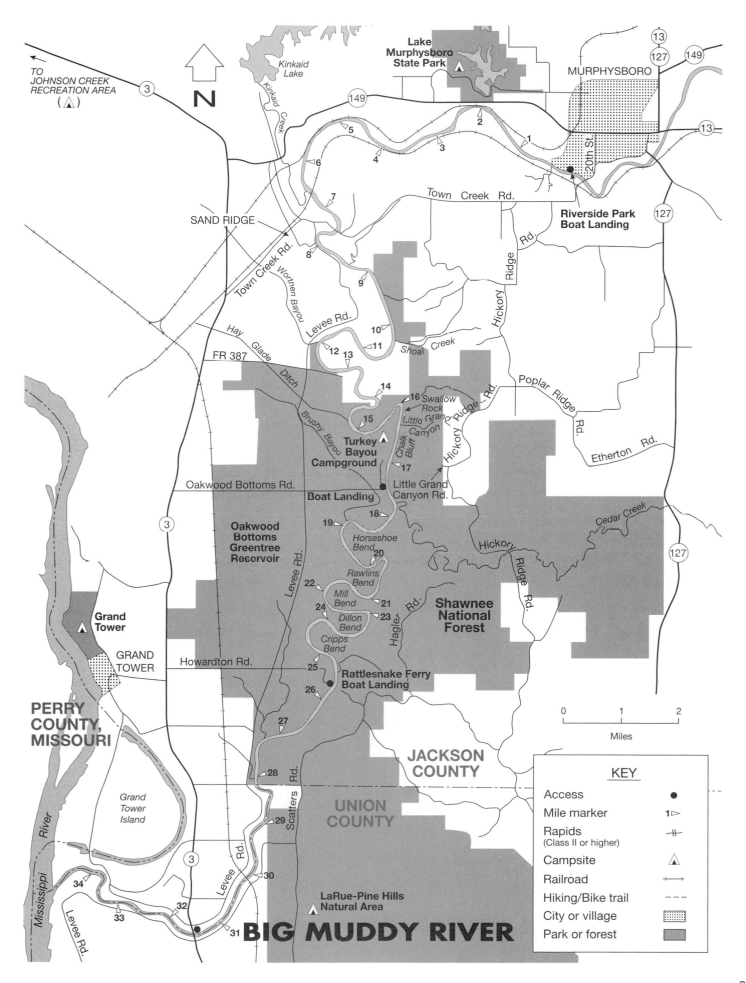

CACHE RIVER 1
Swamp Trail (2.5–5 Miles)

On several of the rivers and streams in this book, you would swear that you're not in Illinois. Nowhere is this more apparent than on the Cache River, which transports you to an environment much like the bayous of Louisiana. The southern tip of Illinois, where the Cache River is located, is actually farther south than Richmond, Virginia, and is the northernmost part of the Gulf Coastal Plain that begins in Louisiana and Florida. Thus, in addition to some of the familiar northern flora and fauna, the Cache River presents a diversity of more "exotic" species such as bald cypress and tupelo gum trees, black vultures, and river otters—all in the largest remaining wetland in the state.

The first trip is unique—an exciting paddle through a true cypress swamp. For those who are intimidated by the prospect of getting lost in a watery "jungle," rest assured that the canoe trail is safe and well marked. There are poisonous snakes, certainly, but they're seldom seen, and all you need to do is exercise reasonable caution. Starting out at an excellent canoe landing, the trail winds through a clearing cut by the DNR through buttonbush and other thick wetland vegetation. The surface of the water is covered by light-green duckweed, as you paddle by one huge cypress tree after another, each with the characteristic

Canoeists visit a 1,000-year-old bald cypress on the swamp trail.

flared buttresses at its base. The trail is a wonderful place for bird-watching: great blue herons, black and turkey vultures, red-winged blackbirds, pileated woodpeckers, and various kinds of warblers are common. In the open part of the trail (the so-called Long Reach and Short Reach), bluegill and crappies are caught.

A big advantage of the trail is that it gives you the option of paddling in the traditional point-to-point fashion (i.e., starting out at one end and ending at the other, with a car-shuttle arrangement), or paddling out-and-back without a shuttle. The latter is the more convenient

way to go; putting in at the public access area, you can take your time exploring the swamp trail, going as far as you wish, then returning to your starting point.

Excellent public **camping** is available to the southwest at Horseshoe Lake Conservation Area (a scenic oxbow cutoff from the Mississippi River) and to the north at Ferne Clyffe State Park (which features many fantastic rock formations).

The **gradient** is negligible.

Water levels. Rock dams on the Cache River (upstream and downstream from the swamp trail) assure that there will always be sufficient water to paddle. The environs are most pleasant at low to medium levels. General water level information (low, medium, or high) may be obtained by calling the DNR office at the Cache River State Natural Area (Belknap, 618-634-9678) or the U.S. Fish and Wildlife Service at Cypress Creek National Wildlife Refuge (Ullin, 618-634-2231).

Put in at the gravel canoe landing at the public access area a mile south of Perks Road. (To reach Perks Road off Interstate 57, take the Ullin exit, turn east on Shawnee College Road, then go north on Long Reach Road; or turn onto Perks Road from Highway 37.) Toilets and parking are provided at the access area, which is also the trailhead for a 2.5-mile hiking trail through the swamp. At the landing, you paddle immediately into a cleared channel through cypress trees and thick buttonbush; at various places on the trail, the channel varies from 6 to 30 feet wide, and is always marked with signs or with yellow markings painted on trees above the high-water level. Occasional wildlife boxes are seen. After the initial leg to the south, the trail comes to a loop; turning right will take you northwest to a side channel where a huge, 1,000-year-old cypress tree is located.

Then, continuing around the upper leg of the loop, you eventually paddle west into the Short Reach, where the channel is deep and quite wide. Near the end of the Short Reach is a big island, marked by a craggy old cypress in the water. At this point you can go to the right and proceed northwest to the northern end of the island. Look carefully for a sign pointing to a very narrow trail through the brush, leading to the Eagle Pond Natural Area, which is owned by the Nature Conservancy. Here you'll find many old cypresses, some with huge root formations called "knees." A circuitous swamp-trail leads from the west end of Eagle Pond to the Long Reach of the Cache River, a broad channel leading to the Long Reach Road bridge south of Perks. A landing is available at the bridge. The return trip goes back up the Long Reach and Short Reach, then through the south trail of the swamp loop, and back to the canoe landing. The whole route as described is approximately 5 miles. You can vary the route in many ways, depending upon how far you want to go and how much time you have.

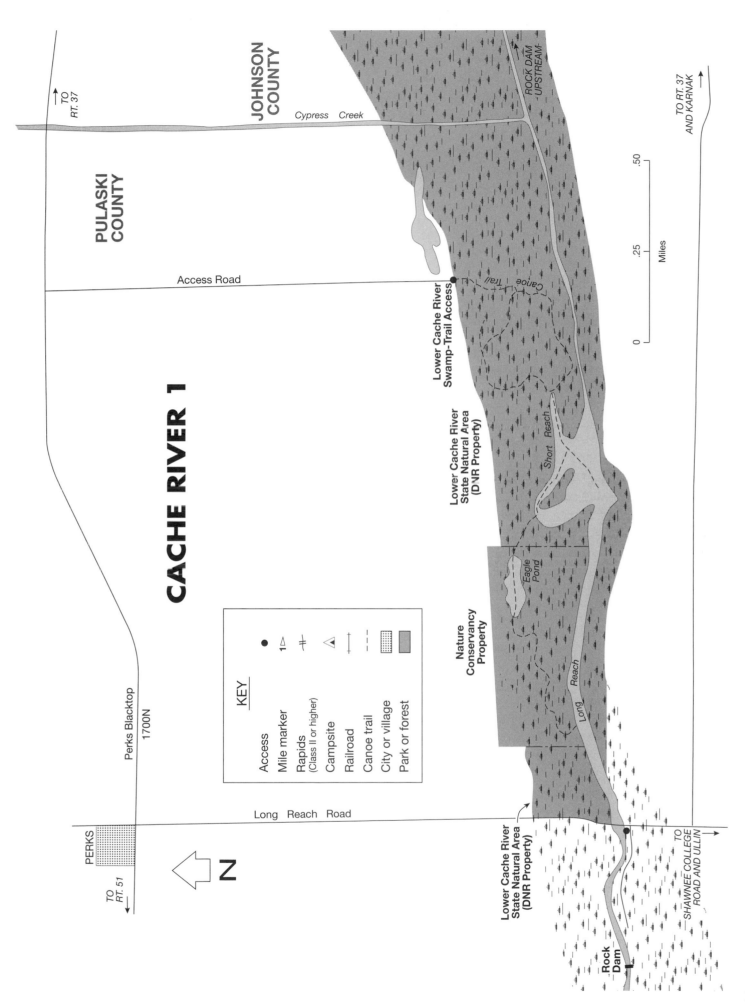

CACHE RIVER 1

JOHNSON COUNTY

PULASKI COUNTY

↑ TO
RT. 37

Cypress   Creek

Access Road

Lower Cache River
Swamp-Trail Access

Canoe Trail

Lower Cache River
State Natural Area
(DNR Property)

Short Reach

ROCK DAM
-UPSTREAM-

TO RT. 37
AND KARNAK
↑

0   .25   .50

Miles

Eagle
Pond

Nature
Conservancy
Property

Long Reach

KEY

Access   ●
Mile marker   1△
Rapids   ≠
(Class II or higher)
Campsite   ◁
Railroad   ┼┼
Canoe trail   – – –
City or village   ▦
Park or forest   ▨

Perks Blacktop
1700N

Long   Reach   Road

Lower Cache River
State Natural Area
(DNR Property)

TO
SHAWNEE COLLEGE
ROAD AND ULLIN
→

PERKS

TO
RT. 51
←

N

Rock
Dam

CACHE RIVER 2
Mississippi Cutoff to Highway 51 (5.8 Miles)

The second day trip on the Cache River takes you within a few miles of the old mouth of the river. In the early 1700s, one of the first Frenchmen who passed this way on the Ohio River observed that the mouth was almost closed off by brush. "Cette crique est caché," he said, meaning "This creek is hidden"—thus, the name. Today, its original mouth is indeed hidden because of a diversion channel constructed in 1950 to hasten the river's flow into the Mississippi River—another effort to reduce flooding in the Cache basin. Early in the 1900s, another diversion farther upstream (the Post Creek Cutoff) had sent most of the upper river into the Ohio, thus cutting the Cache in half. The trip described here gives you an opportunity to paddle the old river channel, thus seeing what the Cache River was like before man's handiwork. There is generally sufficient water for comfortable canoeing.

The river here is rather wide—between 70 and 200 feet—so deadfall is usually not a problem, although one spot can be difficult. The easy-to-follow, winding channel passes wooded banks, floodplain forest, and cultivated fields. Not as isolated or swampy as the Perks-area trip, this stretch is nevertheless quite peaceful, with lots of ducks, turkey buzzards, herons, beavers, muskrats, turtles, and other wildlife. Occasional stands of bald cypress, together with patches of duckweed on the surface, remind you that you're at the southern tip of Illinois. Accesses at both ends are comfortable and easy to get to, with good parking. The old channel is owned by the U.S. Fish and Wildlife Service, as part of the Cypress Creek National Wildlife Refuge project. Like the swamp route (Cache River 1), this section is home to poisonous snakes, so be cautious.

For nearby **camping,** see Cache River 1.

The **gradient** is less than 1 foot per mile, and **water levels** are generally sufficient for comfortable canoeing.

Shuttle route (5.4 miles). The easiest way to paddle this section is to put in at either end, go as far as you wish, and then return (current is usually almost nonexistent). If you don't want to cover the same stretch twice, the trip can easily be done in the traditional point-to-point fashion with a car shuttle. If you're paddling from the western end, drive down Levee Road from the public landing to Highway 3, then east on Levee Road to Golden Lily, and north on Highway 51. After you cross the river, an easy-to-miss gravel access road goes down to an upstream-left landing. Less than a mile to the north of the landing is the Mound City National Cemetery, which was established during the Civil War and still displays the gravestones of almost 5,000 casualties of that war, together with many who died in later conflicts. This part of the state was quite important for the Union cause during the Civil War: Cairo was a big troop-staging center, and Mound City was a naval base for the Union's river fleet.

Put in at either end, but the description here runs from west to east. There is an excellent gravel boat landing (with parking area) alongside the levee, near the location where the river has been diverted southwest into the Mississippi.

Fairly narrow at the beginning, the old channel winds around for awhile, widening to 100–150 feet. At the beginning of a right bend, a sizable creek enters on the left. At this point, deadfall tends to accumulate, and you may have difficulty squeezing through the floating trees and limbs. The creek is a good place for an exploratory side trip, but fallen trees usually keep you from getting very far.

After the creek mouth, plowed fields alternate with woods, and the river gets as wide as 250 feet at times as it heads through a series of bends and straightaways. After an impressive old, iron-trestle railroad bridge and several bends, the Interstate 57 bridges come into view. Shortly thereafter is Highway 51, where the channel flows through a huge, square concrete culvert.

Take out upstream-left at Highway 51, where there's a gravel landing and room to park several cars. Downstream from Highway 51, the old channel winds around to a levee where floodgates control inflow from (and outflow to) the Ohio River.

The Much-Tampered-With Cache River

From its headwaters near the small community of Cobden, the Cache River winds for 110 miles, draining most of the southernmost portion of the state. Since white settlers first entered the area in the early 1800s, the vast swamps and bottomland forests have been severely reduced and altered—first by logging, then by clearing, draining, channelization, dredging, and levee-building. Moreover, shortcut channels constructed in 1912–16 and 1950 divert the river to two new mouths on the Ohio and Mississippi Rivers. One result of such changes has been widespread bank erosion and logjams that make canoeing difficult if not impossible in many places, especially the section upstream from Karnak. Fortunately, major strides have been taken in recent years by the DNR, U.S. Fish and Wildlife Service, Nature Conservancy, and other organizations to preserve and restore thousands of acres along the river for recreation and ecosystem protection. The two day trips described here are among the beneficial results of this joint effort.

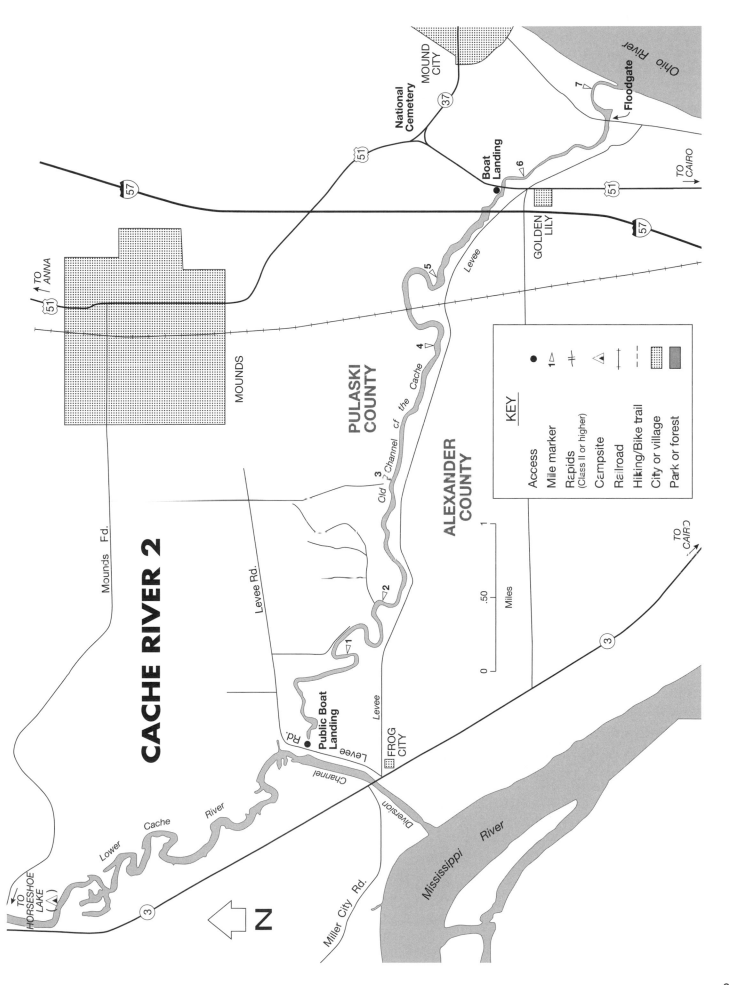

CACHE RIVER 2

CHICAGO RIVER–NORTH BRANCH
Willow Road Dam to Whelan Pool (9.9 Miles)

No river in Illinois is more historically significant or has undergone more dramatic changes than the Chicago River. From the late 1600s through the early 1800s, early fur traders and missionaries entered the mouth of the river from Lake Michigan, paddled up the South Fork, then portaged across wetlands to the Des Plaines River; from there they traveled down the Illinois River to the Mississippi River. In 1848, the Illinois and Michigan Canal linked the Chicago and Illinois rivers and provided impetus for the exponential growth of Chicago.

Today portions of the river are an excellent recreational resource in the midst of the hustle and bustle of Chicago. On the day trip described here (unofficially known as the Ralph Frese Trail in honor of the owner of Chicagoland Canoe Base, a long-time promoter of paddling), Cook County Forest Preserves and other green corridors often give you the impression that the city is far away. The river is narrow, winding, and intimate, and fallen trees sometimes block all or part of the channel; thus, maneuvering ability is required in order to get around limbs here and there. There are also three small dams to portage.

There are no nearby **campgrounds**, but many camping opportunities are available in the Greater Chicago area, including Chain O' Lakes State Park near Spring Grove, Illinois Beach State Park near Zion, and Channahon State Park, together with several private campgrounds such as Windy City Camping Resort near Tinley Park and Gages Lake Campground near Gurnee.

Canoe and kayak rentals are available at Chicagoland Canoe Base, 4019 N. Narragansett Avenue, Chicago, IL 60634 (773-777-1489). Rentals for other sections of the river are available at Chicago River Canoe & Kayak in Chicago and Skokie (773-704-2663 or 847-414-5883 or www.chicagoriverpaddle.com).

The **shuttle route** (9.8 miles) from the put-in goes a short distance south on Forest Way Drive to Willow Road, then west to Interstate 94; go south on I-94, west on Touhy Avenue, south on Caldwell Avenue, and west on Devon Avenue. Turn right at the sign into the Whelan Pool/Caldwell Woods Forest Preserve, and park near the back of the parking lot behind the swimming pool complex.

The **gradient** is a gentle 1.5 feet per mile.

For **water levels**, check the gauge at Niles (station #05536000) on the USGS Web site listed in the introduction.

Park alongside Forest Way Drive and carry your boat down a gravel path to the dam north of Willow Road. **Put in** at the concrete steps downstream-left. Initially you'll be paddling on the Skokie River until its confluence with the Middle Fork, where the North Branch begins. The river starts about 40 feet wide, with a mud, sand, and gravel bottom. Storm drain outflows soon begin appearing in the banks. Within view of the Winnetka Avenue bridge, the first dam has a drop of about a foot; portage past the concrete platform on either side.

After the dual bridges of Interstate 94, then the Happ Road bridge, there is a picturesque railroad trestle where deadfall often accumulates. Then, just before the mouth of the Middle Fork on the right, a biking/hiking trail bridge crosses the river. Downstream-left from the Lake Avenue bridge, in Blue Star Memorial Woods, is a grassy bank (near a parking area) that can be used as an access. After Lake Avenue, the river becomes even prettier, narrowing to only 20–25 feet and winding circuitously.

At Glenview Road, Harms Woods begins, noted for its profusion of lovely wildflowers in the spring. Downstream from Golf Road, the Chick Evans Golf Course lies on both sides, with two footbridges over the winding streambed, and many ancient oaks within view. In a sharp left bend, the West Fork enters on the right along a morainal ridge. Two more footbridges follow; under the second is another low dam, which can be portaged on the left. Shortly thereafter, you pass under the Beckwith Road bridge and enter Linne Woods. A large grated outflow on the left is near the Linne Woods Forest Preserve parking lot and can be used as an access.

After Dempster Street, much old-growth forest can be seen in St. Paul Woods and Miami Woods. Downstream from the Howard Street bridge, the environs become rather suburban in nature, with retaining walls and some buildings. As you come around a sharp right bend, alongside a brick building on the left, the third dam appears, with a drop of about 2 feet; portage on the right. The river now becomes canopied and twisty again in the last stretch. Finally, in a right bend, a biking/hiking trail bridge crosses overhead. The easy-to-miss **take-out** (a small, open patch on the mud bank) is about 100 yards downstream from this bridge on the right, where the river begins turning sharply to the left. A short path leads up to the nearby parking lot near Whelan Pool.

Other trips. Upstream from the Willow Street dam, the Skokie Lagoons provide an opportunity to observe wildlife on the small, interconnecting lakes that were once part of a huge, postglacial wetland. For brief descriptions of several other trips, see the Friends of the Chicago River Web site at <www.chicagoriver.org/>; or David M. Solzman's *The Chicago River: An Illustrated History and Guide to the River and Its Waterways* (Chicago: Loyola Press, 1998); or www.openlands.org/watertrails.asp.

One of the small dams on the North Branch

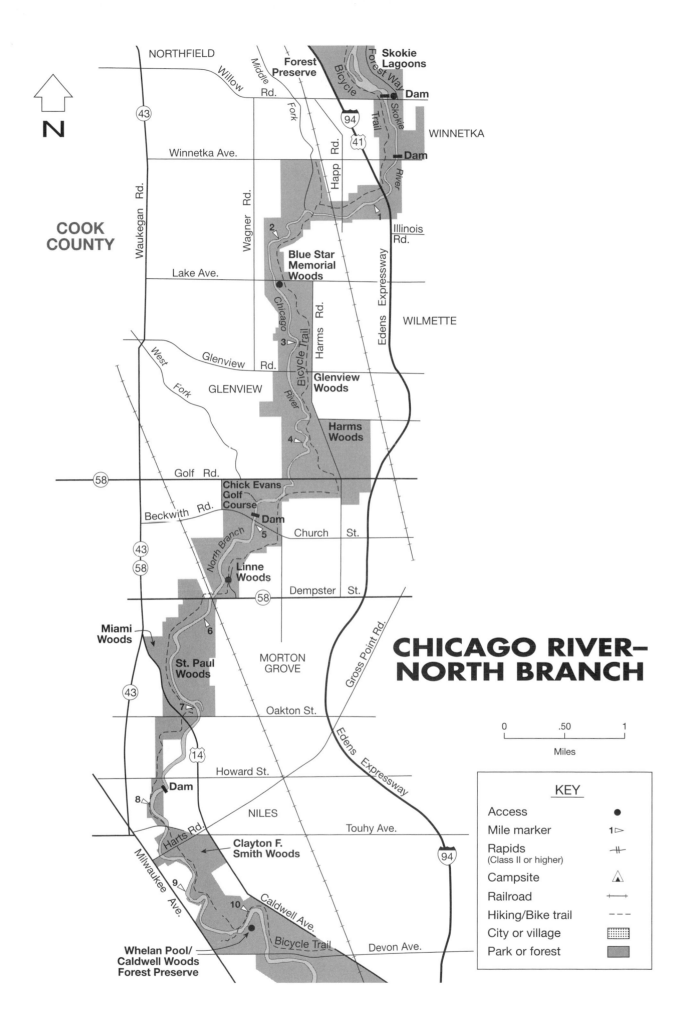

CHICAGO RIVER– NORTH BRANCH

NORTHFIELD

COOK COUNTY

WINNETKA

WILMETTE

GLENVIEW

MORTON GROVE

NILES

Forest Preserve

Skokie Lagoons

Blue Star Memorial Woods

Glenview Woods

Harms Woods

Chick Evans Golf Course

Linne Woods

Miami Woods

St. Paul Woods

Clayton F. Smith Woods

Whelan Pool/ Caldwell Woods Forest Preserve

Willow Rd.

Winnetka Ave.

Lake Ave.

Glenview Rd.

Golf Rd.

Beckwith Rd.

Church St.

Dempster St.

Oakton St.

Howard St.

Touhy Ave.

Devon Ave.

Waukegan Rd.

Wagner Rd.

Happ Rd.

Harms Rd.

West Fork

North Branch

Chicago River

Middle Fork

Skokie River

Gross Point Rd.

Edens Expressway

Milwaukee Ave.

Harts Rd.

Caldwell Ave.

Bicycle Trail

Forest Way Bicycle Trail

Skokie Trail

Illinois Rd.

Dam

Dam

Dam

Dam

Dam

43

58

43

58

43

58

14

94

41

94

KEY

Access	●
Mile marker	1▷
Rapids (Class II or higher)	―#―
Campsite	▲
Railroad	―+―
Hiking/Bike trail	- - -
City or village	▦
Park or forest	▨

0   .50   1
Miles

N

DES PLAINES RIVER 1
Russell Road to Wadsworth Road (6.8 Miles)

From Wilds to Towns

"Take a canoe trip down the upper Des Plaines River from just north of the Wisconsin border south to the Cook County town of Lyons, and you can see the history of urbanization in Illinois laid out like a diorama. As the river moves through parts of Lake, Cook, and Du Page Counties, farms give way first to bedroom suburbs, then to 1990s-style 'edge cities.' Along the crowded southern part of the upper Des Plaines, 'urban uses'—airport terminals to Toys 'R' Us—are ten times more concentrated than in Illinois as a whole and cover as much as 70 percent of the land.

No other natural Illinois river runs through such an urbanized watershed; no other urban river still has so much nature left in and around it. The upper Des Plaines basin thus is uniquely situated to find answers to a new question about an old dilemma: If nature cannot be restored to its old place in Illinois' natural order, can it at least be admitted to a place in the new human one?" (James Krohe Jr., *The Upper Des Plaines River Basin: An Inventory of the Region's Resources*. Springfield: Illinois DNR, 1998).

Thanks to the efforts of the Lake County Forest Preserve District, the northernmost portion of the Des Plaines River in Illinois flows through a natural, undeveloped environment that is one of the state's most pleasant canoeing locales. Since its formation in 1958, the district has acquired 7,000 acres along the river, creating an almost continuous greenway of floodplain forests and wetlands and thus protecting over 80 percent of the land along the river in Lake County for wildlife habitat, recreation, and nature preservation. A major factor in the comeback of the once-heavily polluted river, the greenway also helps control flooding and teems with wildlife—especially marsh-loving birds. Anglers say the fish population includes northern pike and largemouth bass.

From the beginning, the river is extremely peaceful and isolated, especially the section upstream from Highway 173. Aside from an infrequent peek at the bike trail, there is no sign of civilization most of the time. Because of the narrow streambed, wooded banks, and numerous turns, there are occasional obstructions that must be maneuvered around or through, but total blockages are uncommon. Open wetlands can often be seen behind the tree line and the low banks. At one point, the river comes close to Sterling Lake, a former quarry converted by the forest preserve district to a beautiful recreational area.

Camping. Except for a youth campground north of the put-in, there is no camping in the forest preserves. The closest public campgrounds are at Illinois Beach near Zion (to the east), and Chain of Lakes State Park near Spring Grove (to the west). Private camping, at Gages Lake Campground, is located to the south.

Canoe rentals are available at Offshore in Vernon Hills (847-362-4880) and at Chicagoland Canoe Base in Chicago (773-777-1489).

The **shuttle route** (5.5 miles) heads east on Russell Road, then south on Kilbourne Road and west on Wadsworth Road.

The **gradient** is negligible.

For **water levels**, check the gauge at Russell (station #05527800) on the USGS Web site listed in the introduction.

Put in at the forest preserve canoe landing, downstream-left from the Russell Road bridge. The river begins fairly wide in a big right bend, then narrows. This section seldom exceeds 50 feet in width, and gets as tight as 25 feet. Lily pads and arrowhead plants begin appearing soon, with considerable willow and other marshland vegetation. Small grassy islands split the river occasionally. The river bends back and forth in a lowland environment, generally with marsh grass on both sides, and overhanging trees often canopy the water. As you might expect, beaver lodges are not uncommon, and you're likely to see great blue herons, egrets, red-winged blackbirds, muskrats, and turtles as well. Sometimes the trees retreat from the river for awhile, creating an open area.

In the approach to the Highway 173 bridge, you pass under two bridges—first a wooden one for the biking/hiking path, then an attractive vehicular bridge within Van Patten Woods Forest Preserve. The river is at its widest in the area of the bridges. A straight stretch follows Highway 173. In a left bend, a big house can be seen on the right bank—the only one of the whole trip. Except for one clay cutbank (about 8 feet high), the banks are mostly low and marshy, and you can see some good examples of oak savanna (prairie with scattered trees). The river continues to twist back and forth, sometimes quite sharply.

Eventually, you can see Highway 41 on river-right for a short time. The last part of the trip includes a couple of relatively straight stretches, but it remains marsh-like and natural to the end. Finally, the river bends to the left alongside Wadsworth Road, then makes an abrupt right turn to the bridge. **Take out** downstream-left at the canoe landing.

Other trips. Some paddlers put in farther upstream in Wisconsin, at Highway 165 or Highway C; neither is a designated access, and the latter is difficult (narrow shoulders and no room to park). This part of the river is quite attractive but is even smaller than Des Plaines River 1 and more prone to deadfall.

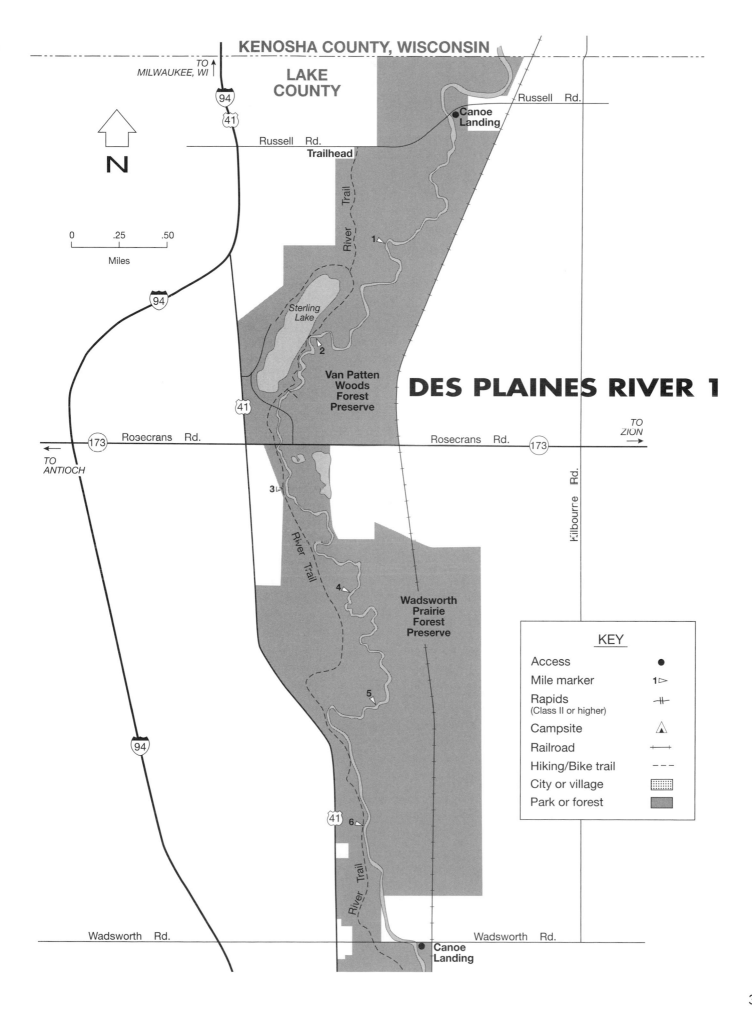

DES PLAINES RIVER 1

KENOSHA COUNTY, WISCONSIN

LAKE COUNTY

TO MILWAUKEE, WI

94
41

N

0   .25   .50
Miles

94

Russell   Rd.

Canoe Landing

Russell   Rd.
Trailhead

River   Trail

1

Sterling Lake

2

41

Van Patten Woods Forest Preserve

173   Rosecrans   Rd.

TO ANTIOCH

Rosecrans   Rd.   173

TO ZION

Kilbourne   Rd.

3

River   Trail

4

Wadsworth Prairie Forest Preserve

5

94

41   6

River   Trail

Wadsworth   Rd.

Wadsworth   Rd.

Canoe Landing

KEY

Access	●
Mile marker	1▷
Rapids (Class II or higher)	—╫—
Campsite	▲
Railroad	—┼—
Hiking/Bike trail	- - -
City or village	▦
Park or forest	▒

DES PLAINES RIVER 2
Wadsworth Road to Oak Spring Road (13.8 Miles)

The River of Maples

Since the early days of French exploration, maps have designated the river by a variety of names, including the Maple River and the *Au Plaine*. Apparently, the current name is derived from the French *eau pleine*, meaning "full of water" in reference to the sap-filled maples that grew plentifully along the banks. This is consistent with the Potawatomi name, which means "river of the tree that flows." To this day, maple trees remain abundant along the river, together with many other species—especially those that thrive in the floodplain environment prevailing along the upper Des Plaines River.

Originating in Wisconsin west of Racine, the Des Plaines River flows through a large Illinois watershed of 855,000 square miles, the majority of which has been developed for urban, agricultural, and industrial use. In the 1900s, urban runoff, industrial waste, and the destruction of wetlands made the river less than clean and more subject to flooding. In recent years, however, efforts by forest preserve districts, sewerage districts, and others have improved the situation considerably. While there is still a long way to go before the Des Plaines River's problems are solved, it has nevertheless improved immensely in water quality, recreational use, fish population, and other measures of river vitality.

Woods fill most of the shoreline on the second recommended day trip, and there is very little development. There are some houses here and there, several bridges, and overhead power lines, but the overwhelming impression is one of wildness. Most of the river here flows through forest preserves, with frequent glimpses of wetlands. The banks are usually rather low and muddy, and good stopping places are infrequent. This section tends to be broader than the upstream stretch, getting as wide as 80 feet, but most of it is still fairly narrow and winding. Downed trees are not uncommon; you can usually paddle around them, but a carry-around is sometimes necessary. First-rate landings are available at the beginning and end of the trip, and other accesses along the way make it easy to vary trip length.

For **camping,** see the description of Des Plaines River 1. Additional private campgrounds are located near Volo (Fish Lake Beach Camping Resort) and west of Wauconda (Fox Valley Campground).

For **canoe rentals,** see Des Plaines River 1.

The **shuttle route** (12.9 miles) from the put-in goes west on Wadsworth Road, south on Highway 41, south on Highway 21, east on Highway 137, south on St. Mary's Road, and west on Oak Spring Road. Shoppers and youngsters in your entourage also will be interested to know that the shuttle route passes near the Gurnee Mills shopping mall and Six Flags Great America theme park.

The **gradient** is negligible (less than a foot per mile).

For **water levels,** check the gauge at Gurnee (station #05528000) on the USGS Web site listed in the introduction.

Put in at the Lake County Forest Preserve landing at Wadsworth Road, downstream-left. The river starts rather wide and marshy, with maple and willow trees, cattails, and other wetland vegetation. From the beginning, wildlife is frequent, including geese, ducks, egrets, and herons. A bike trail runs along the left shore. Before long, the river narrows, quickens, flows under a biking/hiking trail bridge, and passes wetland restoration projects on both sides. A couple of times, Highway 41 can be seen off to the right. For awhile, the river flows attractively through woods and relatively open lowland, then goes through a dense floodplain forest, narrowing at times to 40 feet. A house, some power lines, and bankside railroad tracks serve as momentary reminders of civilization. After another house, the Highway 41 bridge appears, followed by many homes and grassy lawns on the right shore.

After the Grand Avenue bridge (Highway 132), dense woods begin again. On river-left, there's a canoe landing at Gowe Memorial park (Gurnee Park District). No more houses are found all the way to Washington Street, where there's an adequate access downstream-left. Then, after the Interstate 94 bridge, the river widens a little, and high banks appear on the left for the first time. The river environs are quite lovely here. Bending right, the river flows alongside Belvidere Road, where there's another unofficial landing downstream-left from the bridge.

At Day Break Farm Road, the two bridges are quite low, especially the second, and can be **quite hazardous** when the water is too high to allow clearance; be ready to portage if necessary. Downstream, the river widens again and passes through a lowland before higher banks reappear. Occasional fallen trees continue to require maneuvering. Upstream from Buckley Road, on river-left, the Independence Grove Forest Preserve canoe landing appears.

A steel retaining wall appears on the left in a sharp right turn, and houses begin appearing on the left, leading to the Oak Spring Road bridge. **Take out** downstream-right at the excellent canoe landing, with good parking nearby.

Other trips. For descriptions of several other sections, see www.openlands.org/watertrails.asp.

Mom's day out on the Des Plaines

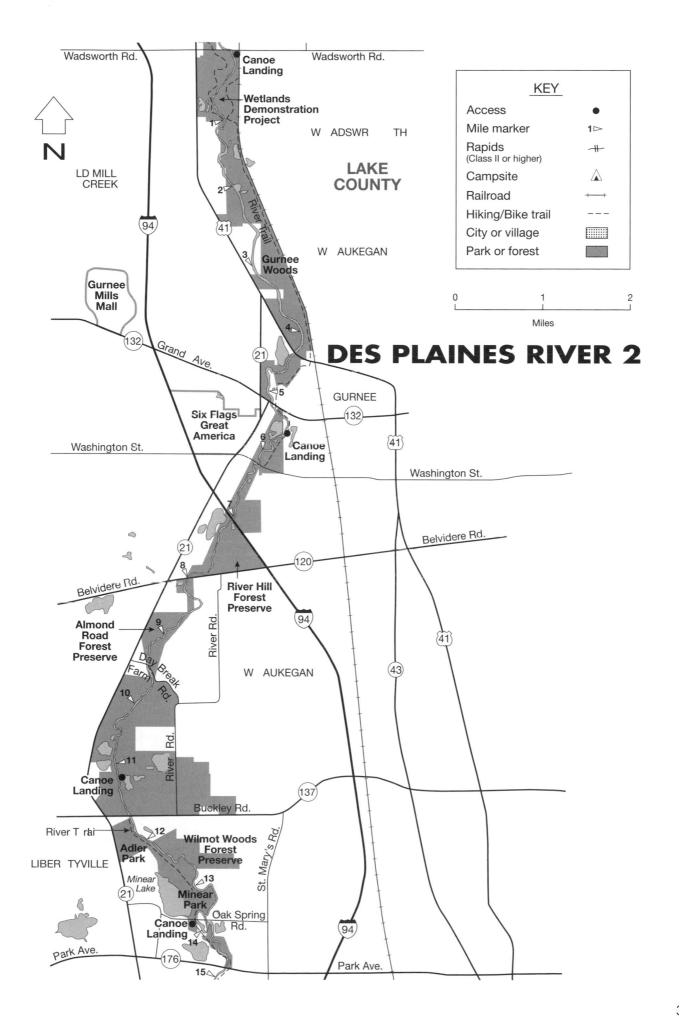

DES PLAINES RIVER 2

KEY

Access	●
Mile marker	1▷
Rapids (Class II or higher)	╫
Campsite	▲
Railroad	┼┼┼┼
Hiking/Bike trail	- - -
City or village	▦
Park or forest	▨

0   1   2
Miles

Wadsworth Rd.   Wadsworth Rd.

Canoe Landing

Wetlands Demonstration Project

W ADSWR TH

LAKE COUNTY

LD MILL CREEK

94

River Trail

41

W AUKEGAN

Gurnee Mills Mall

132

Grand Ave.

3

Gurnee Woods

4

21

GURNEE

5

132

41

Six Flags Great America

Washington St.

6

Canoe Landing

Washington St.

7

21

Belvidere Rd.

120

8

Belvidere Rd.

River Hill Forest Preserve

94

Almond Road Forest Preserve

9

River Rd.

Day Break Farm Rd.

W AUKEGAN

43

41

10

River Rd.

11

Canoe Landing

137

Buckley Rd.

St. Mary's Rd.

River Trail

12

Wilmot Woods Forest Preserve

Adler Park

LIBER TYVILLE

Minear Lake

21

13

Minear Park

Oak Spring Rd.

94

Canoe Landing

14

Park Ave.

176

15

Park Ave.

DES PLAINES RIVER 3
Willow Springs to Isle a la Cache (12 Miles)

After winding southward from Wisconsin to the Lyons area and flowing over its next-to-last dam, the Des Plaines River bends alongside the Illinois and Michigan and Chicago Sanitary and Ship Canals and heads southwestward through an ancient glacial outwash valley. In the days of canal building, much of the river in this stretch was channelized in order to accommodate the three parallel bodies of water; thus, the lower river exhibits little of the intimate, small-stream character of the upper portion. Nevertheless, the lower river is not without charms for the canoeist.

First, of course, is the marvelous history of the river—traveled for centuries by Native Americans, then voyageurs, as a major thoroughfare in the network of canoe routes in the Great Lakes region. Another plus is the surprisingly wild environment along much of the lower river, thanks to the large tracts of forest preserves. And finally, this third recommended trip on the Des Plaines River begins and ends with excellent accesses. The takeout at Isle a la Cache is especially memorable, with a splendid museum where you can learn more about the lives of early Native Americans, the routes of the fur traders, and other aspects of river history.

Public **camping** is available to the south at Channahon State Park and the Des Plaines Conservation Area. Private camping is located approximately 18 miles south of the put-in at Windy City Camping Resort (private) near Tinley Park.

Canoes may be rented at Chicagoland Canoe Base in Chicago (773-777-1489) and at Offshore Marine in Vernon Hills (847-362-4880).

The **shuttle route** (approximately 14 miles) from Columbia Woods Forest Preserve goes south across the river on Willow Springs Road, west on Highway 171, and west on 135th Street (Romeoville Road) to the Isle a la Cache Museum parking lot.

The **gradient** is negligible (less than a foot per mile).

For **water levels**, check the upstream gauge at Riverside (station #05532500) on the USGS Web site listed in the introduction.

Put in at the Columbia Woods Forest Preserve canoe landing, downstream-right from the Willow Springs Road bridge. (As soon as you cross the bridge going north, take the first road to the west into the forest preserve.) The river begins about 80 feet wide, with a big, gentle bend to the right, but soon widens to about 100 feet and straightens out. Early in the trip, wildlife becomes apparent, especially herons, egrets, hawks, and songbirds of many kinds. For a while, the scene is quite isolated, with few signs of civilization. Several bends and a couple of small islands put you within sight of the Highway 83 bridge, where there's an excellent public boat landing upstream-right (near the end of Madison Street south of Burr Ridge).

A low limestone shelf appears just upstream-right from the bridge, but—unfortunately—an auto junkyard along the right shoreline is a terrible eyesore. Finally, the wild, forested environment resumes. A long straightaway is interrupted only by a slight right turn, and eventually the next bridge can be seen in the distance. Trees on the right give way to a long marshy area, then a huge lagoon that lies immediately to the south of the Argonne National Laboratory (a famous energy research institution). As you approach the three bridges at Lemont, where there's a low shelf of stratified limestone, the shoreline becomes less wild. Be careful at the railroad bridge, where deadfall tends to get caught in the five old piers. The next bridge is at Lemont Road, and the third is at a frontage road that leads to Des Plaines River Road. Immediately after the third bridge is an undeveloped gravel landing, downstream-left.

The river now becomes quite wild-looking again, with low floodplain banks (often marshy) on one side and higher forested banks on the other. Eventually, a very long, gentle left bend begins and the river widens to 200 feet. After briefly narrowing, the river widens even more into a long, often windy lake, with the towers of a refinery visible in the distance. Finally the river narrows to about 100 feet, then widens again in the approach to Isle a la Cache, a huge island with an identifying sign on its upstream end. Take the attractive right channel around the island, paddle under the 135th Street bridge, and **take out** at the gravel landing near the museum parking lot.

Other trips. (1) A canoe landing upstream at Stony Ford (off Joliet Road, just west of Highway 43 in Lyons) makes it possible to paddle 7.5 miles to Columbia Woods. (2) The stretch after Isle a la Cache includes many islands and (downstream from Highway 7) the Fishnet Rapids. Before the river joins the Chicago Sanitary and Ship Canal south of Lockport, the gradient steepens considerably (12.2 feet per mile between Isle a la Cache and Lockport), with riffles, waves (sometimes quite large), and Class I rapids as it flows through a fishnet pattern of islands. Take out in the Lockport Prairie Forest Preserve at the Division Street bridge (river-right), or 1.5 miles upstream at the Highway 7 bridge (downstream-right). After Lockport the river is more urban and is dammed again at Rockdale, near Joliet.

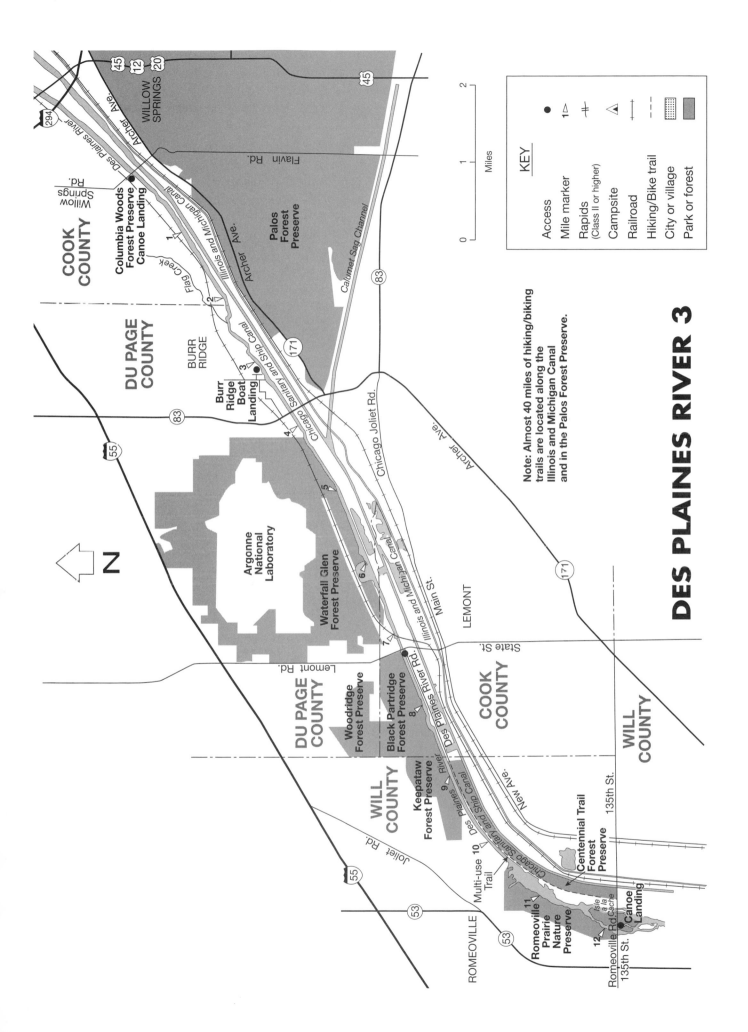

DES PLAINES RIVER 3

KEY

●	Access
△ 1	Mile marker
╫	Rapids (Class II or higher)
◁	Campsite
┼	Railroad
- - -	Hiking/Bike trail
▦	City or village
▨	Park or forest

0   1   2
Miles

Note: Almost 40 miles of hiking/biking trails are located along the Illinois and Michigan Canal and in the Palos Forest Preserve.

N

COOK COUNTY

WILLOW SPRINGS

DU PAGE COUNTY

BURR RIDGE

Palos Forest Preserve

Argonne National Laboratory

Waterfall Glen Forest Preserve

Columbia Woods Forest Preserve Canoe Landing

Burr Ridge Boat Landing

Woodridge Forest Preserve

Black Partridge Forest Preserve

LEMONT

WILL COUNTY

Keepataw Forest Preserve

Romeoville Prairie Nature Preserve

Centennial Trail Forest Preserve

Canoe Landing

ROMEOVILLE

Multi-use Trail

Isle a la Cache

DU PAGE RIVER 1
St. Charles Road to Mack Road (8 Miles)

A Smashing Experience

Located immediately to the west of this first section of the Du Page River is one of the top scientific installations in the world—the Fermi National Accelerator Laboratory. Teams of physicists from all over the world come to this renowned facility to conduct experiments that probe the fundamental nature of matter and energy. Many subatomic particles have been discovered here, repeatedly forcing scientists to revise their theories. Much of the 6,800-acre site is occupied by a huge subterranean ring where magnets accelerate protons and hurl them at target material, smashing it into pieces that often yield new discoveries. Fermilab is named after Dr. Enrico Fermi, whose scientific team created the world's first self-sustaining atomic chain reaction in 1942 at the University of Chicago.

In addition to touring this cutting-edge nuclear research facility, you can also hike or bike a 4-mile paved trail, view a bison herd, or visit a tallgrass prairie. To get there, take Batavia Road west.

Although it flows through several of Chicago's western suburbs, the West Branch of the Du Page River has the feel of a rural stream. Small and intimate, it winds delightfully through forest preserves in an often tree-canopied setting. The Du Page County Forest Preserve District does a good job of removing trees and limbs that fall into the river, but you may have to maneuver or carry around a recently fallen blockage here and there. Banks are generally 3 to 4 feet high and grassy, and the river bottom is a mix of sand, gravel, and mud. Waterfowl, birds, deer, muskrat, and other wildlife are often encountered. Named after a French trader who once operated in the area, the river at one point passes the site of ancient burial mounds. The trip recommended here has an excellent landing at the end, together with a pleasant intermediate access that allows paddlers to stop for lunch or to vary trip length.

Public **camping** is available at Blackwell Forest Preserve near the take-out. For other campgrounds farther south, see the description of Du Page River 2. Several campgrounds also are located to the southwest near the Fox River (see Fox River 1 and 2).

Canoe rentals are available at Chicagoland Canoe Base in Chicago (773-777-1489); the Canoe Shack in St. Charles (630-584-8017); and at the Du Page County Forest District (630-933-7248).

The **shuttle route** from the put-in goes west on St. Charles Road, south (briefly) on Prince Crossing Road, northwest on North Avenue, south on Highway 59, and east on Mack Road.

The **gradient** is almost 5 feet per mile.

For **water levels**, check the West Chicago gauge (station #05539900) on the USGS Web site listed in the introduction.

Put in at the St. Charles Road bridge, downstream-right. The river is quite narrow here—only about 15–20 feet—and stays narrow throughout the trip, sometimes widening to 40 feet. Shortly after the put-in, the North Avenue bridge appears, with old piers immediately preceding it. Farther downstream are a couple of biking/hiking trail bridges. A few houses can be seen on the right, high up on a bluff. Surprisingly, you notice little

vehicular noise as the river passes through a heavily wooded floodplain.

Approaching Geneva Road, the river widens, and Kline Creek enters on the left just before the bridge. Another biking/hiking trail bridge follows. At this point, the dome-shaped Winfield Mounds are located on the right (built by Late Woodland Native Americans between A.D. 600 and 1,000), and Winfield Road runs fairly close to the river on the left. For some time, the imposing buildings of Central Du Page Hospital can be seen from river level. Eventually, you pass the city of Winfield on the left, the first obviously urban setting of the trip. Condominiums and a grassy lawn appear on the right just before the High Lake Road bridge, where the river is rather wide. Just downstream from the railroad bridge is Riverside Park, which has a convenient canoe landing. This is a wonderful spot to stop for relaxation and lunch.

The river now winds around a great deal and more houses appear before Roosevelt Road (Highway 38). After the bridge, Highway 59 is close by on the right and traffic occasionally can be seen. Gary's Mill Road (the next bridge) is named after Erastus Gary, an early settler who operated a grist mill just east of the river where Blackwell Forest Preserve is now located. Gary later helped found the city of Gary, Indiana, and the U.S. Steel Company. Finally, a pleasant paddle through the forest preserve takes you to an excellent landing at the Mack Road bridge, with plenty of parking. **Take out** downstream-left.

Other trips. For descriptions of several other sections, see www.openlands.org/watertrails.asp

Maneuvering through limbs on the West Fork of the Du Page

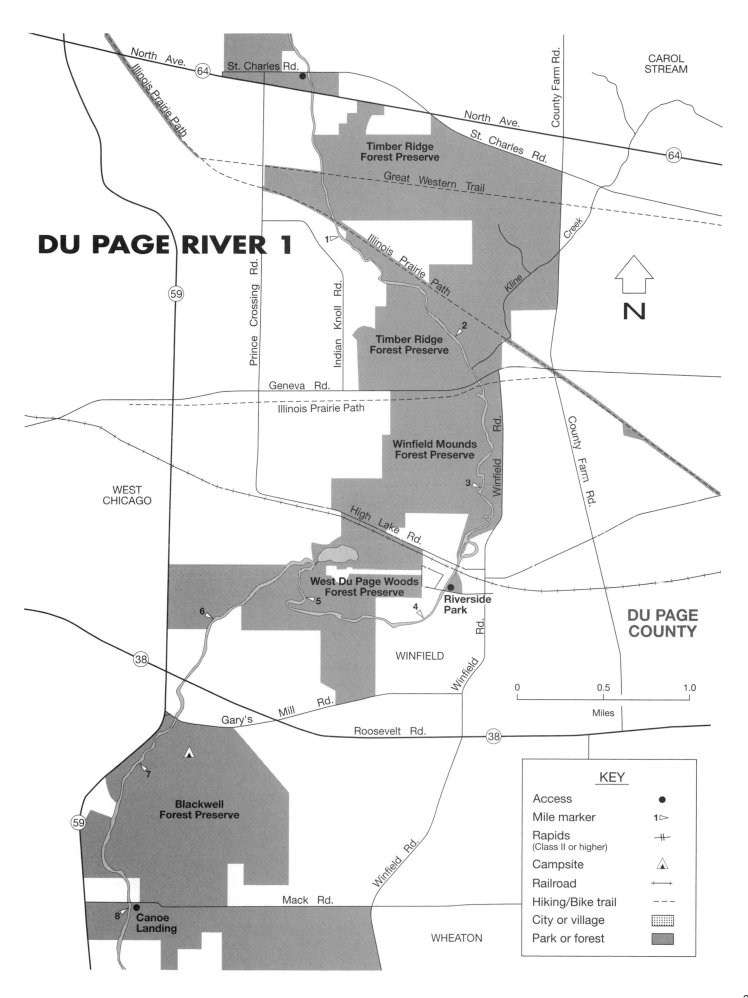

DU PAGE RIVER 1

CAROL STREAM

North Ave.

St. Charles Rd.

North Ave.

St. Charles Rd.

County Farm Rd.

Timber Ridge
Forest Preserve

Great Western Trail

Illinois Prairie Path

Kline Creek

N

Timber Ridge
Forest Preserve

Prince Crossing Rd.

Indian Knoll Rd.

Geneva Rd.

Illinois Prairie Path

Winfield Mounds
Forest Preserve

Winfield Rd.

County Farm Rd.

WEST
CHICAGO

High Lake Rd.

West Du Page Woods
Forest Preserve

Riverside
Park

DU PAGE
COUNTY

WINFIELD

Winfield Rd.

| 0 | 0.5 | 1.0 |

Miles

Gary's Mill Rd.

Roosevelt Rd.

Blackwell
Forest Preserve

Winfield Rd.

Mack Rd.

Canoe
Landing

WHEATON

KEY

Access	●
Mile marker	1▷
Rapids (Class II or higher)	—#—
Campsite	⛺
Railroad	—+—
Hiking/Bike trail	— — —
City or village	▦
Park or forest	▓

DU PAGE RIVER 2
Hammel Woods to Channahon (9.5 miles)

Before flowing into the Des Plaines River near Channahon, the final section of the Du Page provides considerable variety for canoeists. Generally wooded, it is occasionally urban in nature, with many homes along the way. The banks are usually fairly low, and the last part of the trip is through a marshy area. Rock outcroppings line the river's edge here and there. Until the end, the river isn't very wide, averaging 90 feet, but is wide enough to make deadfall blockages unlikely. Exciting riffles enliven the trip, especially between Interstate 80 and Shepley Road. Accesses are good at both ends of the trip, although paddlers must be cautious in taking out at the Channahon dam. With its greater width and numerous houses, this section is quite unlike the first recommended stretch on the Du Page, but is enjoyable nevertheless. Fishermen catch bass, crappie, bluegill, catfish, and bullheads.

Public **camping** is available near the put-in at Hammel Woods Forest Preserve, near the take-out at Channahon State Park, and south of Channahon at McKinley Woods Forest Preserve. Hammel Woods and McKinley Woods are part of the Will County Forest Preserve District.

Canoe rentals are available at Chicagoland Canoe Base in Chicago (773-777-1489).

The **shuttle route** (9.2 miles) from Hammel Woods Forest Preserve goes south on Brook Forest Avenue, east on Highway 52, south on Interstate 55, west on Highway 6, and south on Canal Street to the Channahon State Park.

The **gradient** is 5.3 feet per mile.

For **water levels,** check the Shorewood gauge (station #05540500) on the USGS Web site listed in the introduction.

Put in at the landing downstream-right from the dam in Hammel Woods Forest Preserve. Enter the forest preserve from Brook Forest Avenue in Shorewood, and follow the signs back to Grinton Grove. Carry boats from the parking area down a path and across a footbridge to the landing.

Immediately after putting in, you pass under two bridges, and houses line both sides for awhile. Then, about 400 yards downstream from a graceful metal footbridge arcing over the river, there's a low concrete dam (several inches high) that can be run through the slots cut into the concrete. The river here is over 100 feet wide and rather shallow. Houses continue as the river bends left, then right; in the right turn, a straight line of boulders runs across the river (runnable on the right side). Limestone shelves appear on the left as the County Farm Road bridge approaches.

A park at the bridge is a good place to stretch your legs. A huge island follows, and River Road pulls close to the river on the right. Houses continue to be numerous. A straightaway leads to the Mound Road bridge, and the river then curves toward the Interstate 80 bridges. More homes follow.

In a very pretty part of the river, limestone shelves appear again throughout a left curve. The river quickens, bends right, then continues narrow and riffly all the way to a railroad bridge where there are some rocks and good waves. Excellent riffles (big waves at higher water levels) are continuous for awhile after the bridge, and another attractive limestone shelf runs along the left shoreline to the Shepley Road bridge, where there's a good access downstream-right. Some cabins and trailers follow, together with a dirt-and-gravel landing on the right, alongside Minooka Road.

The river now goes into a secluded lowland setting where the trees are no longer close to the water. After a series of large islands and a private sportsmen's club on the right, grassy wooded banks appear again on both sides. The river is deeper and the current slacker. After a long, isolated stretch, houses appear again and continue all the way to the Channahon Road bridge and beyond. Finally, after a left turn that begins the southeastward approach toward Channahon, the river environs become quite wild; marsh grasses are plentiful on both sides all the way to the end. The Highway 6 bridge is a good place for an alternate **take-out,** with easy access downstream-right; a wide area along the shoulder accommodates several cars.

As you approach the dam, **stay to the left** and **take out** near the old Illinois and Michigan Canal Lock 6. Be **very careful** not to get caught in the current and swept over the dangerous spillway. From the take-out, carry boats up the bank to the nearby park, where there's a large parking lot. Be sure to take the time to visit the historic lock and adjacent lock tender's house. The mouth of the river is only a mile downstream from the dam.

Meeting of the Waters

Once called Snifton, the community at the confluence of the Du Page and Des Plaines Rivers was renamed Channahon (the Native American word for "meeting of the waters"). In 1848 a third waterway was added to the combination when the I&M Canal was completed. The canal-builders' problem of getting across the Du Page was solved by damming the river and constructing two locks where barges could exit the canal, float across the river impoundment, then reenter the canal. You can still see the scenic old lock tender's house alongside Lock 6, near Channahon State Park. About 100 feet upstream-right from the dam is a small, gated diversion structure that sends water from the Du Page into the canal.

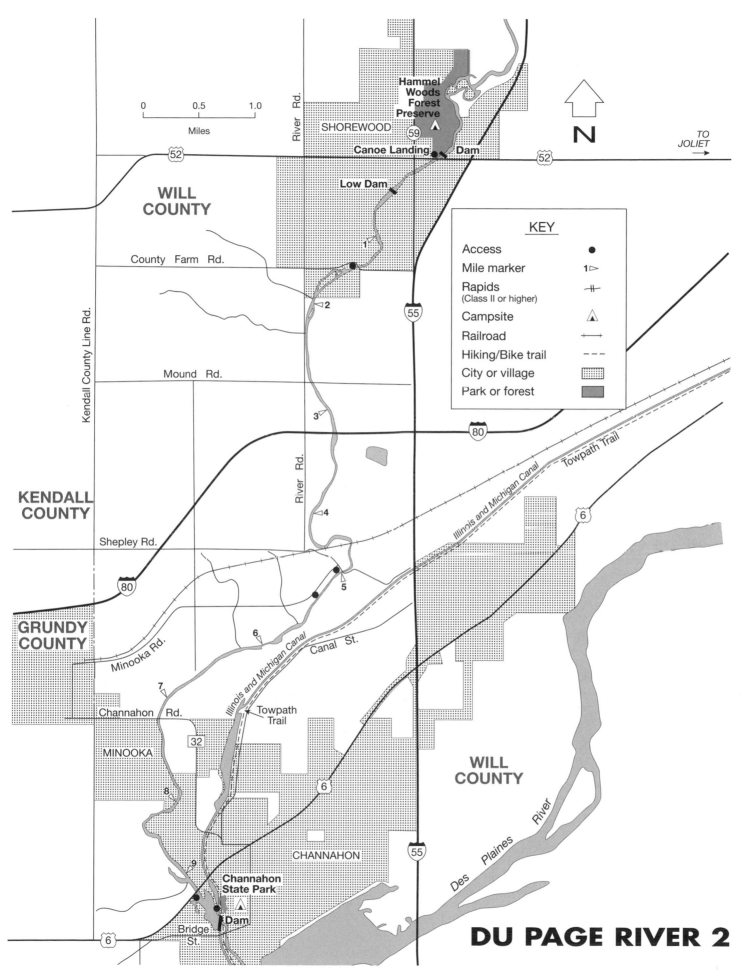

KEY

Access	●
Mile marker	1▷
Rapids (Class II or higher)	╫
Campsite	⚠
Railroad	┼─┼
Hiking/Bike trail	- - -
City or village	▒
Park or forest	▓

Hammel Woods Forest Preserve

SHOREWOOD

Canoe Landing   Dam

Low Dam

WILL COUNTY

County Farm Rd.

River Rd.

Mound Rd.

KENDALL COUNTY

Shepley Rd.

River Rd.

Illinois and Michigan Canal   Towpath Trail

GRUNDY COUNTY

Minooka Rd.

Illinois and Michigan Canal   Canal St.

Channahon Rd.

Towpath Trail

MINOOKA

WILL COUNTY

CHANNAHON

Channahon State Park

Dam

Bridge St.

Des Plaines River

Kendall County Line Rd.

N

TO JOLIET

DU PAGE RIVER 2

EMBARRAS RIVER 1
Lake Charleston to Fox Ridge State Park (8.8 Miles)

Lincoln Attractions

Just a few miles from Fox Ridge State Park is a special historic site that's worth an hour of your time during your visit to the Embarras. On the eighty-six acres of the Lincoln Log Cabin site, the last home of Abraham Lincoln's father and stepmother is preserved. After a horrible winter in the Lincoln family's first Illinois cabin near Decatur (1830–31), Abraham struck out on his own and lived in New Salem for several years. His parents, however, moved to Coles County, eventually settling at this site near the Embarras in 1840. Both Thomas and Sarah Bush Lincoln died here. During the summer, costumed interpreters help re-create the 1840s atmosphere of the Lincoln farm. Several other historic buildings are located nearby.

The cabin is not the only Lincoln lore associated with the area. For example, Lincoln practiced law in Charleston as part of his circuit, debated Stephen Douglas there, and visited his parents at their farm.

The nearby city of Greenup is named after the man who supervised the construction of the portion of the National Highway (the Cumberland Trail) that runs from the Indiana border to Vandalia.

A long river, the Embarras (pronounced AM-braw) originates just south of Champaign-Urbana and flows southeastward for 174 miles through the mostly flat terrain of eastern Illinois before joining the Wabash River near Vincennes, Indiana. Most of its course is through thinly forested farmland, with little development anywhere and a pervasive feeling of isolation. From its source to Lake Charleston the river repeatedly earns its name—*embarras* means "obstruction" in French. After Charleston, however, it is usually 80–100 feet wide, and logjams are seldom a problem.

The streambed is sand and silt, and the banks are fairly steep, with occasional wooded bluffs and a few small rock outcroppings. The farther downstream you go, the more sand and sandbars you see. Between Charleston and Greenup, accesses are excellent, making a variety of trip lengths possible. Adding to the attractions of the 26.5-mile section below Charleston is the river's edge location of Fox Ridge State Park, a beautiful place to use as a base camp for a weekend of paddling on the Embarras.

Public **camping** at Fox Ridge State Park is located 8 miles south of Charleston, on the rugged hills of a glacial moraine. Among the features of Fox Ridge are deep, wooded ravines, challenging hiking, and two canoe landings on the Embarras. Another public campground is found north of Charleston at Walnut Point State Fish and Wildlife Area (also on the Embarras), together with a couple of private camprounds—Hebron Hills Camping and Springhaven. There also is a KOA campground near Casey.

The **shuttle route** for Embarras River 1 (6.5 miles) goes south on Highway 130 from the Lake Charleston dam to the signed entrance road at Fox Ridge State Park, then to the south canoe landing.

The **gradient** is gentle: only 1.5 feet per mile.

For **water levels,** check the gauges at Camargo (station #03343400) and Ste. Marie (#03345500) on the USGS Web site listed in the introduction.

Put in at the landing downstream-right from the dam, accessed by a short road off Highway 130 just south of Charleston. The river here is about 90 feet wide, and will be approximately this width for the whole trip. Soon after Highway 130, the river passes under a picturesque, old arched bridge, then bends to the right between thinly wooded, steep banks. Downstream, cultivated fields are often seen near the river, and the countryside is flat. Thus, if there's wind, you'll feel it. After a sizable island in a sharp left turn, some wooded bluffs appear on the left—the first of many between here and Greenup. Eventually, a sign on the left announces the northern boundary of the state park. Shortly thereafter, in a right curve, is the north canoe landing; be on the lookout for it because it's easy to miss. A paved road runs through the park to a parking lot, from which a gravel path leads to the landing. This is a good place to stop, relax, and perhaps have lunch.

In the left bend after the landing, a gravel road can be seen coming down the bluff on the right, then back up again. The banks continue to be steep and muddy. For awhile, the wooded bluffs recede from the river, which winds back and forth in a lowland area, unprotected from wind.

Take out at the Fox Ridge State Park south landing, which appears on river-left after a straightaway, just before a sharp right turn. Concrete riprap on the high left bank makes it easy to spot the landing site. If you'd like a longer trip, you can continue downriver and take out at the concrete boat landing at County 1200N (downstream-right).

Portaging around a logjam: an infrequent situation south of Lake Charleston

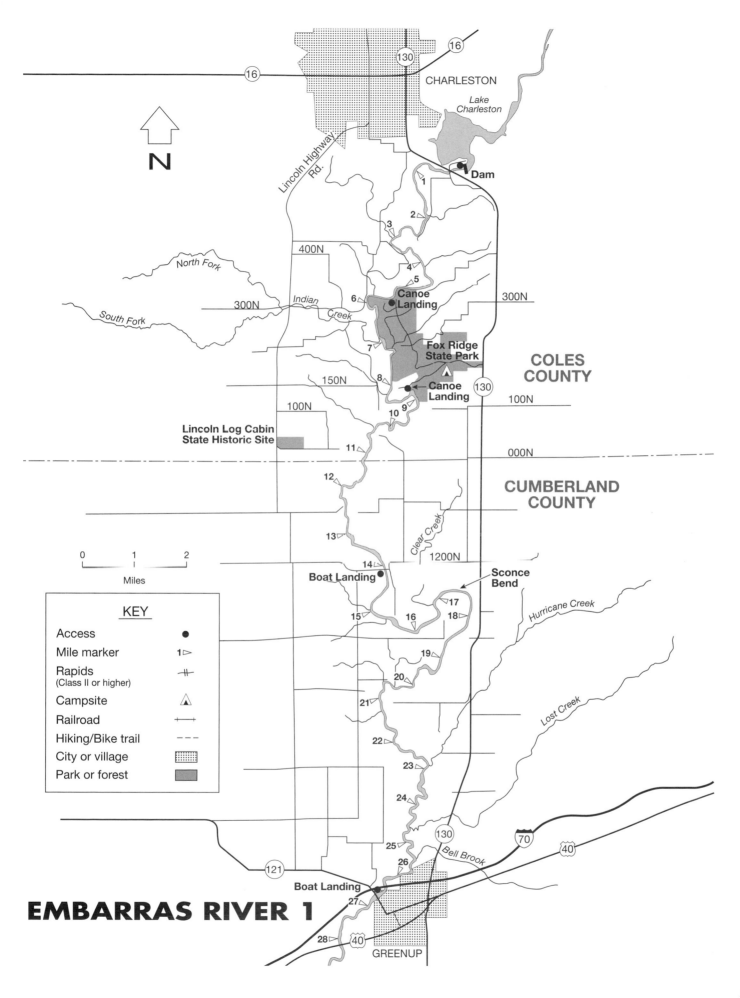

EMBARRAS RIVER 1

EMBARRAS RIVER 2
Fox Ridge State Park to Greenup (17.7 Miles)

An American Hero

The area of the lower Embarras River is associated with the exploits of one of America's greatest heroes, George Rogers Clark. In 1778, the 26-year-old Clark stunned the British by floating down the Ohio to Fort Massac (near modern-day Metropolis, Illinois) with fewer than 200 men, then marching overland to capture the important outpost at Kaskaskia. Then, even more incredibly, he set out in February 1779 toward Vincennes, hoping to surprise the British and their Indian allies. For eighteen miserable days Clark and his men struggled through more than 150 miles of wet terrain, including the swollen Big Muddy and Little Wabash Rivers. The final obstacles were the Embarras, then the Wabash—both flooded for miles around. Somehow Clark and his hardy men got through, rushed the fort in chest-high water, and stunningly secured the Illinois Country for the new American government.

The Embarras won't overwhelm you with scenery, but its remoteness from cities and other development makes it an attractive place to paddle for a day or two. In our second recommended stretch, steep mud banks continue to limit access to the shoreline along the way, but there are convenient landings at the beginning, middle, and end of the trip. Pretty wooded bluffs often parallel the river, and brief rocky shelves lend a little variety to the setting. Sheer cutbanks are often seen, ranging from 1 to 20 feet high. There are few signs of habitation (just a few houses and farm buildings), the dogwood and wildflower display is beautiful in the spring, and wildlife sightings are frequent—especially ducks, geese, owls, hawks, turkey vultures, squirrels, and deer. The average width of 100 feet usually provides plenty of room to maneuver around fallen trees, but there's always a chance of a blockage, especially in sharp bends.

Camping is plentiful in the area. See the description of Embarras River 1.

The **shuttle route** (13.6 miles) begins at the south canoe landing in Fox Ridge State Park, then heads south on Highway 130 from the park entrance, turns west onto Highway 121 at Greenup, and proceeds to the boat landing on the edge of town. A shorter trip can be arranged by putting in at the County 1200N boat landing, or by paddling from the park's north landing to 1200N.

The **gradient** is only 1.7 feet per mile.

For **water levels,** see Embarras River 1.

Put in at the south canoe landing of the park. A paved road leads through the beautiful ridges and ravines of the park to a parking area near the landing, which can be muddy in the spring and after rainfall. At the put-in, the river turns sharply right, then left, and signs soon indicate the end of park property. A series of gentle curves follows, with many cutbanks. Sand appears occasionally in the banks, and at one point there's an expanse of stratified shale and sandstone. Beaver activity is obvious in the numerous tooth-sculptured trees. Wooded bluffs often adjoin the river.

Only a couple of farm buildings are seen until 1200N, where a house on the left precedes the bridge. Downstream-left is a canoe livery, and across the river is an excellent concrete boat landing. Because the prevalent mud banks make it inconvenient to get out of your boat most of the time, this landing is a good place to stop for relaxation or lunch; a pleasant grassy area is located nearby. After 1200N, the river is less winding for awhile, with several straightaways, but bankside vegetation continues to be thick.

Not long after a big island, a radio tower can be seen in the distance, then the Greenup water tower. Both banks are rather low now, and the hills are distant. Riverside woods thin out somewhat. After a set of power lines pass overhead, traffic noise can be heard downstream. Then, in a right bend, wooded bluffs appear alongside the river again, and there's a 10-foot thick shale outcropping for several hundred yards in a southwestward straightaway. Suddenly Interstate 70 runs alongside until the river turns left to pass under the two bridges. Then a gentle right bend takes you to Highway 121. **Take out** at the concrete landing upstream-right. A short dirt access road leads from the highway to the landing.

Other trips. Accesses aren't as convenient downstream, but local canoeists report that paddling is good all the way to the Ste. Marie area. There's some channelization in the lower river.

Sheer exposed bluffs on the Embarras

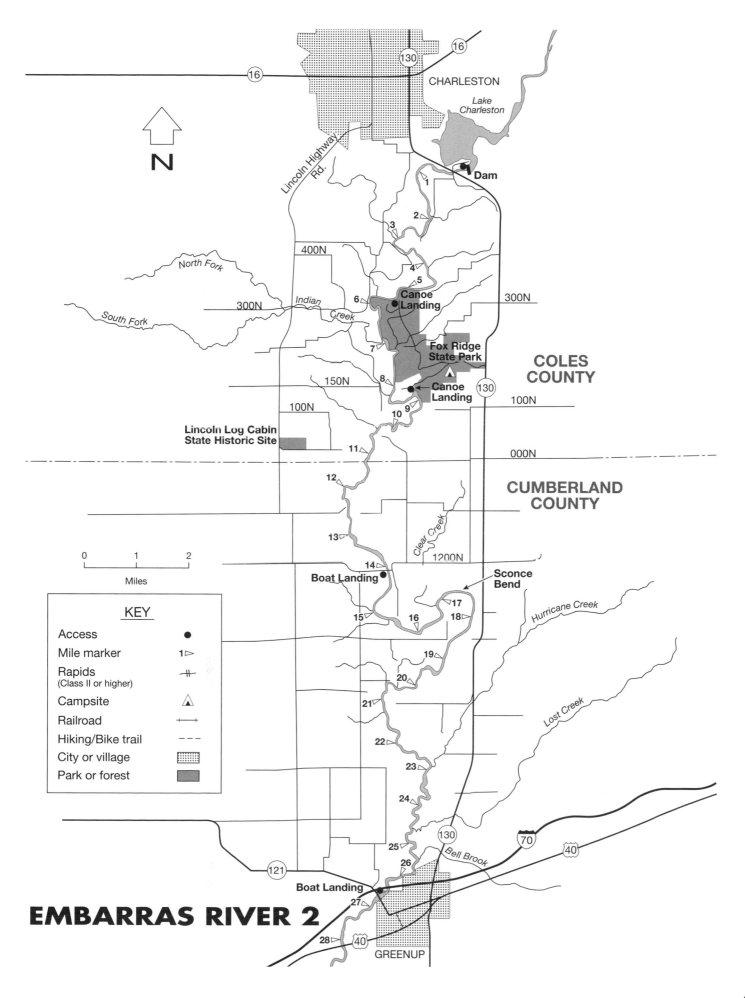

EMBARRAS RIVER 2

N

CHARLESTON

Lincoln Highway Rd.

Lake Charleston

Dam

North Fork

400N

Indian Creek

300N

South Fork

Canoe Landing

Fox Ridge State Park

COLES COUNTY

150N

Canoe Landing

100N

Lincoln Log Cabin State Historic Site

000N

CUMBERLAND COUNTY

Clear Creek

1200N

Boat Landing

Sconce Bend

Hurricane Creek

Lost Creek

KEY

Access	●
Mile marker	1▷
Rapids (Class II or higher)	#
Campsite	▲
Railroad	—+—
Hiking/Bike trail	— — —
City or village	▓
Park or forest	▓

0   1   2
Miles

Bell Brook

Boat Landing

GREENUP

FOX RIVER 1
South Elgin to St. Charles (7.5 Miles)

From its source near Waukesha, Wisconsin, the Fox flows through the glacial Chain O' Lakes and many wetlands after entering Illinois, then passes through one urban community after another until swinging west at Oswego. From there to its mouth near Ottawa, it goes through a rural environment. Parts of the river upstream from Oswego are canoed, but there are many dangerous dams to be avoided; altogether, there are fifteen dams on the Fox in Illinois. A relatively large river, the Fox is generally several hundred feet wide, and is often slow because of dam impoundments. Nevertheless, there are many attractive areas on the upper river, even in the vicinity of some large population centers.

The following trip, for example, begins and ends within sizable cities, but along the way moves through pretty countryside and past attractive parks. Be forewarned that motorboats are often seen on this section, especially on weekends. Incidentally, the annual Mid-America Canoe Race (15 miles) is held in this area in June.

Public **camping** is available to the southwest at Silver Springs State Fish and Wildlife Area near Yorkville and at Bliss Woods Forest Preserve near Aurora, and to the north at Buffalo Park Forest Preserve near Algonquin, at Burnidge Forest Preserve/Paul Wolff Campground near Elgin, and at Chain O' Lakes State Park near Spring Grove. Also see the description of Fox River 2.

Canoe rental and shuttle service are available at the Canoe Shack near St. Charles (630-584-8017). Canoes also may be rented at Chicagoland Canoe Base in Chicago (773-777-1489).

The shuttle route. From the put-in at Seba Park in South Elgin, go west on State Street, then south on Highway 31 into St. Charles, to the public parking lot near the Carroll Towers (upstream-right from the Hotel Baker and the St. Charles dam). For a slightly shorter trip that avoids taking out in St. Charles, turn in to Ferson Creek Park north of town, off Highway 31.

The **gradient** is only 1.3 feet per mile.

For **water levels,** check the gauge at South Elgin (station #05551000) on the USGS Web site listed in the introduction.

Put in at the unimproved gravel landing alongside Seba Park in South Elgin, near a small shopping center.

A good example of a "horizon line": just upstream from the Fox River dam in St. Charles

Parking is available at the park, which runs alongside South Water Street. The put-in is downstream from State Street, which in turn is about 100 yards downstream from the dam. The 7.5 river miles between here and St. Charles make this one of the longest stretches between dams on the upper Fox.

The stretch begins (and continues) quite wide, with houses on both sides. The shoreline environment is urban for awhile. Not far downstream on the right shore is the Fox Valley Trolley Museum, a fascinating place where you can view a large collection of antique electric trolleys and take a ride on railroad tracks alongside the river. A clump of islands follows, then a long railroad bridge. Houses cease for awhile after the bridge. On the right shoreline, bicyclists can be seen on the Fox River Trail, a much-used bike route that follows the river between Aurora and Crystal Lake and connects with several other popular trails.

After the railroad bridge, the river makes a big right bend, then a big left one. In the right turn, the Fox River Trail passes overhead on an old railroad bridge that spans an island. Just downstream from the bridge, on the right, a canoe landing in Blackhawk Forest Preserve is a pleasant place to stop for awhile. Another clump of islands follows the bike bridge. When the river heads south for the remainder of the trip, the shoreline remains largely undeveloped and wild, despite the fact that Highway 31 is never far away on the right.

Eventually, a park appears on the right, with a good canoe landing. This is Ferson Creek Park, operated by the St. Charles Park District. The landing is immediately downstream from the mouth of Ferson Creek and comes just before a small bay. This is the best and safest **take-out.** If you want to continue to St. Charles, head downstream, where you'll next pass the Boy Scout Island Landing on the right. Here the ramp is primarily intended for motorboats, and a fee is required. Across the river is Potawatomi Park.

Immediately after Potawatomi Park, you paddle under a railroad bridge and some power lines, and past a riverside restaurant. **Take out** on river-right at a concrete shelf at water's edge alongside the Carroll Towers senior apartment building, about 150 yards upstream from the dam. Stairs run down from the adjacent public parking lot. **Don't get any closer to the dam—a lethal danger.**

Other trips. The upstream section from Algonquin to Elgin (Voyageurs Landing Forest Preserve) is often paddled, but you must portage the dam at Carpentersville. Canoe rental and shuttle service are available from Schmidt's Canoeing Service in Elgin (847-697-1678 or www.canoetrips.net). For descriptions of several other sections, see www.openlands.org/watertrails.asp.

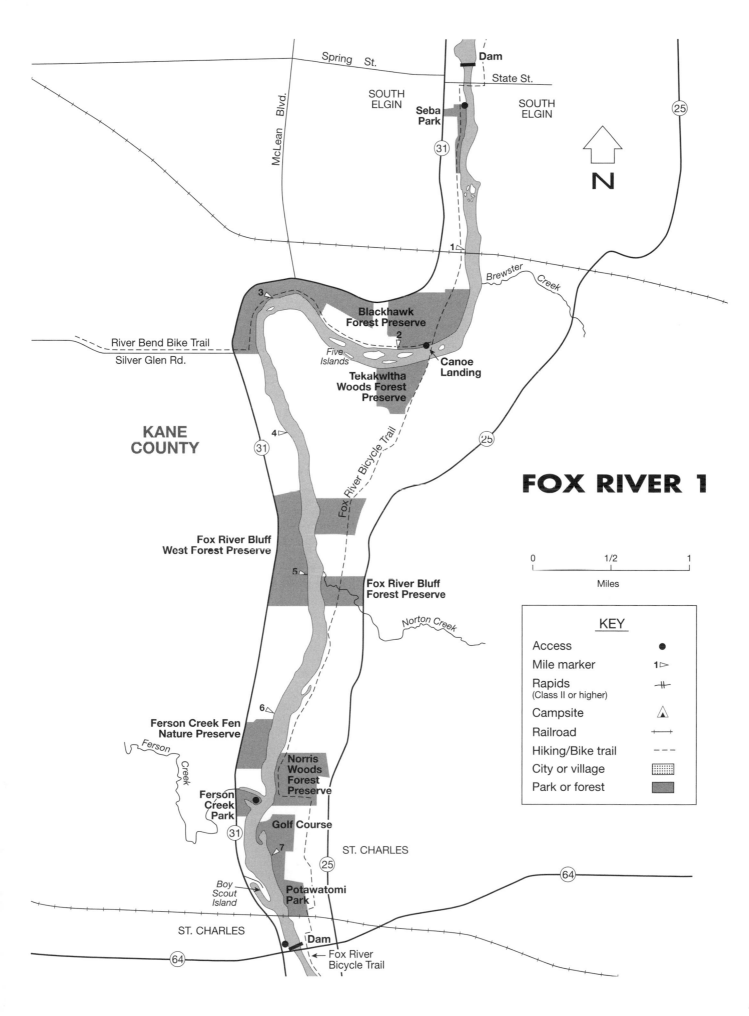

Spring St.
Dam
State St.
SOUTH
ELGIN
**Seba
Park**
SOUTH
ELGIN
McLean Blvd.
31
25
1
Brewster Creek
3
**Blackhawk
Forest Preserve**
River Bend Bike Trail
2
Silver Glen Rd.
Five
Islands
**Canoe
Landing**
**Tekakwltha
Woods Forest
Preserve**
Fox River Bicycle Trail
**KANE
COUNTY**
4
31
25

FOX RIVER 1

**Fox River Bluff
West Forest Preserve**
5
**Fox River Bluff
Forest Preserve**
Norton Creek

0   1/2   1
Miles

6
**Ferson Creek Fen
Nature Preserve**
Ferson Creek
**Norris
Woods
Forest
Preserve**
**Ferson
Creek
Park**
31
Golf Course
7
25
ST. CHARLES
64
Boy
Scout
Island
**Potawatomi
Park**
ST. CHARLES
Dam
64
Fox River
Bicycle Trail

KEY
Access	●
Mile marker	1▷
Rapids (Class II or higher)	-H-
Campsite	⚠
Railroad	+---+
Hiking/Bike trail	- - -
City or village	▦
Park or forest	▨

FOX RIVER 2
Yorkville to Sheridan (15.5 Miles)

Why "Fox"?

The Fox River is named after the tribe that originally lived along the Fox and Wisconsin Rivers in Wisconsin and later established a presence in Illinois. Known as *mesquaki* (the "red earth people") or *outagami* ("people of the other shore") in Algonquin, they were called *Renards* by the French and *Fox* by the English. These names (and many others) are reflected in early maps, where the river is also called the *Riviere des Renards*, the *Pistakee* ("buffalo"), and the *Riviere du Rocher* ("Rock River" because of the stone cliffs).

After St. Charles, more dams check the flow of the Fox every couple of miles until the dam at Montgomery, where a relatively long (10.5-mile) stretch leads to the next dam at Yorkville. Here begins the most beautiful part of the Fox: 27 free-flowing miles of densely wooded shoreline, interesting historical sites, convenient accesses, and gorgeous sandstone cliffs. From Yorkville downstream, the river just keeps getting more and more impressive. It's no wonder that this is one of the most popular canoeing areas in Illinois.

The section between Yorkville and Sheridan doesn't have the massive rock formations of the downstream "Fox Dells" stretch, but is definitely an attractive place to paddle. Scattered homes found along the river don't take much away from the mostly wild setting. Islands, birds, and waterfowl are abundant. Fishermen say they catch largemouth and smallmouth bass, catfish, walleye, bluegill, carp, and drum. Generally at least 300 feet wide, the river has some light riffles in low-water conditions.

Several **campgrounds** can be accessed from the river, making canoe-camping trips easy and fun. Silver Springs State Park is just a few miles downstream from Yorkville, and two private riverside campgrounds are located near Sheridan—Mallard Bend and Rolling Oaks. Off river, the Hide Away Lakes Campground is just south of Yorkville, and Yogi Bear Jellystone Park is near Millbrook.

Canoe rentals and shuttle service for trips beginning at Yorkville are available at Freeman's Sports in Yorkville (630-553-0515). Canoes may also be rented at Chicagoland Canoe Base in Chicago (773-777-1489), and kayaks at Geneva Kayak in Geneva (630-232-0320).

The easiest **shuttle route** (17.5 miles) from the Yorkville put-in goes south on Highway 47, west on Highway 71, west on Sheridan East Road into Sheridan, then north on Robinson Street to the bridge. Shuttling closer to the river via River Road, etc., is more involved but shorter. Trip length can be varied by taking out at Silver Springs, Millbrook, Mallard Bend Campground, or Rolling Oaks Campground. Camping overnight at Mallard Bend or Rolling Oaks makes an excellent two-day trip, breaking the Yorkville-to-Wedron section roughly in half.

The **gradient** is a pleasant 2.9 feet per mile.

For **water levels,** check the downstream gauge at Dayton (station #05552500) on the USGS Web site listed in the introduction.

Put in at the Yorkville public boat landing, downstream-left from the Highway 47 bridge, on Hydraulic Street. Plentiful parking is provided. Located upstream from the bridge, the Yorkville dam is 31 miles from the final (and biggest) dam on the Fox, at Dayton. Several islands lie in the middle of the river at the beginning, and homes are seen on both sides for awhile. The shoreline is heavily wooded, including many maples and oaks. Shortly after the second set of power lines and just before the first bridge, the Silver Springs canoe landing appears on the left. Picnic facilities, toilets, and other amenities make Silver Springs a good place to stop. Upstream-right from the bridge is a popular tourist attraction, the Farnsworth House designed by Mies van der Rohe.

After the canoe landing and bridge, the river swings to the southwest. Downstream-left is a wooden staircase leading up the bank to the park's carry-in camping area. Big Rock Creek enters on the other side of the river; a half mile upstream is Meramech Hill, site of a long-standing Native American village in the eighteenth and nineteenth centuries. Some contend that the hill was the site of a 1730 battle in which the French and their allies massacred 300 Fox Indians.

Soon the remnant of the old Millhurst dam appears, with the lovely stone mill—now an inviting bed-and-breakfast—alongside it. Run the narrow, wavy channel to the left of the dam. After the mouth of Hollenbeck Creek, the river curves gently to the left. North of Millbrook, two bridges cross the river, the first of which is a picturesque structure restored by the Kendall County Historical Society. An access is found upstream-right at the old bridge—a good **take-out** for a short trip.

Densely wooded shoreline continues, with occasional houses, to the Millington Road bridge (no access). Downstream is a long stretch of 7-foot cutbanks on the right and a series of small islands. Then a sign indicates the access to Mallard Bend Campground on the right (a small inlet), followed by a huge island. A long succession of trailers now covers the left shore, often with unsightly riprap. Soon the gravel landing for Rolling Oaks Campground is seen on the right.

After a straightaway, then a huge island, the Sheridan bridge appears. **Take out** downstream-left at the steep concrete boat ramp behind the tavern, which charges a nominal fee for use of the landing and parking lot. The Mallard Bend and Rolling Oaks landings can also be used as take-outs by noncampers for a small fee.

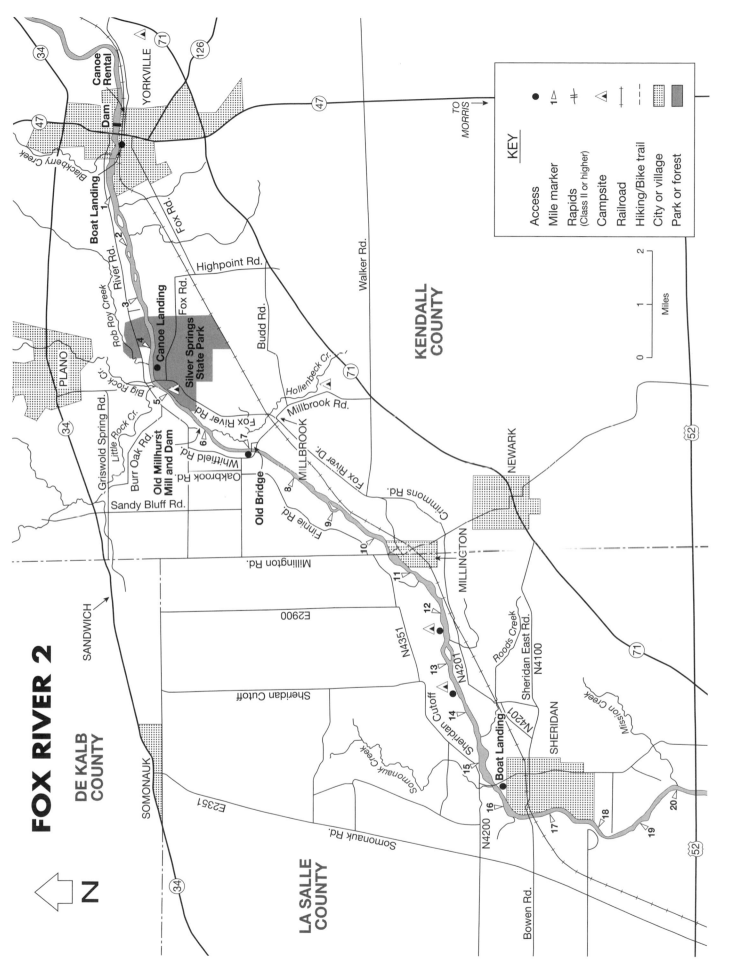

FOX RIVER 2

FOX RIVER 3
Sheridan to Wedron (11.5 Miles)

Swallow colonies honeycomb many cliffs on the Fox.

Upon being asked to name the three or four most beautiful sections of river in Illinois, any knowledgeable canoeist would have to include this one. The many riverside cliffs of St. Peters Sandstone—especially in the stretch downstream from Highway 52—are among the most breathtaking you'll see anywhere. The floral display is almost as impressive, including pine, cedar, and yew trees, ferns and mosses, and profuse wildflowers, including delicate columbines peeking out of the cliff faces. Swallows commonly swirl about the cliffs as you pass by, and sand-and-gravel bars occasionally create riffles and make great places to stop and dawdle. This is a section liberally sprinkled with islands, large and small. Although homes and cottages are not uncommon, the river environs are generally wooded, clean, and unspoiled. Add to all of this the fact that, upstream from Wedron, the river is usually too shallow for motorboats. There are several active sand-and-gravel pits in the area, however, and you may occasionally hear mechanical noise from them.

Camping. In addition to the campgrounds listed in the description of Fox River 2, two public campgrounds are located within 20 miles of Wedron, at Illini State Park near Marseilles and Starved Rock State Park near Oglesby.

Canoe rental and shuttle service for this section are available at Ayers Landing, half a mile upstream from Wedron (815-434-2233 or 800-540-2394), at C&M Canoe Rental in Wedron (815-434-6690 or www.cmcanoerentalcom) and at River Adventures in Dayton (815-481-2142 or www.canoethefox.com).

The **shuttle route** is approximately 9.5 miles. From the put-in, go north across the Sheridan bridge, west on County N4200, then south on Somonauk Road to Wedron. If you are taking out at Ayers Landing, turn north on County E2089 in Wedron on the west side of the river. If taking out downstream at the Fox River Tavern (C&M), cross the river to the east side and turn south on County E2062. Shuttling via Sheridan Road, Highway 71, and Wedron Road is farther, but takes you through the interesting little community of Norway, the first permanent Norwegian settlement in America, where a commemorative marker tells the "Norsk story."

The **gradient** of 3.2 feet per mile lends itself to good current and pleasant riffles.

For **water levels,** see Fox River 2.

Put in (for a small fee) at the steep concrete boat ramp behind the tavern at the southwest corner of the Sheridan bridge. If you've spent the previous night at the Mallard Bend or Rolling Oaks campgrounds, put in at your campground landing. Both campgrounds allow noncampers to use their landings for a small fee.

Directly across from the landing at the bridge is the mouth of Somonauk Creek. After bending left and clearing a big island, you see the first sandstone cliff of the trip on the right, topped with houses. Beautiful pine trees precede the Bowen Road bridge, followed by an interesting railroad bridge on limestone and steel piers. After a slender island and a couple of gentle bends, a pretty little box canyon is seen on the right. Cabins, small islands, and low stone outcroppings appear occasionally.

After a very long left bend, the river heads back to the right near the mouth of Mission Creek, and the Highway 52 bridge comes into view—a graceful structure with four spans. There's a good access upstream-left, with a dirt road leading down to the shore.

The river now heads into a straightaway, then veers right, where a lovely grassy area with picnic tables and toilets is located near an earth home (private). Farther into the curve is a canoe landing on the left (also private), followed by houses on top of steep banks. After the river bends left, then right, lovely cliffs appear on the left again, with coniferous trees on top. Low shorelines now prevail for awhile, and the river goes into a long westward straightaway.

Within view of more cliffs, another big island appears, preceded by power lines. The yew-topped cliffs continue for a quarter mile and are the prettiest so far. Another big island quickly follows, with pleasant riffles in the right channel, and beautiful cliffs resume. Note the undercutting of the lowest layers of stone, the plentiful swallow nests in cliffside cavities, and the occasional small "caves."

After a swing to the left, there are many small islands. In the southward approach toward Wedron, cliffs begin again on the left—the most glorious of all—and continue all the way to Ayers Landing and beyond. At Ayers Landing **take out** downstream-right from the mouth of Indian Creek, an unusually beautiful place to end your trip because of the nearby cliffs. There is a small landing-and-parking fee for canoeists using their own boats. After Ayers Landing, the rock formations soon end and the slack water from the Dayton Dam begins. If you wish to take out 0.75 mile farther downstream, paddle past the Wedron bridge, then the silica-processing plant, to the Fox River Tavern landing on river-left.

After Wedron, the Fox flows 9 miles before emptying into the Illinois River near Ottawa, 185 miles from its source in Wisconsin.

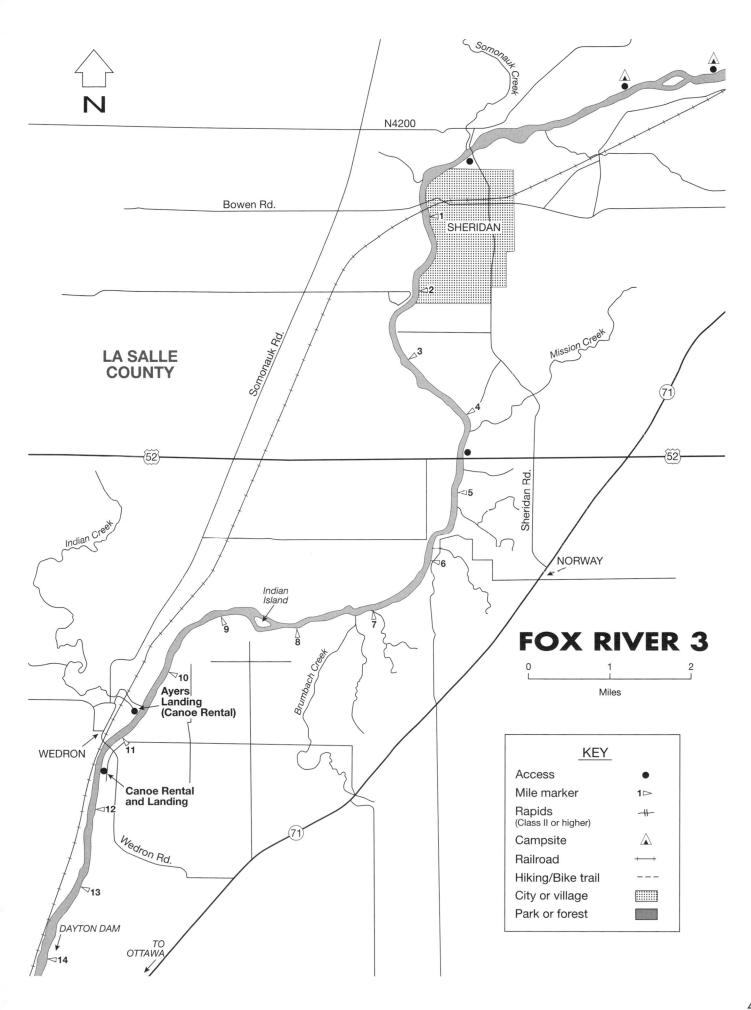

N

N4200

Bowen Rd.

SHERIDAN

1

2

LA SALLE
COUNTY

Somonauk Rd.

3

Mission Creek

4

71

52

52

Sheridan Rd.

5

NORWAY

Indian Creek

6

Indian
Island

9

8

7

FOX RIVER 3

Brumbach Creek

0   1   2

Miles

10

**Ayers
Landing
(Canoe Rental)**

11

WEDRON

**Canoe Rental
and Landing**

12

Wedron Rd.

71

KEY	
Access	●
Mile marker	1▷
Rapids (Class II or higher)	─╫─
Campsite	△
Railroad	┼─┼
Hiking/Bike trail	- - -
City or village	▦
Park or forest	▬

13

DAYTON DAM

TO
OTTAWA

14

GALENA RIVER 1
Buncombe Road to Galena (13.5 Miles)

Cross the Border, Change the Name

As with other Illinois rivers, history has given many names to the Galena. Among the many designations on early maps are *Riviere des Mines* ("River of Mines") and *Riviere au Feve* ("River of Beans"), but the name that stuck was Fever River (perhaps because the French word for "bean" was misinterpreted, perhaps because of a smallpox outbreak in the Native American population). Some citizens were upset with the disease connotations of the long-standing name, and persuaded the state legislature in 1854 to adopt the name Galena (after the lead ore mined there). Wisconsin still calls the part north of the border the Fever River.

The Galena River—originating in Wisconsin, then flowing to the southwest across Jo Daviess County to the Mississippi—is one of the prettiest rivers in the state. Like the Apple, it is located in the unglaciated driftless area of northwestern Illinois. Quite narrow and clear until it approaches the city of Galena, it is loaded with pleasant riffles, wooded bluffs, cliffs, and smallmouth bass. Dangerous when high, the upper part requires boat control even under normal water conditions and should be limited to experienced canoeists. Because part of the shoreline is pastureland, you may encounter wire strung across the river; do not disturb it any more than you have to, and give cattle a wide berth. The section described here is almost entirely adjoined by private property, so please respect the rights of landowners. Also, be careful driving on the steep, twisting roads in the area.

Public **camping** is located a few miles to the east at Apple River Canyon State Park (north of Stockton), and to the south at Mississippi Palisades State Park (near Savanna) and at Blanding's Landing Recreation Area (west of Hanover). The private Palace Campground is located north of Galena.

Canoe rentals are available at Fever River Outfitters in Galena (815-776-9425 or www.feverriveroutfitters.com).

The **shuttle route** (10.6 miles) from the put-in goes west (briefly) on Buncombe Road, south on Ensch Road (which becomes Birkbeck Road in Illinois), west on West Council Hill Road, and south on Highways 84 and 20 to Galena.

The **gradient** on this stretch averages 2.4 feet per mile; most of the drop (3.9 feet) comes before Buckhill Road.

Water levels. Normally, there is sufficient water to paddle only in the springtime and after sustained rainfall.

Put in at the river-right landing off Buncombe Road, 0.6 mile north of the Illinois-Wisconsin state line. To get to the put-in, go north on Birkbeck Road, then Ensch Road in Wisconsin. At the T, go east on Buncombe Road; as soon as you cross a bridge over a creek, a dirt lane leads to a wooden-step landing. The property owner (upstream-left) has given permission for its use.

Riffles begin immediately as you paddle into a left curve past a couple of creek mouths. The river here is only 30 feet wide and very clear, with a sand-and-gravel bottom. Flowing in a succession of pools and riffles, the river bends back and forth in a long pastureland, passing the stone abutments of a defunct railroad line that used to run through a tunnel in a nearby hill. Eventually a tall wooded bluff with attractive stone outcroppings forces the river abruptly to the right. Huge chunks of limestone have fallen into the long riffly stretch here.

Downstream from the Birkbeck Road bridge the river curves, then heads straight for another tall bluff, which sharply deflects the stream to the left. Here begins another breathtaking stretch: overhanging trees, quick current, and tremendous peacefulness. Pastureland and a few low, grassy islands follow. Twice more the river is abruptly turned aside by tall bluffs, accompanied by boulders and riffles. Impressive cliffs loom along the river, and coniferous trees appear for the first time. The West Council Hill Road bridge can be accessed downstream-right (parking is almost nonexistent, however, and the nearby curve in the road is blind).

After the bridge the streambed widens a little and winds back and forth between high stone cliffs and wooded bluffs. Twice more the river veers to the right at tall bluffs, with the usual stone chunks and riffles, followed by an abandoned bridge. Then, after several sharp bends and grassy islands, the Buckhill Road bridge appears (accessible downstream-right, but with little parking).

Riffles, high cutbanks, sharp turns, and the only house of the trip follow the bridge, together with numerous gravel bars. In a big left arc, the river enters its last beautiful stage: intimate, peaceful, and wooded. Finally, however, after a right turn where railroad tracks begin to be seen on the left, the last riffle occurs and the high, steep banks have a ditchlike appearance that will continue all the way to Galena. Current diminishes considerably, and by the time you pass under the high, old Stagecoach Road bridge, it has almost disappeared.

Big, gentle bends follow Stagecoach Road. Although the banks are monotonous, the setting remains wild. As the city approaches, a noisy foundry appears on the right, followed by a metal pedestrian bridge, then another. Soon the beautiful brick-and-stone buildings of Galena can be seen on the right—a lovely vista! **Take out** downstream-right from the Highway 20/84 bridge at a small gravel landing alongside a sizable parking lot.

Clear, sparkling water on the upper Galena

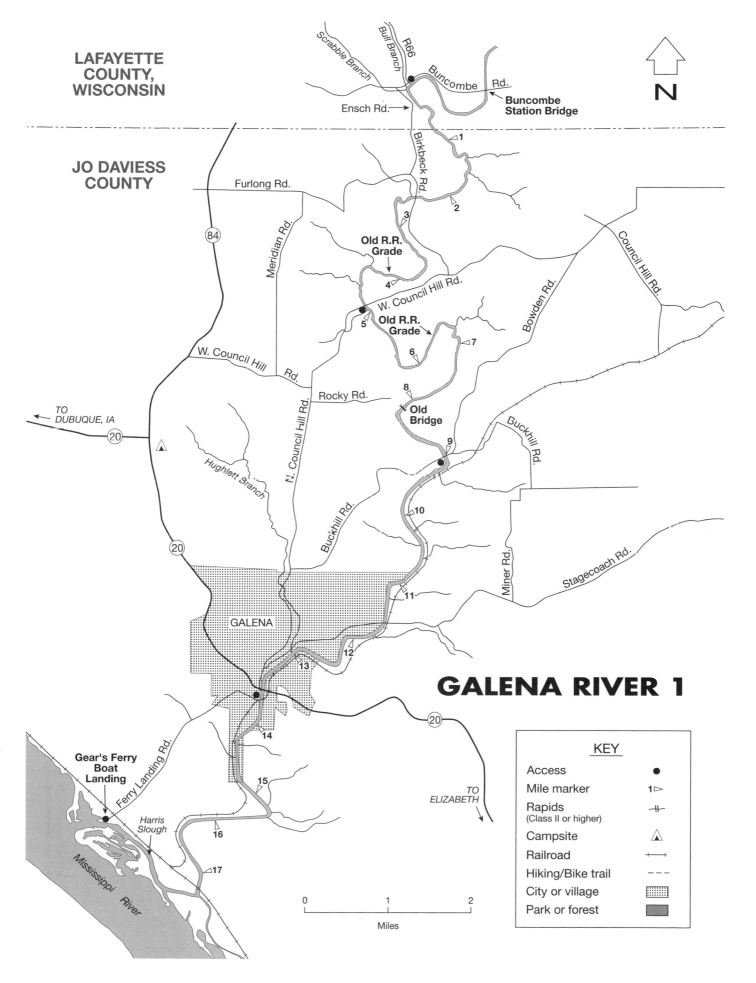

LAFAYETTE
COUNTY,
WISCONSIN

JO DAVIESS
COUNTY

Scrabble Branch

Bull Branch

R66

Buncombe Rd.

**Buncombe
Station Bridge**

Ensch Rd.

Birkbeck Rd.

1

Furlong Rd.

84

Meridian Rd.

2

3

**Old R.R.
Grade**

4

W. Council Hill Rd.

5

**Old R.R.
Grade**

7

6

Council Hill Rd.

Bowden Rd.

W. Council Hill Rd.

N. Council Hill Rd.

Rocky Rd.

8

**Old
Bridge**

9

Buckhill Rd.

TO
DUBUQUE, IA

20

Hughlett Branch

Buckhill Rd.

10

Miner Rd.

Stagecoach Rd.

11

GALENA

12

13

GALENA RIVER 1

20

14

Gear's Ferry
Boat
Landing

Ferry Landing Rd.

Harris
Slough

15

16

TO
ELIZABETH

Mississippi River

17

KEY	
Access	●
Mile marker	1▷
Rapids (Class II or higher)	╫
Campsite	△
Railroad	┼┼
Hiking/Bike trail	- - -
City or village	▦
Park or forest	▓

0   1   2

Miles

GALENA RIVER 2
Galena to Gear's Ferry Landing (5.5 Miles)

The Halcyon Days of Galena

In the boomtown days when the region was producing most of the nation's supply of lead (fifty-four million pounds came from the area in 1845), Galena was a significant river port, and one of the most important cities in Illinois. Steamboats regularly plied the waters between St. Louis and Galena, easily making the 5-mile trip upriver from the Mississippi. Looking at the Galena River now, it's difficult to believe that it was 250 feet wide a century and a half ago. Unfortunately, there was a tremendous amount of erosion from hillside farming and from timber being cut as fuel for the steamboats and lead smelters. The river gradually silted in, making it shallower, narrower, and more prone to flooding. Eventually, a lock and dam was built in 1890 near the mouth to facilitate riverboat traffic (this structure lasted until 1921), and dikes and floodgates were constructed in 1951 to protect the city from flood damage.

Today, only canoes and motorboats travel on the Galena River, but the many fine mansions and commercial buildings of the 1800s still remain (including the home of Ulysses S. Grant), together with the rolling hills, mounds, and valleys that draw throngs of tourists to this gorgeous, unglaciated part of the state. The scenery is beautiful wherever you go.

The most attractive part of the Galena River is the stretch upstream from Buckhill Road (see Galena River 1), but its relatively high gradient and small watershed make it unpaddleable much of the year. This is not the case, however, with the final leg of the river. Averaging about 100 feet wide, the final miles of the Galena aren't especially scenic but provide an enjoyable two-to-three-hour paddle. Although the mud banks are generally rather steep and inaccessible, the environs are pleasantly wooded, and no houses are seen from beginning to end. The width makes serious obstructions unlikely. A highlight of the trip is the concluding stretch on a narrow backwater of the Mississippi River. Both accesses are quite good, and the shuttle is quick and easy.

For nearby **camping** and **canoe rentals,** see the description of Galena River 1.

The **shuttle route** (only 2.6 miles) from the put-in goes west on Gear Street, then south on Ferry Landing Road to the public boat ramp.

The **gradient** is negligible (less than a foot per mile).

Water levels. There is almost always enough water to paddle.

Put in downstream-right from the Highway 20/84 bridge, near a public parking lot where a short path leads to a small gravel landing. You're likely to see a few motorboats moored along the river at the outset, and there's a metal railroad bridge soon after the put-in.

The initial right bend is followed by a straightaway. Power lines cross where the river heads back to the left, and railroad tracks parallel the right bank. The river continues to bend back and forth, with intervening straight stretches. At one point, where railroad tracks appear again on the right, there's some broken rock on the right shore in a big left bend.

The current is normally minimal, and the water muddy-colored. The farther you go, the wider becomes the river, the lower the banks, and the more densely vegetated the shoreline.

After a quick right bend, then left, a railroad bridge appears, preceded by a short rocky shelf on the right—the location of the old lock and dam.

A couple hundred yards downstream from the bridge, you come to a T. Go to the right, and paddle up the Mississippi backwater channel (Harris Slough) toward the Gear's Ferry Landing. Some canoeists enjoy exploring the maze of backwater islands, but you should have an Army Corps of Engineers map with you if you wish to do so; otherwise, it's easy to get lost. The channel arcs gently to the right, then left, gradually increasing in width. Much of the shoreline is marshy. Eventually the buildings of the ferry landing come into view, with many docks and motorboats. Paddle past most of the docks and **take out** at the concrete-and-asphalt boat ramp on your right.

In the nineteenth century, Galena was a major port for steamboats (photo courtesy of the Galena–Jo Daviess County Historical Society).

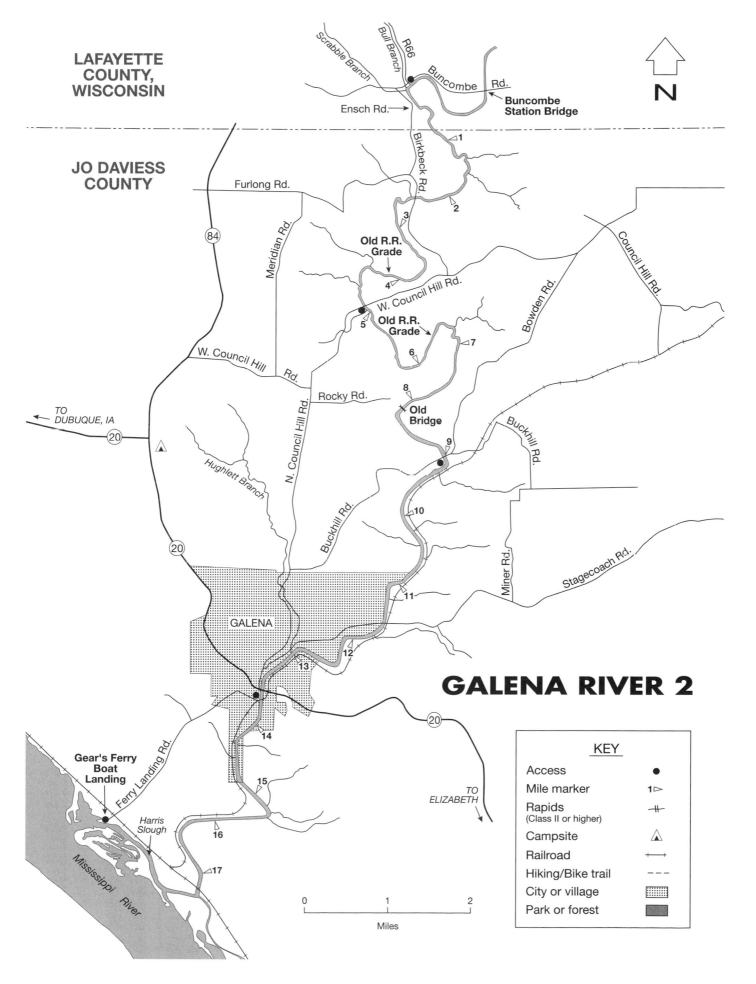

LAFAYETTE
COUNTY,
WISCONSIN

JO DAVIESS
COUNTY

Scrabble Branch

Bull Branch

R66

Buncombe Rd.

Buncombe
Station Bridge

Ensch Rd.

Birkbeck Rd.

1

Furlong Rd.

2

84

3

Meridian Rd.

Old R.R.
Grade

4

W. Council Hill Rd.

5

Old R.R.
Grade

7

6

W. Council Hill Rd.

Rocky Rd.

Bowden Rd.

Council Hill Rd.

8

Old
Bridge

TO
DUBUQUE, IA

20

N. Council Hill Rd.

9

Buckhill Rd.

10

Hughlett Branch

Buckhill Rd.

20

Miner Rd.

Stagecoach Rd.

11

GALENA

12

13

GALENA RIVER 2

20

14

TO
ELIZABETH

Gear's Ferry
Boat
Landing

Ferry Landing Rd.

15

Harris
Slough

16

17

Mississippi
River

0   1   2

Miles

53

HENNEPIN CANAL 1
Feeder Canal: Highway 40 to the Main Canal (26 Miles)

The Illinois-Mississippi Canal—better known as the Hennepin—is a 104-mile waterway. Exiting the Illinois River 2 miles upstream from the city of Hennepin, the canal heads west for 75 miles to the Rock River, which soon joins the Mississippi just south of Rock Island. Water for the main canal comes from the Rock River at Rock Falls, coursing southward through a feeder canal that joins the east-west waterway at the "summit pool." Thirty-three locks were constructed on the canal: one at the head of the feeder to protect the canal from high water, and the other thirty-two along the main canal to compensate for the drop from the summit pool to the Illinois and Mississippi rivers. Some of the locks (16, 22, 23, 24, and 33) have been restored so visitors can examine their interesting structure.

Except for the last few miles of the eastern leg, the whole canal is canoeable, although the large number of locks east of Lock 21 (near Wyanet) makes this section impractical. Most of the canal is in good condition, and is popular with the public; you're likely to see fishermen at the day-use areas, hikers and cyclists on the towpath trails, and fellow canoeists on the water.

As you might expect, glorious scenery is not a characteristic of the Hennepin. Much of the canal is separated from the adjoining countryside by a levee that limits your view of the surroundings. The waterway is often rather straight, with grassy banks, but a surprising amount of the shoreline is wooded. Typically 80 feet wide, the canal averages 3–5 feet in depth. There is virtually no current most of the time, but whenever you emerge from one of the "tubes" (i.e., bridges that have been replaced with 12-foot steel culverts), you can tell that the water is moving. Of the

original nine aqueducts built to carry the canal over obstacles (such as the Green River or Big Bureau Creek), six remain; five are located on the canoeing sections recommended here. Paddling across an aqueduct is an unusual experience.

The canal is a great place for beginning paddlers: there are no obstructions, tricky current, or sharp turns. The only places that pose any danger are the small spillways on the upstream side of locks where water runs down to the lower level, and the "waterfalls" that are formed where locks have been replaced by concrete bulkheads. Both are easily avoided by taking out well upstream from locks.

The three maps included here present all of the stretches that can be paddled without lock portages. Most of the bridges on the maps provide easy access, so you can put in or take out wherever you wish, designing trips of variable length. First, we'll look at the feeder canal.

For **camping** opportunities, see the description of Hennepin Canal 2.

Shuttle routes for trips on the feeder canal are easily arranged by using Highway 40 as the primary route.

Water levels. There is always enough water to paddle.

The two obvious trips on the feeder, both using designated boat ramps, are (1) from Highway 40 near Rock Falls to Highway 92 (14.6 miles), and (2) from Highway 92 to County 2000N (9.8 miles), but the first is definitely on the long side. Another good trip begins at 2000N, then turns east into the main canal and ends at the boat ramp near the Hennepin Canal Parkway State Park Visitor Center (6.2 miles). One big advantage of paddling the Hennepin is that the slow current permits you to put in anywhere, paddle for awhile, then return to your starting point.

The Highway 40 boat landing just south of Rock Falls is the northernmost access on the feeder. While you're in the area, a trip into Rock Falls will enable you to see the lock alongside the Rock River dam where the feeder originates. The dam also is the trailhead of the paved biking/hiking trail that runs alongside the canal all the way to Highway 92.

A highlight of the feeder route is the nearby town of Tampico, at County 300N and Highway 172. President Ronald Reagan was born here in an apartment over the bank, then spent his boyhood in nearby Dixon. Farther south on the feeder, the aqueduct over the Green River is the longest on the canal, and is equipped with submerged emergency gates to prevent canal dewatering in case of a break in the banks. The aqueducts are big concrete troughs supported by concrete piers and steel beams.

Bikers and hikers use the Hennepin Canal towpath heavily.

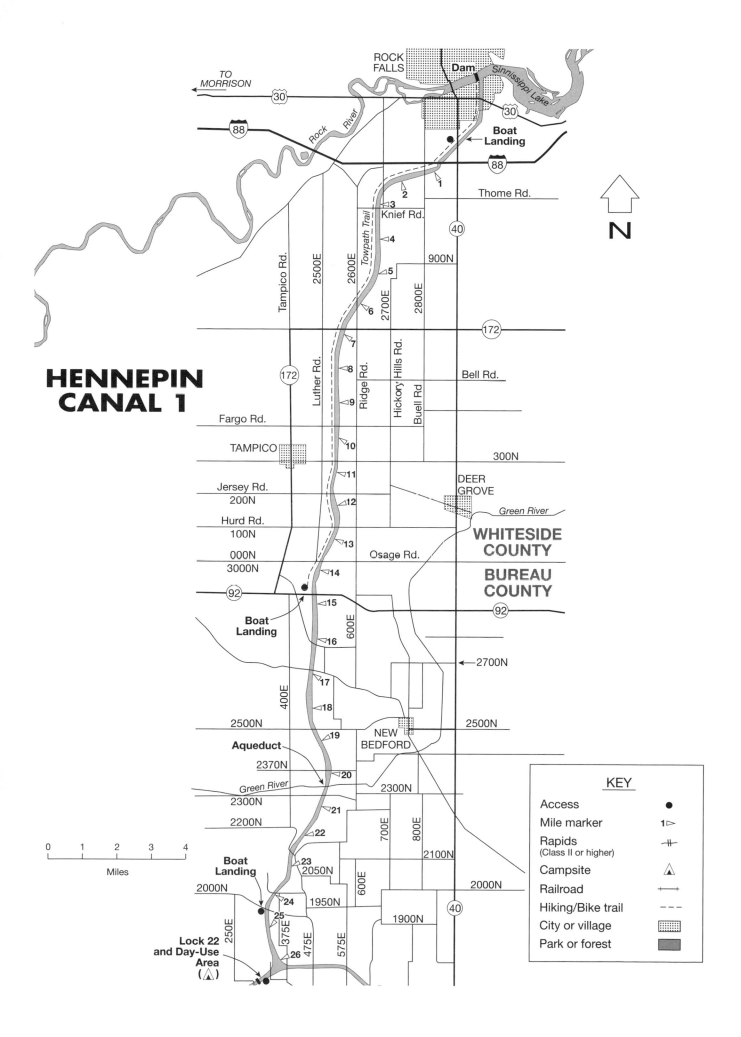

HENNEPIN CANAL 1

KEY

Access	●
Mile marker	1▷
Rapids (Class II or higher)	╫
Campsite	◬
Railroad	┼┼
Hiking/Bike trail	---
City or village	▦
Park or forest	▬

HENNEPIN CANAL 2
Main Canal: Highway 78 to Lock 21 (17.5 Miles)

In its long southward route from Rock Falls to the T where the main canal branches to the east and west, the feeder canal has a total drop of only 1 foot. After the feeder joins the mainline, there is a low-gradient, 11-mile section of the main canal between Locks 21 and 22—called the summit pool or feeder basin. On either side of the summit pool, however, the fall is considerable: 196 feet in the 17.5 miles from Lock 21 to the Illinois River, and 93 feet in the 46.3 miles between Lock 22 and the Mississippi.

This gradient necessitated many locks to enable barges to ascend the canal from the Illinois, then descend to the Mississippi. Altogether, there were thirty-two locks on the main canal (twenty-one east of the feeder, eleven west of it), each measuring 170 feet by 35 feet. East of Lock 21 (near Wyanet), the locks average less than a mile apart; thus, canoeing that part of the canal is suitable only for boaters who enjoy frequent portages. Besides, the easternmost portion of the canal past Lock 6 (south of Princeton, on Highway 2160E) is now dry.

Camping is allowed at a number of places along the canal, including the four locations indicated on the maps (near Locks 21, 22, and 23, and the Highway 78 bridge). Camping is permitted alongside the canal towpath, except the section on the feeder from Highway 92 north to Rock Falls. Public camping is also available at Johnson Sauk State Park south of Annawan, Morrison-Rockwood State Park northwest of Rock Falls, Green River Conser-vation Area southeast of Rock Falls, and Prophetstown State Park. A number of private campgrounds are found in the area, too, including Geneseo Campground, along-side the canal north of Geneseo on Highway 82.

Shuttle routes depend upon the trip that you select, and are readily determined from the map. In addition to the designated boat landings (indicated on the map), most bridges provide good access. Remember, too, that out-and-back trips are an option: you never have to worry about bucking the current on your way back.

Water levels. There is always enough water to paddle.

On the eastern leg of the canal, the most obvious trip originates near the feeder junction (at County 2000N or Lock 22, for instance) and ends at Lock 21—or vice versa—totaling 11–12 miles. This is one of the most attractive sections of the canal. A big highlight is the Hennepin Canal Parkway State Park Visitor Center, a great place to stop for lunch. Be sure to see the excellent displays in the center; they'll give you a deeper appreciation and understanding of the canal's past. Near the boat ramp west of the visitor center is a picturesque metal truss bridge (no longer used), a reminder of the bridges that once crossed the canal before being replaced by modern structures and "tube" bridges.

Much of this section is beautifully wooded and creeklike. Between the visitor center and the Highway 6/34 bridge, there are a couple of miles where the canal was built over a peat bog; this stretch tends to be shallow, but canoeists have no problems with it. The Lock 21 landing and day-use area are located immediately south of Highway 6/34. Like all of the day-use areas on the canal, Lock 21 has toilets and plenty of parking.

Good canoeing on the western end of the canal begins at Lock 22, where there's another comfortable day-use area and boat ramp. From Lock 22 to the Highway 78 landing is 6 miles, while a longer trip to Lock 23 is 9 miles.

Taking out at locks is usually easy. In five locations, convenient boat ramps are found close by. In situations where there is no boat ramp, you can simply pull your boat up alongside the 4–5-foot grassy bank and carry it ashore—either ending your trip at that point or portaging around the lock if you wish to continue.

Paddling through one of the many "tubes" on the Hennepin—huge culverts that have replaced old bridges.

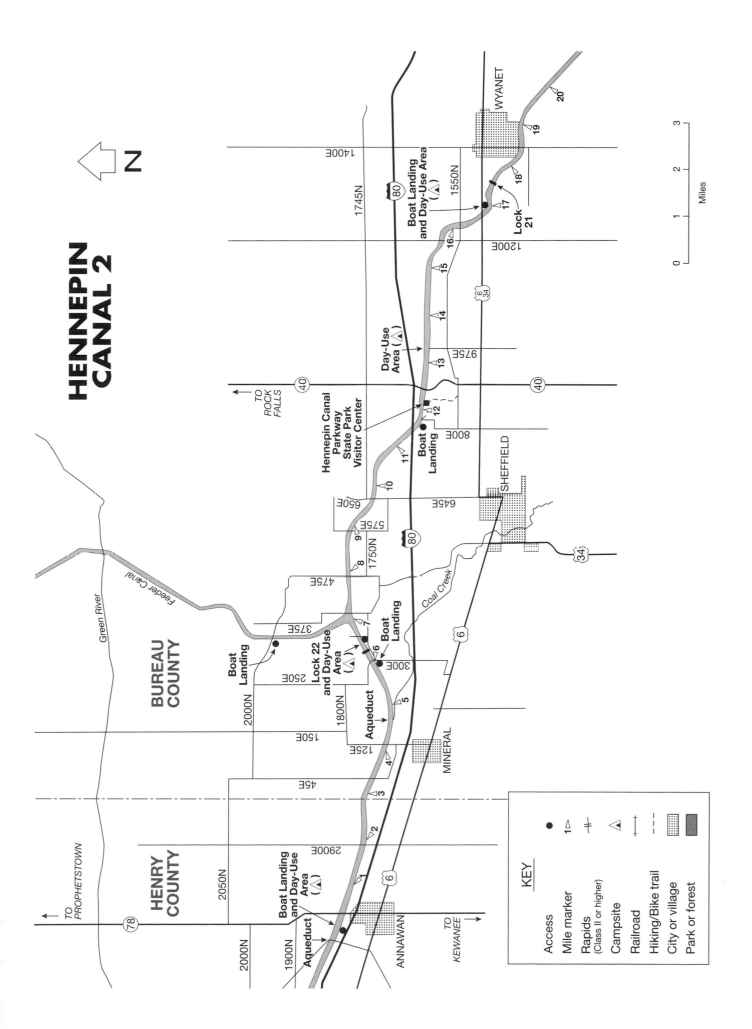

HENNEPIN CANAL 2

N

TO PROPHETSTOWN

Green River

Feeder Canal

BUREAU COUNTY

HENRY COUNTY

TO ROCK FALLS

WYANET

Boat Landing
and Day-Use Area (△)

Lock 21

Day-Use Area (△)

Hennepin Canal Parkway State Park Visitor Center

Boat Landing

SHEFFIELD

Coal Creek

Boat Landing

Lock 22 and Day-Use Area (△)

Aqueduct

Boat Landing

MINERAL

Boat Landing and Day-Use Area (△)

Aqueduct

ANNAWAN

TO KEWANEE

TO PROPHETSTOWN

1400E
1745N
80
1550N
17
18
19
20
1200E
6 34
15
16
14
13
975E
40
40
800E
12
11
10
650E
645E
575E
9
1750N
80
8
475E
7
375E
34
6
6
5
300E
250E
2000N
1800N
150E
125E
4
45E
3
2
2900E
6
1
2050N
1900N
2000N
78

SHEFFIELD

Miles
0 1 2 3

KEY

●	Access
△1	Mile marker
╫	Rapids (Class II or higher)
◁	Campsite
⊥	Railroad
---	Hiking/Bike trail
▦	City or village
▦	Park or forest

HENNEPIN CANAL 3
Main Canal: Highway 78 to Lock 25 (17 Miles)

Too Little, Too Late

The Illinois-Mississippi Canal was first proposed in the 1830s as a way of cutting 419 miles off the river route from Lake Michigan to Rock Island on the Mississippi. After the political wrangling dragged on for half a century, work finally began in 1890 and was strung out for another seventeen years. When the canal finally opened in 1907, it was already a white elephant. Its dimensions were bigger than those of the previously completed Illinois and Michigan Canal, but not big enough for the barges that later transported goods down the Chicago Sanitary and Ship Canal and the "improved" Illinois River. Thus, the Hennepin never carried more than 1/600 of its anticipated capacity, and was eventually abandoned as a commercial enterprise in 1951. Fortunately, however, the canal has continued to serve an important purpose as a recreational resource. In 1970 the Army Corps of Engineers turned the waterway over to the Illinois DNR, which subsequently has managed it as an important locale for fishing, picnicking, hiking, bicycling, canoeing, camping, horseback riding, and other uses.

Because the western leg of the Hennepin Canal isn't nearly as steep as the eastern portion, the stretches between locks tend to be longer. Starting at Lock 22 near the feeder junction, the interlock intervals are 9, 9, and 5 miles. Farther westward to the terminus of the canal at the Rock River, the intervals shrink, ranging from 1 to 2.5 miles. Several concrete boat ramps are located west of the feeder, and four aqueducts convey the canal over intersecting streams. Attractive day-use areas at Locks 22, 23, and 24 provide excellent accesses, with picnic facilities, toilets, and plenty of parking.

Fishermen are a common sight near the locks and day-use areas, angling for largemouth and smallmouth bass, walleye, bluegill, crappie, channel cat, bullhead, flathead, drum, and carp. Wildlife is more common than you might expect, especially in the wooded areas. In fact, one park official characterizes the canal corridor as a linear wildlife refuge through corn-and-bean country, with plentiful quail, pheasant, partridge, deer, squirrels, possums, and raccoons.

Because the canal's locks aren't functional (navigation was officially ended in 1951), the old wooden gates have been removed and a concrete head wall built at the upstream end, creating a damlike drop.

Five locks have been restored, however, to provide visitors a close-up view of the original construction, and three of the restorations are located in this section: Locks 22, 23, and 24. Lock 22 is particularly noteworthy because of the picturesque girder lift bridge on its downstream end. (A comparable bridge also can be seen at Lock 21 on the eastern leg of the canal.) Be careful on the upstream end of all locks: both the head wall of modified locks and the intake spillway of restored locks can be hazardous.

For **camping,** see the description of Hennepin Canal 2.

Out-and-back **canoe rentals** are available at the Geneseo Campground (309-944-6465), situated alongside the canal just north of the Highway 82 bridge, between Locks 24 and 25; trips begin and end at the campground.

Shuttle routes are easily arranged along Highway 6, where signage clearly indicates the county roads leading north to the canal bridges and day-use areas. Miniscule current makes it possible to dispense with a shuttle by beginning at one point and paddling back to it.

Water levels. There is always enough water to paddle.

As usual, you can access the canal from virtually any bridge, boat landing, or day-use area. There are three obvious between-lock trips: (1) Lock 22 to Lock 23 (9 miles), or shorter trips using the intermediate boat landing at Highway 78; (2) Lock 23 to Lock 24 (9 miles), shortened to 8 miles if you use the boat ramp at Highway 2300E; and (3) the Highway 1500E bridge to the boat ramp just east of Lock 25 (4.5 miles), shortened to 4 miles if the two boat ramps between Locks 24 and 25 are used.

A picturesque lift bridge at one of the Hennepin Canal locks

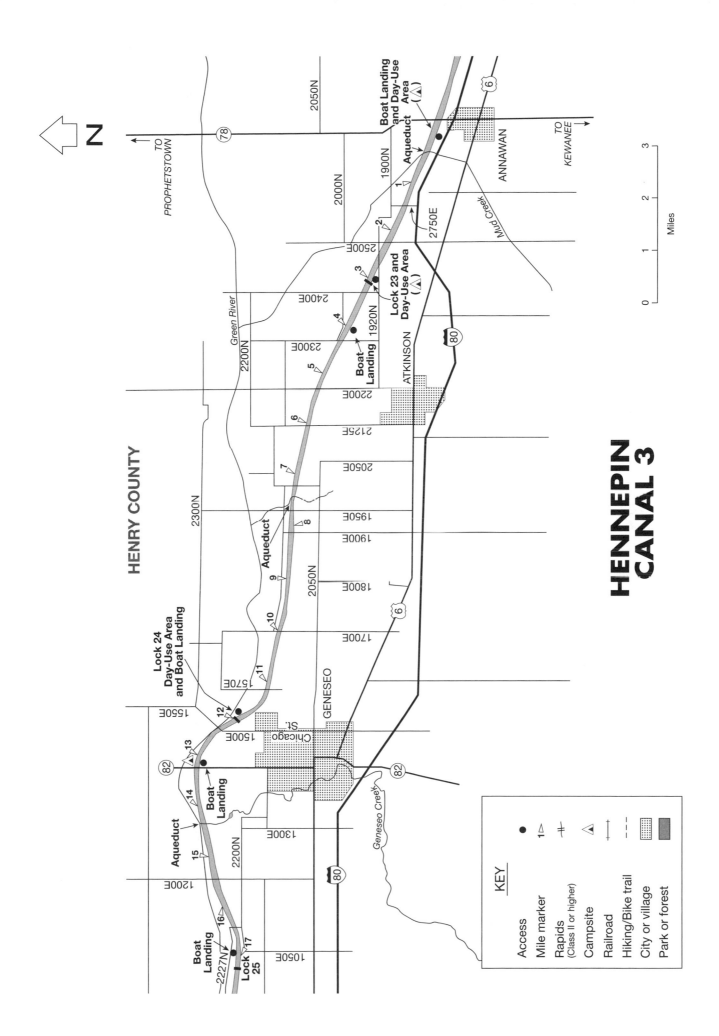

HENNEPIN CANAL 3

HENRY COUNTY

KEY

- Access •
- Mile marker 1△
- Rapids (Class II or higher) ╪
- Campsite ◁
- Railroad ┼
- Hiking/Bike trail ┄
- City or village ▦
- Park or forest ▨

N

TO PROPHETSTOWN

TO KEWANEE

Miles
0 1 2 3

Boat Landing and Day-Use Area (◁)

Aqueduct

ANNAWAN

Mud Creek

Lock 23 and Day-Use Area (▲)

Boat Landing 1920N

ATKINSON

Green River

Aqueduct

GENESEO

Chicago St.

Lock 24 Day-Use Area and Boat Landing

Boat Landing

Aqueduct

Geneseo Creek

Boat Landing

Lock 25

2050N
2000N
1900N
2750E
2500E
2400E
2300E
2200E
2125E
2050E
1950E
1900E
1800E
1700E
1570E
1550E
1500E
1300E
1200E
1050E

2300N
2200N
2050N
2200N
2227N

1
2
3
4
5
6
7
8
9
10
11
12
13
14
15
16
17

78
6
6
80
82
82
80

ILLINOIS AND MICHIGAN CANAL 1
Channahon to Aux Sable Lock 8 (8 Miles)

After Louis Joliet and Father Jacques Marquette made their historic exploratory trip in 1673, including an arduous portage between the Des Plaines and Chicago Rivers, Joliet suggested a canal be cut between the neighboring rivers, thus opening up a water route between the Great Lakes and the Mississippi. Nearly two centuries later, his idea came to fruition with the opening of the Illinois and Michigan Canal, a waterway that was a prime impetus for the development of the Midwest and the rapid growth of Chicago as a center of transportation and commerce.

After 12 years of construction, the I & M opened in 1848, paralleling the Des Plaines and Illinois Rivers and stretching 96 miles from Chicago to LaSalle. Because there was an elevational difference of 141 feet between the Chicago and Illinois rivers, fifteen locks were required along the canal, together with four aqueducts over creeks and rivers. Sixty feet wide at water level and 6 feet deep, the canal allowed long, narrow boats to carry huge quantities of grain, lumber, meat, stone, coal, salt, and manufactured goods to and from Chicago. Eventually, however, competition from railroads and the canal's inadequate dimensions caused it to decline, and its use for shipping ended in 1933 with the opening of the Illinois Waterway (a combination of the Chicago Sanitary and Ship Canal and "improved" Des Plaines and Illinois rivers).

Fortunately, the historical, cultural, and recreational value of the canal has been preserved as the I & M Heritage Corridor. The Illinois DNR has had jurisdiction over the canal since 1974, maintaining a 55-mile biking/hiking trail where the towpath was once located, together with several state parks and other facilities along the way. Fishing, bicycling, hiking, and picnicking are popular, and two stretches lend themselves to canoeing: 14.5 miles between Channahon and Morris, and 5 miles between Utica and LaSalle.

Camping is available at Channahon State Park, Gebhard Woods State Park, McKinley Woods Forest Preserve (Will County Forest Preserve District), and the Des Plaines Conservation Area.

Canoe rental is available at Chicagoland Canoe Base in Chicago (773-777-1489).

The easiest **shuttle route** for the Channahon-to-Aux-Sable stretch goes west on Bridge Road, west on Highway 6, south on Tabler Road, and west on Dellos Road. Shuttling via Bridge Road, Hansel Road, and Cemetery Road is a little shorter. Because there is virtually no current in the canal, boaters can also paddle from Aux Sable to Channahon, or begin at either end and paddle back.

Water levels. There is always enough water to paddle.

Put in at the sandy landing downstream-left from the bridge on Bridge Road, adjacent to a large parking area. Lock 7 is located a short distance upstream from the bridge, near the Du Page River dam, and a gated diversion structure sends water from the river into the canal. On the other side of the Du Page are Lock 6, the lock tender's house, and Channahon State Park—all accessed via the walkway on top of the dam, and well worth a visit. Incidentally, the original dam was built to enable canal boats to float across the impoundment from Lock 6 to Lock 7.

Farm buildings appear on the right for a short time, then disappear as the canal bends right, then left. Low banks on the right are succeeded by lovely wooded hillsides. Curving back and forth, the waterway often seems more like a rural creek than a canal. At McKinley Woods Forest Preserve, a wooden footbridge crosses the canal, with a canoe landing upstream-right and a nearby picnic shelter. After McKinley Woods, the environs of the canal continue to be quite beautiful—densely vegetated, with wooded bluffs on the north side. At one point, the trail on the south bank crosses a small bridge with a spillway under it. A very narrow strip of land—sometimes as little as 15 feet—now separates the canal from the Des Plaines.

A red barn on the right (north) bank is on the site of the old town of Dresden—the barn, a house, and a cemetery are all that remains of Dresden, once a stopping place for stagecoach riders and later for canal travelers. If you'd like to see the Dresden Island Lock and Dam and nearby nuclear plant, take out on the left bank opposite the red barn and walk to the Des Plaines from the trail. Incidentally, you are now near the point where the Des Plaines and Kankakee come together to form the Illinois River.

At McLindon Road, two bridges cross the canal—an old, no-longer-used truss bridge, then the new one. Between the bridges, on the south bank, is a small parking lot, with toilets and a good place to access the canal. To the west, power lines and a railroad bridge cross the canal, which continues to be woodsy and intimate.

About 100 yards west of the Tabler Road bridge, the canal crosses Aux Sable Creek in a concrete-and-steel aqueduct (a modern replacement for the original stone-and-wood structure), then comes to Lock 8 fifty yards later. **Take out** on either bank before the lock; parking lots are located nearby, on both Dellos Road and Cemetery Road. The Aux Sable area is quite interesting and picturesque, and is popular with tourists and fishermen. A lock tender's house sits on the south bank, all that remains of the village of Aux Sable.

Aux Sable Lock 8

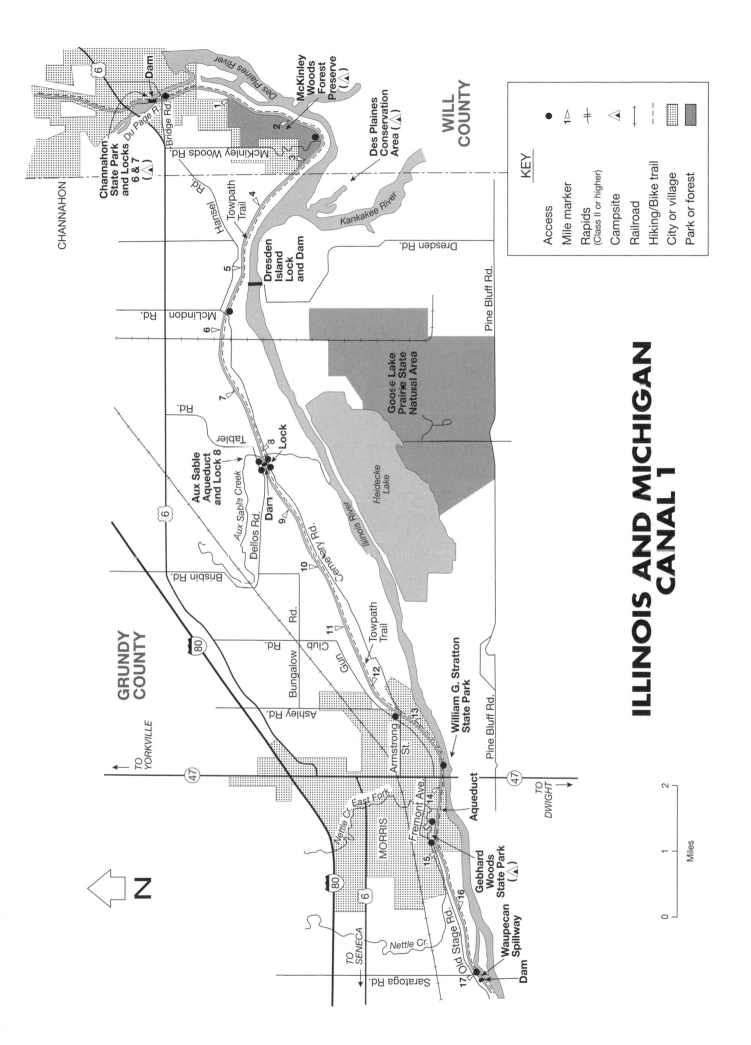

ILLINOIS AND MICHIGAN CANAL 1

ILLINOIS AND MICHIGAN CANAL 2
Aux Sable Lock 8 to Gebhard Woods State Park (6.5 Miles)

For canoeists and kayakers, the best place to experience the historic Illinois and Michigan Canal firsthand is the 14.5-mile section from Channahon to Morris. There have been a few changes since the heyday of the canal—such as replacement of wooden lock gates with concrete ones—but the canal is otherwise much like the waterway that shippers used from 1848 to 1933.

"Breakouts" have always been the bane of canal managers, and the I & M experienced a bad one in 1996 when floodwater on the Du Page River destroyed the dam at Channahon, resulting in the dewatering of the canal. By the time the dam was rebuilt in 1998 and the canal rewatered, the DNR had removed considerable debris and silt from the waterway. Cattails, algae, and other aquatic vegetation have grown thickly in several parts of the 14.5-mile stretch since 1998, however, requiring periodic removal by DNR personnel to keep a channel open for paddlers, especially in the 6.5-mile section west of Lock 8. Thus, boaters are advised to call the I & M Canal Information Center at Morris beforehand to make sure the channel is clear (815-942-0796). Another way to check out the canal close-up is to take a quick bike trip from Channahon to Gebhard Woods State Park (or vice versa) on the excellent trail along the south bank. This part of the canal isn't quite as attractive as the previous section; it's straighter, for example, has no wooded hillsides, and passes through a partly urban setting. But it has charms of its own and is worth paddling if the in-stream plant life permits.

For **camping** and **canoe rental**, see the description of I & M Canal 1.

The shortest **shuttle route** from the designated put-in goes west on Cemetery Road, west on Armstrong Street, south on Highway 47, west on Fremont Avenue, and south on Shabbona Street to the entrance of Gebhard Woods State Park. You can paddle either direction, of course, or can begin and end at the same place.

Water levels. There is always enough water to paddle.

Put in downstream from Lock 8 on either bank; small parking lots are located along Dellos Road on the north and Cemetery Road on the south. Two informative historical signs tell the story of the I & M and the little settlement here that disappeared after the decline of the canal. About 100 yards downstream from the lock is a charming old truss bridge (now closed to traffic) from which farmers once loaded grain into barges through a trapdoor. A half mile farther downstream, some houses can be seen on the north side of the canal, and later a group of houses sits along the canal on the left. For the most part, however, the setting is wild and wooded.

After the Armstrong Street bridge, the city of Morris is close by on the north bank. A canoe landing is located nearby. William G. Stratton State Park soon appears on the left, after a wooden vehicular bridge that leads to the eastern end of the park from Morris. The park is a popular motorboat access on the nearby Illinois River, but also makes a good access for canoeists on the canal; there's a huge parking lot near the left (south) bank, immediately east of the Highway 47 bridge. The canal now passes under the north end of the bridge. Farther west, near an attractive metal footbridge that crosses from the Morris business district, an aerating sprinkler creates a fountain in the canal.

After two more bridges, a small aqueduct carries the canal over Nettle Creek. Then the graceful metal footbridge downstream indicates that you are in Gebhard Woods State Park. Gebhard Woods is a lovely park with picnic shelters, campground, toilets, a playground, and a nature trail. The information center (headquarters for the I & M Trail) has excellent displays and literature on the canal, and is an interesting place to visit. In addition to Armstrong Street and Stratton Park, there are 4 canoe landings that can serve as **take-outs**: (1) Canal Port Plaza three quarters of a mile east of Gebhard Woods in Morris, (2) Gebhard Woods itself, (3) Mud Bridge one block west of Gebhard Woods in Morris, and (4) the Waupecan Spillway west of Morris.

Other trips. Approximately 5 miles of the canal between Utica and LaSalle (Lock 14) are also canoeable in the spring and early summer before aquatic growth makes paddling difficult. One highlight of this stretch is Split Rock, an impressive dolomite-and-sandstone escarpment alongside the canal. This section, too, can be scouted beforehand by bicycling the trail. **Canoe rental** and shuttle service for this section are available at Canoe the Vermilion, north of Streator (815-673-3218).

A Glimpse of Illinois's Prairie Heritage

Before settlement by Europeans in the 1800s, Illinois was mostly prairie—as much as 60 percent of its area was covered with such prairie grasses as big bluestem, Indian grass, cordgrass, and switchgrass, sometimes as high as 12 feet. Traveling through the dense vegetation, together with the wetland that often fostered it, was quite intimidating for the first settlers, who initially preferred to locate their homesites in wooded groves. Today you can still get an idea of what it must have been like back then, by visiting the Goose Lake Prairie State Natural Area, a few miles east of Morris. The 2,500 acres of Goose Lake are the largest remnant of prairie left in Illinois, and you can experience it by walking its 7 miles of trails and visiting the information center. (See the map.)

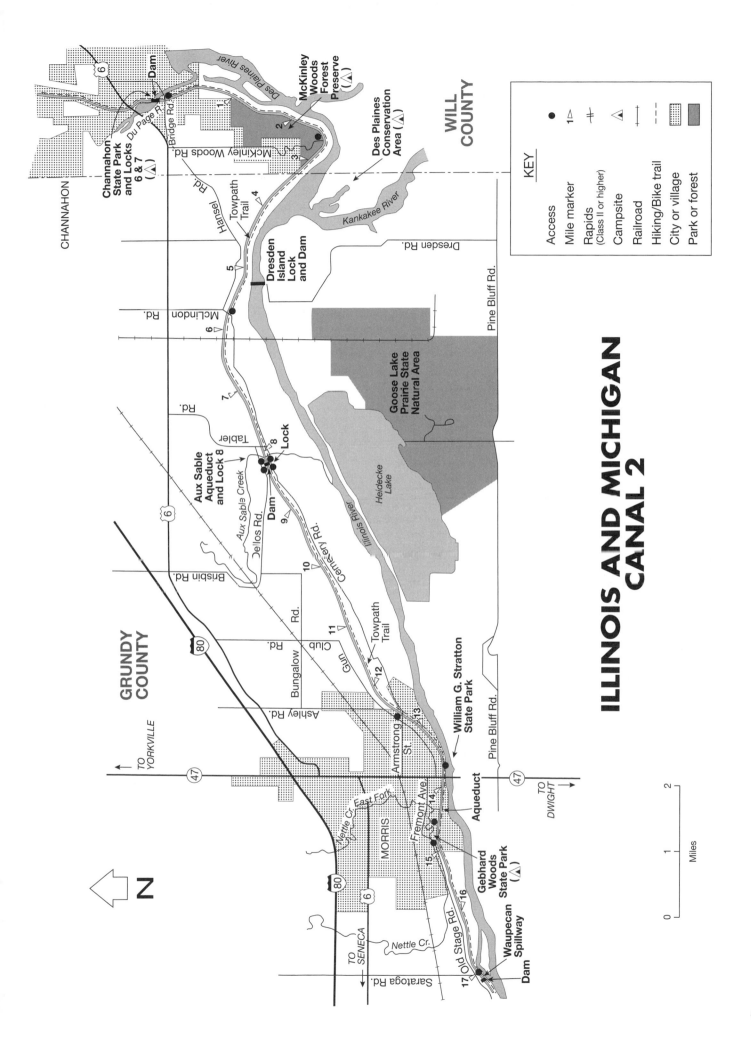

ILLINOIS AND MICHIGAN CANAL 2

IROQUOIS RIVER 1
Watseka to Plato Bridge (15.2 Miles)

Invasion from the East

No Illinois tribe had much success in resisting the periodic raids of the Iroquois. This confederation of tribes (Mohawk, Oneida, Onondaga, Cayuga, and Seneca) from the New York area was never very populous, but their political, organizational, and military skills were always superior to those of other Native American nations. In the 1600s, one Algonquin tribe after another fled their ferocity and resettled in the Midwest—including the Potawatomi, Ottawa, Ojibwa, Sauk, and Fox. These migrations eventually resulted in conflict with the tribes who already inhabited Illinois—principally the Illiniwek confederation of Kaskaskia, Cahokia, Peoria, Tamaroa, Michigamea, and Moingwena. By the mid-1600s the Iroquois had defeated most of their eastern neighbors, so they turned westward and directed much of their attention to Illinois. For half a century the Illiniwek felt the wrath of the Iroquois—abandoning their huge village on the Illinois River (near modern Utica) and sometimes fleeing across the Mississippi. In the 1700s the Illiniwek dwindled in numbers and power, partly because of the Iroquois but also because of their own disunity. To learn more about Illinois's Native American past, see Wayne C. Temple's *Indian Villages of the Illinois Country* (Springfield: Illinois State Museum, 1987).

Flowing west out of Indiana into Iroquois County, the Iroquois River turns north at the city of Watseka and joins the Kankakee River a few miles southeast of the city of Kankakee. Altogether, it is about 94 miles long, with 55 of its miles in Illinois. The country through which it runs is flat farmland; in fact, 94 percent of the total area of Iroquois County is agricultural, a little higher than the 89 percent of neighboring Kankakee County. The level terrain is reflected in a minimal gradient of less than half a foot per mile for most of the river's length. Before settlement, prairie grass covered the region, and long before that, the area was a glacial lake bed (Lake Watseka). Two or three times a year, on average, the Iroquois is subject to flooding, largely because of the flat terrain.

The river isn't one of the canoeing gems of Illinois, but when the water level is neither too high nor too low, it's a pleasant place to paddle for a day or two. Although the surroundings are almost entirely farmland, wooded shoreline is continuous and gives the river an isolated feeling most of the time. Tranquil and slow, the Iroquois is a good beginner's river: there are almost no riffles, and obstructions are infrequent. The mud banks are generally rather high and steep, and make it difficult to get out of your boat, especially if you must portage around a deadfall obstruction: **be careful!** Although the water gets clearer in the summer, it always has a muddy cast to it. The two sections described here range in width from 80 to 150 feet. The river has a variety of fish, including catfish, smallmouth and largemouth bass, walleye, northern pike, panfish, and drum.

Private **campgrounds** are found to the north on County 6000S (Kankakee South KOA), and east of Momence (Lake Alexander Campground). North of Kankakee is Kankakee River State Park, which has several camping areas.

The **shuttle route** (10.2 miles) for the Watseka-to-Plato-Bridge stretch starts at the West Main Street landing, then heads north on Highway 1 (Jefferson Street), and west on County 2400N (Pittwood Road) to the Plato Bridge. There are no intermediate accesses.

For **water levels**, check the gauge near Chebanse (station #05526000) on the USGS Web site listed in the introduction.

Put in at the public boat landing at the end of West Main Street on the north side of Watseka. There is enough parking to accommodate several cars. This landing is the only practical put-in: upstream, the river is considerably smaller and subject to logjams. The section from Watseka downstream is often canoed; trees occasionally fall in from the banks, but the river's width usually leaves plenty of room to get around them.

At the put-in, the river is relatively small, but after bending to the right it is soon augmented by Sugar Creek. After a short straightaway, a sharp right turn initiates two big loops that are collectively known as Nine-Mile Bend. As a result, you won't go very far "as the crow flies," but will paddle a considerable distance before the take-out. Banks are steep and wooded from the outset, and few buildings are seen on the whole trip. Usually, cultivated fields are fairly close on both sides, separated from the river by a narrow band of trees, and fishing boats are occasionally seen tied along the high banks. The setting changes little as you paddle along.

After completing the first northeastward loop, the river bends to the right to begin a second loop. At this point, the road (1800E) runs along the left bank for awhile. Later, after the second loop has been completed, the road again hugs the left shore all the way to the Fiddler Bridge.

The river now enters another isolated area, curving gently back and forth until it swings left alongside 2400N. As you approach the bridge, numerous trailers appear along the river. **Take out** at the concrete boat ramp downstream-right, just before the entrance to a trailer camp along the river.

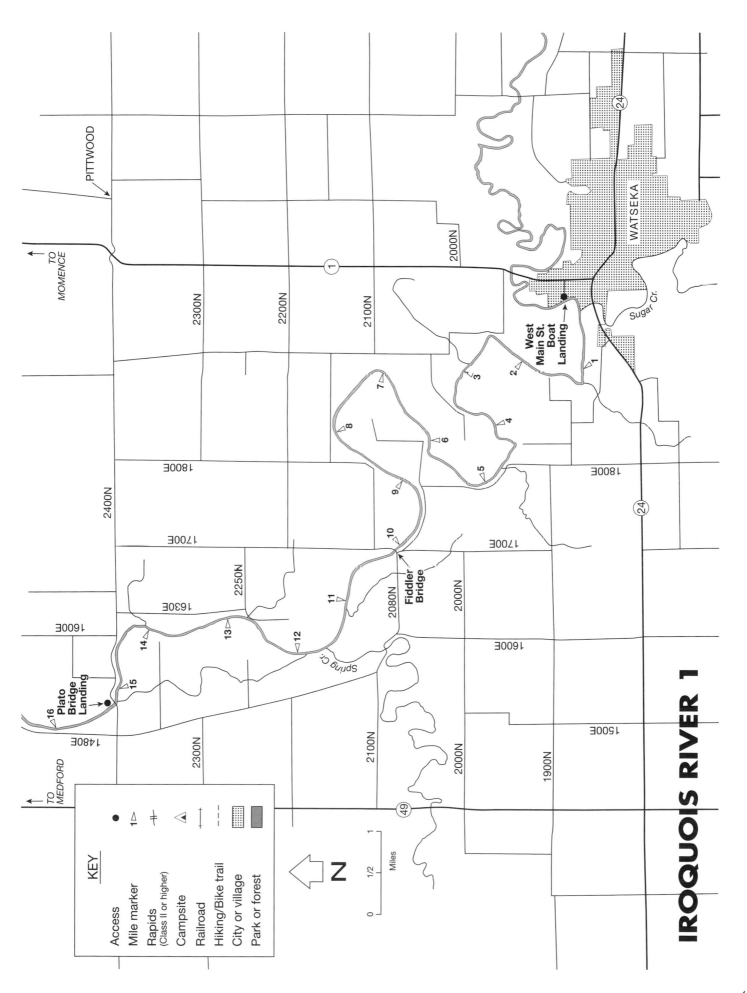

IROQUOIS RIVER 1

IROQUOIS RIVER 2
Plato Bridge to Aroma Park (18.5 Miles)

In its last miles before joining the Kankakee River near Aroma Park, the Iroquois is similar to the previous section from Watseka to Plato. Still placid, it flows in an unaltered channel between wooded, muddy banks over a silt, sand, and gravel bottom. No dams block its low-gradient course, which is generally suitable for inexperienced canoeists except when the water is high. There are a few differences from the upstream portion of the river, however. You'll see more dwellings, for example, and the river will grow progressively wider as you approach the mouth. Overall, this part of the river is straighter, and at one point you'll encounter a long, rocky shoal. Unlike the previous section, which has only one intermediate bridge, this stretch has four—one of which offers an access that enables you to shorten trip length. Two nature preserves are passed in the last few miles of the river. Both the put-in and take-out are convenient concrete boat landings. Logjams are infrequent, but when they do occur, the steep banks make it difficult to get out of your boat.

For **camping** and **water levels**, see Iroquois River 1.

The **shuttle route** for a short trip from Plato to Sugar Island goes west on County 2400N, north on County 1480E/1500E, and east on County 7750S. For a longer trip to Aroma Park, continue past the Sugar Island bridge to County 2500E, go north to County 4000S, east to County 3250E, then north into Aroma Park. The boat landing is in Potawatomi Park, to your left (west) as soon as you cross the Kankakee River.

The **gradient** is a miniscule 0.25 foot per mile.

Put in at the boat landing at Plato Bridge, downstream-right. Now a small riverside community, Plato once was the site of a ferry and post office. Immediately after the landing is a long series of cabins, homes, and trailers, some with boat docks. The road is close by on the left for awhile as the river arcs right. At one point, a rutted gravel road leads down to an access on the bank—once used as a landing by a local sportsmen's club.

Soon the river passes under a couple of bridges—first the modern structure at Highway 52, then a charming, old one-lane truss bridge on County 2700N, near the tiny community of L'Erable. Neither is a good access. Two miles later, another bridge crosses the river at County 2900N. Houses appear near the river occasionally, but are sparse.

Several creeks enter on both sides as the river continues its northward course for several miles toward Sugar Island, where the streambed is a long, rock outcrop that creates a rocky shoal several hundred yards long. In low-water conditions, this is a push-and-scrape area, but riffles and waves are created when the water is higher. Incidentally, the outcrop here serves as a dam of sorts that forms a pool for many miles upstream, all the way to the Watseka area. At the Sugar Island bridge, a short gravel road leads down to the rocky shoreline (downstream-left), where canoe access is easy. By the way, the name "Sugar Island" comes from the large piece of land cut off by a narrow channel just downstream from the bridge.

Within a couple of miles, River Road lies close along the left shore, and houses with docks become more numerous. Iroquois Woods Nature Preserve (with 47 acres of old-growth forest) appears on the right shoreline in a right curve, immediately before the mouth of Minnie Creek on the left.

The river gets wider, the tree line thinner, and houses more numerous as you continue toward the mouth. The current almost disappears as you paddle into the pool created by the Kankakee River dam downstream at Kankakee. Less than a mile from the mouth, a nature preserve occupies the 22 acres of Gooseberry Island, and marshy vegetation begins to appear.

To **take out**, paddle out the mouth of the Iroquois to the opposite shore of the Kankakee, then upstream a short distance to the Potawatomi Park boat landing in Aroma Park (river-right).

The Fur Trader and His Pretty Woman

Early settlement of the Iroquois County area goes back to the 1820s, when a fur trader named Gurdon Hubbard established a trading post a few miles northeast of the present site of Watseka. In subsequent years, he helped establish an important trail between Chicago and Vincennes, Indiana, that came to be called Hubbard's Trace. The trail followed essentially the same route as today's Highway 1. Soon after arriving in the area, Hubbard married a Potawatomi named *Watch-e-kee* ("pretty woman"), for whom the Iroquois County seat was later renamed Watseka.

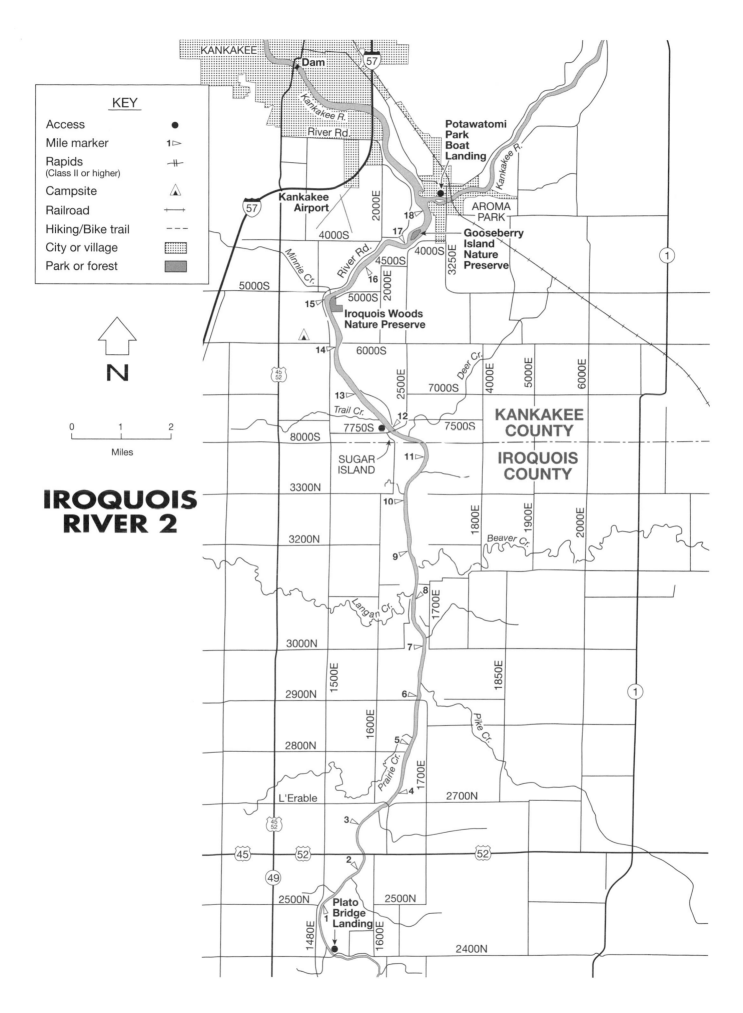

IROQUOIS RIVER 2

KEY

Access   ●

Mile marker   1▷

Rapids   —#—
(Class II or higher)

Campsite   △

Railroad   ——

Hiking/Bike trail   – – –

City or village

Park or forest

N

0 1 2
Miles

KANKAKEE

Dam

57

Kankakee R.

River Rd.

Potawatomi
Park
Boat
Landing

Kankakee R.

Kankakee
Airport

57

2000E

AROMA
PARK

18

17

Gooseberry
Island
Nature
Preserve

4000S

4000S

3250E

1

Minnie Cr.

River Rd.

4500S

2000E

5000S

16

15

5000S

Iroquois Woods
Nature Preserve

5000S

14

6000S

2500E

Deer Cr.

7000S

4000E

5000E

6000E

45
52

13

Trail Cr.

12

7750S

7500S

KANKAKEE
COUNTY

8000S

11

SUGAR
ISLAND

IROQUOIS
COUNTY

3300N

10

3200N

1800E

1900E

2000E

Beaver Cr.

9

8

1700E

Langan Cr.

7

3000N

1500E

6

2900N

1600E

1850E

1

5

2800N

Prairie Cr.

1700E

4

L'Erable

2700N

45
52

3

45

52

52

2

49

2500N

2500N

Plato
Bridge
Landing

1480E

1

1600E

2400N

KANKAKEE RIVER 1
State Line Road to Momence (9.5 Miles)

The Grand Marsh

In its two-state journey, today's Kankakee is much shorter than its original length. When Europeans began settling the area in the early 1800s, there was a limestone outcrop just upstream from where Momence is now located, backing the river up into a vast marshland extending deep into Indiana. The river meandered lazily through half a million acres of the "Grand Marsh," which became a haven for trappers and hunters. In order to turn the swamps and marshes into farmland, channelization of the river and its tributaries was begun in the 1880s, and in 1893 the rock ledge at Momence was dynamited. By the early 1900s, most of the Kankakee in Indiana essentially had been converted into a drainage ditch. Fortunately, the Illinois portion of the river channel has not been straightened, and in the Momence Wetlands it still twists through 1,600 acres of sloughs and swamps.

Initiated in 1998, a project of the U.S. Fish and Wildlife Service seeks to purchase 30,000 acres of remaining wetland along the Kankakee in Illinois and Indiana in order to establish a national wildlife refuge that will preserve a small fragment of the Grand Marsh.

From its source near South Bend, Indiana, the Kankakee crosses into Illinois and flows another 62 miles through the cities of Momence, Kankakee, and Wilmington before joining the Des Plaines near Channahon to form the Illinois River. In the 9.5-mile stretch from the Indiana border to Momence, you can still get a taste of ancient wetlands. Only the Sugar River in northern Illinois and the Cache in the far south offer comparable marshland experiences for paddlers. This section of the Kankakee still runs in its original channel through bottomland forest and swamps populated with beaver, herons, egrets, wood ducks, terns, and a host of other wildlife. Be forewarned that deadfall obstructions are not infrequent.

Riverside **camping** is available at the Lake Alexander Campground east of Momence; it can be reached from the river or from Highway 114. Also in the area are Kankakee River State Park (north of Kankakee) and Kankakee South KOA Campground.

Canoe rental is available from Reed's Canoe Trips in Kankakee (815-932-2663).

The **shuttle route** (9 miles) goes south on State Line Road, west on Highway 114, north on Highway 17/1 into Momence, and east on Fourth Street to the public boat landing. The intersection of State Line Road and Highway 114 is on a dangerous curve, so be careful when turning.

Not surprisingly, the **gradient** is only 1 foot per mile.

For **water levels,** check the gauge at Momence (station #05520500) on the USGS Web site listed in the introduction.

Put in at the boat landing at the rickety old State Line Road bridge (upstream-right), or downstream-left alongside the road. The latter is usually the better option, especially when the water is high enough to make bridge clearance inadequate for canoeists. Fishermen are often seen fishing from the bank here. From the bridge, take a look east at the Indiana portion of the river—unattractively channelized and straight as an arrow.

Take the left (main) channel at the island just downstream from the bridge; the right side is usually choked with deadfall. Narrow at the beginning—only about 60 feet—the river is surrounded by swamps, low banks, and lowland forest. A left curve immediately follows the bridge, then a right turn goes past a cabin; deadfall has a tendency to collect at this right turn.

Dense swampy areas, often with sloughs off the main channel, continue on both sides as the river broadens, becoming especially wide where a series of cabins appears on the left shore, at the end of County 17000E. There are many sandbars.

After a left turn, the houses of Illiana Heights are seen atop the high right bank for a short time. Except for periodic dwellings, the wild surroundings continue. By now, the river has widened to 100 feet. Eventually the river makes an abrupt right turn, then an abrupt left, forming a small peninsula filled with houses and ringed with retaining walls. As soon as you start swinging back to the right, there's an inlet leading to the River Isle Campground. Three old concrete piers follow shortly, then a long stretch with no cabins. Finally, a group of houses appears on the left where streams enter on both sides. In the straight section that follows, you can access Lake Alexander Campground; the landing is an easy-to-miss bare spot on the left shoreline.

Houses become thick on both sides as you approach the city of Momence. **Take out** at the public boat ramp on the right, immediately downstream from a radio tower and a set of overhead wires. The landing is in a big left curve. Paddlers who continue past this point must be aware of a dangerous low-head dam in the right channel of the huge island that begins downstream from the landing. If continuing, head for the left side of the river and stay there until the island has been cleared (after the Highway 17/1 bridge).

Other trips. To extend the trip by 4 miles and to contrast Illinois's natural channel with Indiana's dredged one, you can put in farther east near Highway 41 and paddle through the LaSalle State Fish and Wildlife Area.

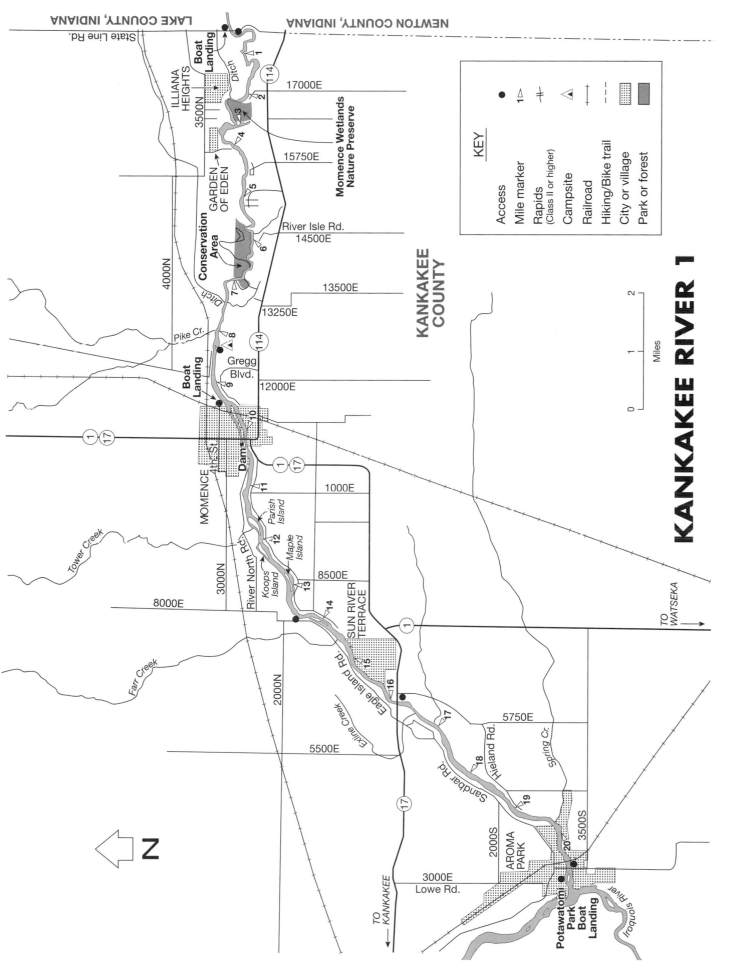

State Line Rd.

Boat
Landing

Ditch

ILLIANA
HEIGHTS

3500N

17000E

Momence Wetlands
Nature Preserve

GARDEN
OF EDEN

15750E

Conservation
Area

4000N

River Isle Rd.

14500E

13500E

13250E

Ditch

7

Pike Cr.

8

114

Boat
Landing

Gregg
Blvd.

9

12000E

10

1   17

4th St.

Dam

MOMENCE

11

1   17

1000E

Parish
Island

12

Maple
Island

River North Rd.

Koops
Island

13

8500E

SUN RIVER
TERRACE

14

3000N

8000E

15

Eagle Island Rd.

2000N

16

17

5750E

Hieland Rd.

Spring Cr.

Exline Creek

18

5500E

Sandbar Rd.

19

2000S

AROMA
PARK

3500S

20

3000E
Lowe Rd.

TO
KANKAKEE

Potawatomi
Park
Boat
Landing

Iroquois River

Tower Creek

Farr Creek

TO
WATSEKA

KANKAKEE
COUNTY

KANKAKEE RIVER 1

N

KEY

Access

Mile marker

Rapids
(Class II or higher)

Campsite

Railroad

Hiking/Bike trail

City or village

Park or forest

Miles

0   1   2

KANKAKEE RIVER 2

Momence to Aroma Park (11 Miles)

Lore of the Kankakee

Called the River of the Miami in the late 1600s because of the Native Americans who lived in the area, the Kankakee was called the *Tioakakee* or *Theakiki* by the Potawatomi who came along later (variously translated as "wolf," "wonderful land," "wonderful river," and "swampy place"). Gurdon Hubbard and his associate Noel Le Vassuer obtained furs from the Potawatomi along the Kankakee and Iroquois in the 1820s. When the Potawatomi ceded their land after the Blackhawk War of 1832, French Canadians settled here, establishing the community of Bourbonnais (named after another fur trader). Historically, the river's chief claim to fame goes back to 1679, when the intrepid explorer LaSalle used it as part of his route to the Mississippi. Unlike Marquette and Joliet, who had earlier used the portage route involving the Chicago and Des Plaines Rivers, LaSalle paddled up the St. Joseph River from Lake Michigan, then portaged 4 miles across to the Kankakee.

From Momence downstream, the Kankakee is like a different river. The surrounding terrain is still flat, but the banks are higher and the river now flows mostly over gravel and bedrock. Although most of the river after Momence remains heavily wooded, houses are much more frequent, roads are never far away, and the streambed is considerably wider. Attractive, forested islands are common. Motorboats are seen more often than in the previous stretch, especially near Momence and Aroma Park, but are usually not a problem for canoeists. The put-in and take-out are both first-rate, and a good intermediate access makes shorter trips possible. Overall, the 20.5 miles from the state line to Aroma Park make a pleasant two-day canoe trip, with an overnight stop at one of the two riverside campgrounds.

For **campgrounds, canoe rental,** and **water levels,** see Kankakee River 1.

The **shuttle route** (11.7 miles) is easier than it sounds. From the public boat ramp in Momence, go west on Fourth Street, south on Franklin Street, west on River North Road, south on County 8000E, west on County 2030N, south on County 7860E, southwest on Eagle Island Road/Sandbar Road, west on Third Street in Aroma Park, south on Bridge Street, and west on Front Street to the landing.

The **gradient** is only 1.4 feet per mile.

Put in at the excellent public boat ramp at the end of Fourth Street in Momence. (The city, incidentally, is named after the Potawatomi chief Momenza, and was once an important stopping place on Hubbard's Trace, the fur-trading route that ran from Vincennes, Indiana, to Chicago. The trail crossed the river at a ford about a mile east of where the Highway 17/1 bridge is now located.)

Homes line both sides of the river at the put-in and will be seen periodically throughout the trip. As soon as you leave the landing, a big island with a park on it can be seen just downstream. Be sure to stay to the left because a dangerous dam (an old mill structure) lies at the end of the right channel. A railroad bridge crosses the island (steer clear of the big concrete piers), followed by some riffles, then the Highway 17/1 bridge. The island ends soon after the highway bridge; take a peek up the right channel at the old dam.

After the bridge, houses continue on both sides for awhile, and the river widens to more than 200 feet. Sizable islands occur where the river bends left; on the right, Van Drunen Farms often gives off a heady scent of chives. A lovely home occupies one island and a bridge crosses the narrow right channel between the island and the right shoreline.

After Van Drunen Farms, houses end and the river environs become wild. Generally, the shoreline consists of low, grassy, and muddy banks with dense trees. Fishermen are occasionally seen along the banks. Finally, the houseless stretch ends with three houses on stilts, on an island (formerly a resort), opposite a private boat ramp on the left. Islands continue, large and small, with many homes on the left. In a long left turn, just before a slender island, a sandy access appears on the right shoreline, off Eagle Island Road. Houses continue off and on, sometimes with boat docks, but trees are always present to maintain a natural appearance.

After a golf course on the left, the river swings right under the Highway 17 bridges, where there's a clay-and-sand access downstream-left. There are few islands after Highway 17, but numerous houses; seldom is the shoreline open, however, as the tree line continues. At one point, the river broadens to several hundred feet and becomes riffly over the rocky bottom. After a lovely old stone house and outbuilding on the left (where a ferry was once located), houses disappear and the shoreline becomes deeply wooded—the wildest part of the trip. Eventually houses resume on both sides as you enter Aroma Park.

In the final left bend, a railroad bridge and highway bridge come into view. There are two **take-outs:** (1) a gravel landing at a small village park immediately downstream-left from the railroad bridge, near a restaurant; or (2) the Potawatomi Park boat ramp, a couple hundred yards downstream-right from the vehicular bridge (stay to the right of the island after the bridge). Located on West Front Street, off South Bridge Street, the park has a big parking lot and pleasant picnic facilities.

In no hurry to get to the Kankakee River take-out

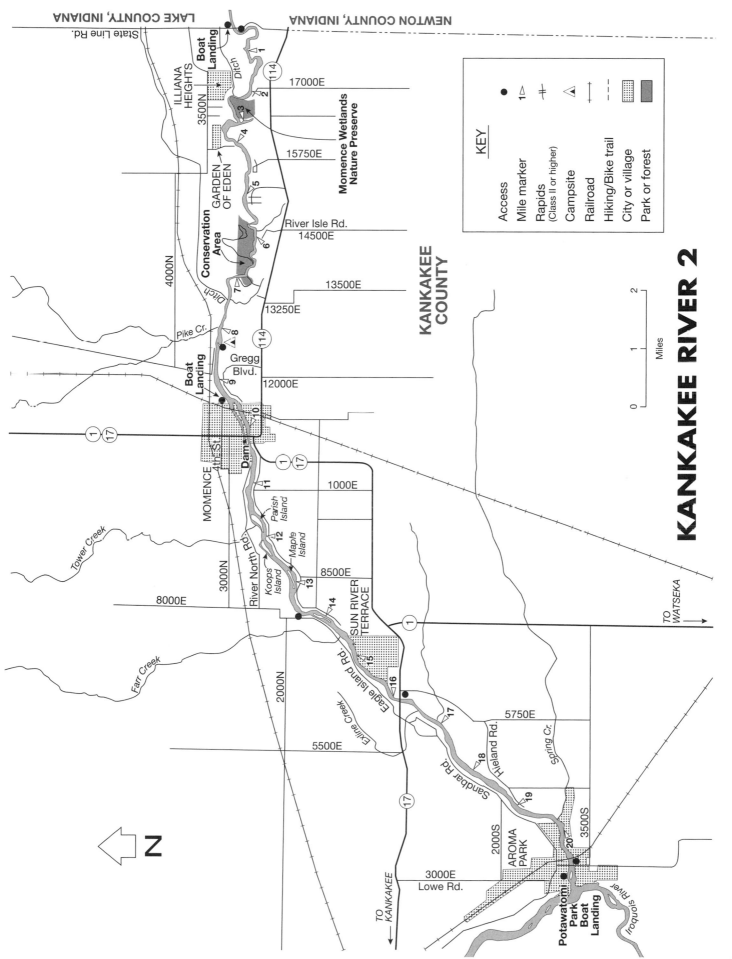

KANKAKEE RIVER 2

KEY

Access ●

Mile marker 1△

Rapids (Class II or higher) ⊣⊢

Campsite ◁

Railroad ⊢⊣⊢

Hiking/Bike trail ┆┄┄

City or village

Park or forest

Miles
0   1   2

N

LAKE COUNTY, INDIANA

NEWTON COUNTY, INDIANA

State Line Rd.

Boat Landing

ILLIANA HEIGHTS

Ditch

1

114

17000E

2

3

3500N

4

15750E

Momence Wetlands Nature Preserve

GARDEN OF EDEN

5

Conservation Area

4000N

River Isle Rd.

14500E

6

Ditch

7

13500E

13250E

114

KANKAKEE COUNTY

Pike Cr.

8

Boat Landing

Gregg Blvd.

9

12000E

10

1 17

MOMENCE

4th St.

Dam

1 17

11

1000E

Parish Island

12

Maple Island

River North Rd.

Koops Island

13

8500E

14

SUN RIVER TERRACE

3000N

8000E

15

Eagle Island Rd.

16

Exline Creek

17

1

TO WATSEKA

5750E

Spring Cr.

18

Hieland Rd.

Tower Creek

Farr Creek

2000N

5500E

19

Sandbar Rd.

AROMA PARK

2000S

20

3500S

TO KANKAKEE

3000E

Lowe Rd.

Potawatomi Park Boat Landing

Iroquois River

KANKAKEE RIVER 3
Kankakee to Warner Bridge (10.4 Miles)

One of the cleanest rivers in the Midwest, the Kankakee is popular with anglers, who find smallmouth and largemouth bass, walleye, sauger, northern pike, and catfish abundant. On this third segment of the river you'll see a number of swift, riffly areas that have smallmouth habitat written all over them. In addition to the good fishing, this section offers excellent canoeing—it's the most frequently paddled stretch on the Kankakee. Part of the reason for its popularity is Kankakee River State Park, which borders the river for 11 miles; the park's 4,000 acres not only preserve a natural environment along the river but also provide great campgrounds, picnic areas, and biking/hiking trails. There is some gorgeous scenery along this part of the river, including rock outcroppings, cliffs, and beautiful islands. Accesses are quite convenient, and the surroundings are mostly wild; homes are generally screened by foliage. Sometimes when rain becomes infrequent, this section gets too low to paddle. Most of the stretch is several hundred feet wide.

For **camping** and **canoe rental,** see the description of Kankakee River 1.

The **shuttle route** (9.9 miles) from Bird Park in Kankakee goes northwest on Highway 113, north on Warner Bridge Road, then west immediately after the bridge toward the boat landing and carry-in campground.

The **gradient** for this section is a relatively brisk 3.4 feet per mile, resulting in several pleasant riffles.

For **water levels,** check the upstream gauge at Momence (station #05520500) or the downstream gauge at Wilmington (#05527500) on the USGS Web site listed in the introduction.

Put in at Bird Park, which is located upstream-left from the Highway 17 bridge in Kankakee. (From the park entrance, a road leads under the bridge to the concrete boat ramp.) A railroad bridge lies just downstream. Houses appear on both sides but soon thin out. After the fenced grounds of the Bradley wastewater treatment facility on the right, houses disappear and the setting becomes quite natural. The banks are fairly high and wooded, and the river flows through one gentle bend after another. Eagle sightings are not uncommon.

Not far downstream from a barn, the river bends left and a creek enters on the right, with a footbridge near its mouth. A short distance up this stream, in a township park, water has carved intricate formations and caves in the limestone. Downstream, in the left bend, a lovely home appears on the right, opposite a 10-foot rocky cliff that continues for several hundred yards.

Houses begin again when the river bends right, and the stratified stone continues on the shoreline. Finally, the bend ends at a huge, rocky island, alongside the Bradley Bourbonnais Sportsmen's Club on the right shoreline. Houses thin out again after the island, and the river widens in a straightaway. Highway 113 now runs alongside for awhile, and riffles appear in the shallower water. After a right curve, the remains of an old stone house are seen on the left, just upstream from some power lines.

Half a mile later is Altorf Island, the biggest of the trip (a nature preserve); on the right shore, a creek cascades down over rocky shelves. Just before the island ends, the river drops over a rocky shoal for 100 yards. More islands follow. On the right shoreline, picnic tables, cars, and fishermen can be seen in the park. After the string of islands, rock shelves and cliffs appear again, and a sand-and-gravel spit juts out into the river from the mouth of Rock Creek on the right. You can land your boat upstream from Rock Creek and walk up to the concession stand, or take out here for a shorter trip. This is a wonderful place to stop: a 3-mile trail along Rock Creek leads you to a lovely limestone canyon and a small waterfall.

Inexperienced paddlers should be careful after Rock Creek: the river is constricted here, making it swift and wavy, sweeping up against the cliffs on the left and creating tricky currents and eddies. The section just downstream from Rock Creek is beautiful, with outstanding stone formations. After a short bend, a wide and straight stretch leads to Warner Bridge. **Take out** a short distance downstream-right at the gravel landing. A primitive campground and large parking area are nearby.

Other trips. The river surroundings are wooded and attractive all the way to Wilmington (10 miles), partly because the state park continues for several miles to the west from Warner Bridge. This stretch is quite wide at times, and slows considerably as you approach the dam at Wilmington. About a mile from the end of the trip, when you see houses on a high bank, you should stay on the right (east) side of the river to avoid the dam. Upstream from the dam, a side channel goes to the right under a bridge; turn into this channel and take out at the concrete ramp at Wilmington Island Park, 100 yards downstream-left from the bridge.

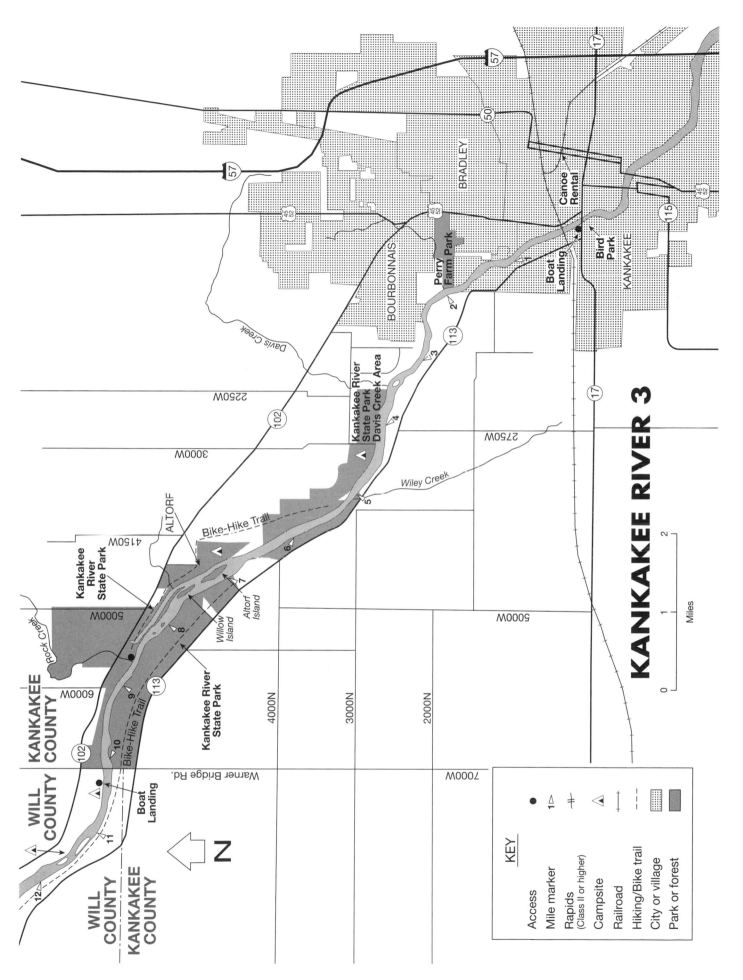

KANKAKEE RIVER 3

73

KASKASKIA RIVER 1
Shelbyville to Moore Bridge (12.5 Miles)

One of the longest rivers in Illinois (almost 300 miles), the Kaskaskia originates near the city of Champaign, then flows diagonally across the southern half of the state to the Mississippi near the site of the first state capital. Along the way, it is dammed to form the first and third largest inland lakes in Illinois—Lake Shelbyville (#3) and Carlyle Lake (#1). Upstream from Shelbyville, canoeists must put up with numerous logjams, but paddling is good all the way from the Lake Shelbyville dam to Vandalia. Portions of the river below Carlyle Lake are also suitable for canoeing, but the last 36 miles of the river have been straightened, widened, and dredged (primarily to allow barges to carry coal out to the Mississippi).

The two sections described here offer surprising variety. Relatively clear and clean under normal conditions, the river generally flows between steep banks, but there are also periodic wooded bluffs and stone formations and numerous sandbars. The river environs are heavily wooded most of the way and convey a feeling of isolation. Except for a trailer camp near the beginning, there are no houses along the river. Many kinds of fish are caught, including catfish, bullhead, walleye, muskie, crappie, and white bass. Overall, the tranquil surroundings encourage relaxed float trips.

An abundance of good **camping** is available in the area. At Lake Shelbyville, for example, there are eight Army Corps of Engineers campgrounds and two Illinois DNR campgrounds. Hidden Springs State Forest, near Clarksburg, also offers camping. Private camping is conveniently located at the put-in (Kaskaskia River Bait and Campground). Additional private camping in the Shelbyville area includes Arrowhead, Cardinal, River Front and Robin Hood Woods Campgrounds.

Canoe rentals and shuttle service are available at Kaskaskia River Bait and Campground (217-774-4721), at the put-in.

The **shuttle route** (6.8 miles) for the first section goes west on Highway 16 into Shelbyville, south on County 1800E (Cedar Street), west on County 925N, then south on County 1700E to Moore Bridge.

The **gradient** is slight—about a foot per mile.

Since **water levels** are largely dependent upon the amount of water being released from the dam, it's a good idea to call for the recorded water-release message at 217-774-2020 (updated daily). Locals indicate that the river starts getting low at 600 cfs and is high at 2,000. You can also check the USGS gauges at Shelbyville (station #05592000) and Cowden (#05592100) on the USGS Web site listed in the introduction.

Put in at the private boat ramp (Kaskaskia River Bait and Campground) downstream-left from the Highway 16 bridge; there is a small launching fee if you aren't renting a boat or staying at the campground. At the beginning the river is only about 60 feet wide; during the trip it will average 75 feet, sometimes wider in bends.

Soon after the put-in, an extremely high, quarter-mile-long railroad bridge passes overhead, spanning the whole river valley. It is said that rookie locomotive engineers quake when they have to cross this awesome structure for the first time. Nearby there was once an old rock dam for a mill. Downstream, in a right bend, a 70-foot clay-shale-and-sandstone cliff appears on the left in a very attractive area. As soon as the cliff stops, a trailer camp begins, continuing for some time along the shore of a big river loop. For awhile, a low rocky cliff runs along the right shore. After a right turn, the long line of trailers ends and the river enters a lovely, narrow, densely wooded section where the trees overhang the water. Here and there, trees have fallen in, but there's usually plenty of room to get around them.

In the long right bend after the trailer camp, high wooded bluffs and stratified rock outcroppings appear occasionally along the shoreline. Copeland Bridge appears 0.75 mile downstream from some power lines, and is a good alternate access, on the left above the bridge. After the bridge, the river widens to about 80 feet and enters a wonderfully quiet, winding, seemingly in-the-middle-of-nowhere section. After a sharp loop, just north of 925N where a few trailers and cabins are seen, another pristine area begins; the quiet is broken only by birdcalls, and trees hang out over the water.

Just before a sharp left turn, Robinson Creek enters on the right—a major tributary. A long series of bends follows, with cutbanks and open areas. Rock formations cease. Finally, within sight of high wooded bluffs in the distance, you approach Moore Bridge. Deadfall can accumulate in the twisty, narrow curve just before the bridge, so be careful. **Take out** on the left, upstream of the bridge, where there's a dirt landing. (Do not block the farmer's access to his nearby field.)

An Interesting Dam Place

Before your canoe trip, take a few minutes to get a close-up view of the imposing Lake Shelbyville dam, located just north of the Highway 16 bridge. Completed in 1970, the dam rises 110 feet over the bed of the Kaskaskia and impounds 11,100 acres of water at the "normal" or "recreation" pool stage. When it is holding back spring rainfall ("flood-control pool"), the lake can cover as much as 25,300 acres. The spillway area below the dam is always a popular area for fishermen. The city of Shelbyville itself is an interesting place to visit. When Abraham Lincoln was a young circuit-riding lawyer, Shelby County was a regular part of his route.

Now, *that's* a dam! (at Shelbyville).

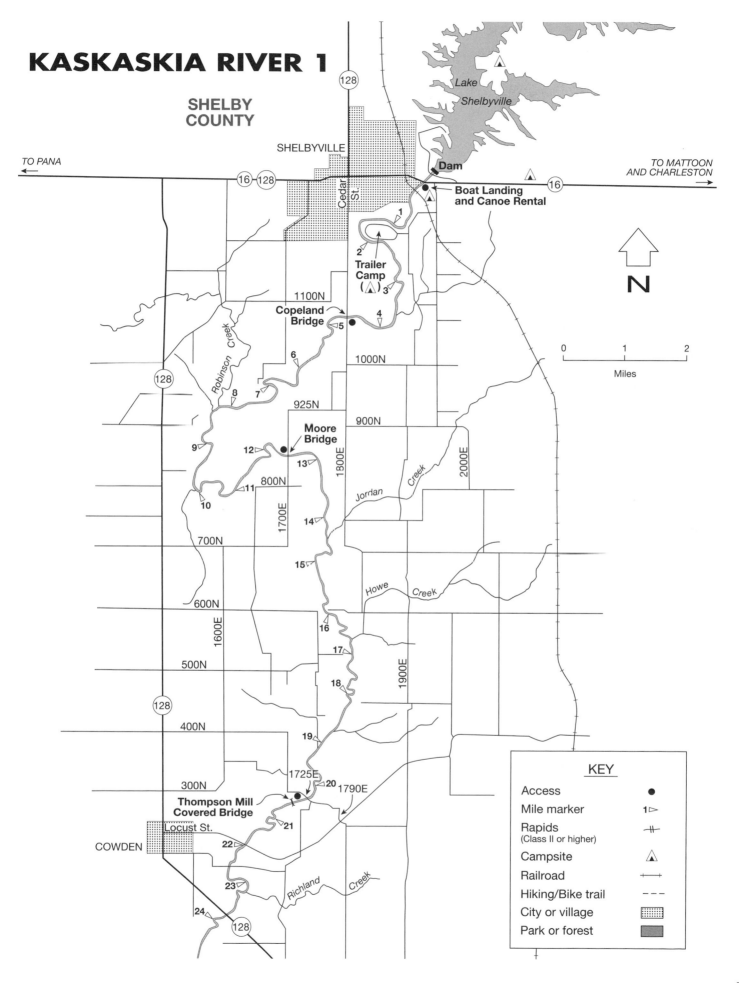

KASKASKIA RIVER 1

SHELBY COUNTY

TO PANA

SHELBYVILLE

Dam

TO MATTOON AND CHARLESTON

Boat Landing and Canoe Rental

1

2

Trailer Camp (⛺) 3

4

1100N

Copeland Bridge 5

6

1000N

7

8

925N

900N

9

Moore Bridge

12

13

1800E

800N

11

1700E

10

14

700N

15

1600E

600N

16

17

500N

18

1900E

400N

19

1725E

300N 20 1790E

Thompson Mill Covered Bridge

Locust St.

21

COWDEN

22

23

24

128

Cedar St.

Robinson Creek

Jordan Creek

2000E

Howe Creek

Richland Creek

Lake Shelbyville

N

| 0 | 1 | 2 |

Miles

KEY

Access	●
Mile marker	1▷
Rapids (Class II or higher)	‖
Campsite	⛺
Railroad	┼┼┼
Hiking/Bike trail	- - -
City or village	▦
Park or forest	▨

KASKASKIA RIVER 2
Moore Bridge to Thompson Mill Covered Bridge (7.8 Miles)

Covered Bridges of Illinois

During the 1800s, as many as 20,000 covered bridges were constructed in the United States, including an estimated 200 in Illinois. Only about 1,000 survive throughout the country (principally in Pennsylvania, Ohio, Indiana, Vermont, New Hampshire, and Oregon), six of which are in Illinois. The rest have fallen to decay, collapse, floods, vandalism, and condemnation in favor of modern structures.

Three of these delightful remnants of the nineteenth century are an important part of three trips in this book: the Thompson Mill Covered Bridge near Cowden (Kaskaskia River 2), the Red Covered Bridge near Princeton (Big Bureau Creek), and the recently reconstructed Wolf Covered Bridge between Dahinda and Maquon (Spoon River 1).

The others are somewhat off the beaten path but can be visited easily. The Sugar Creek Covered Bridge (1880) is found near Glenarm, a few miles south of Springfield and 0.75 mile west of Interstate 55. Not far from the Mississippi, the Henderson Creek Bridge (1845) is now located 2.5 miles south of Oquawka in a park alongside Highway 164. Also near the Mississippi, but much farther south, the Little Mary's River Covered Bridge (1854) is a few miles east of the city of Chester. Also worth visiting is the modern-era covered bridge (1965) over the Sangamon River at Lake of the Woods Park near Mahomet.

A wonderful little 48-page booklet by Leslie C. Swanson, *Covered Bridges in Illinois, Iowa, and Wisconsin* (1985) provides a very readable introduction to the subject.

A relatively short trip, this section of the river makes a good Sunday morning paddle for weekend canoeists who have done the upstream section on Saturday. The stretch begins and ends fairly straight, but the middle portion is a long succession of tight turns. The setting is even more isolated here, with fewer cabins and trailers. There are almost none of the rock formations that are seen upstream, but sandbars are plentiful for relaxation stops. Sightings of deer, raccoons, bank swallows, and other wildlife continue to be frequent. Because the river is typically 80–100 feet wide, total blockages are infrequent, but (as always) paddlers should be careful when they encounter downed trees, especially in bends.

The highlight of the trip, of course, comes at the end, when paddlers take out in the shadow of a graceful, old covered bridge. Named for a mill that was once located nearby, the Thompson Mill Covered Bridge was built in 1868 and is in excellent condition despite its age and the inevitable graffiti. The intricately constructed trusses that support the bridge are protected by a wood-shingled roof and are 105 feet long. A nearby sign indicates that the bridge was located on a once-important road between Springfield and Effingham. At the end of a day's paddle, the bridge provides a good background for photographs of your fellow canoeists.

For **camping** and **canoe rentals**, see the description of Kaskaskia River 1. Camping is also available within 20 miles of Cowden at Ramsey Lake State Park, off Highway 51 between Pana and Vandalia.

The **shuttle route** (11.9 miles) from Moore Bridge goes south on County 1700E, west on County 700N, south on Highway 128 to Cowden, east on Locust Street, and north on County 1790E.

The **gradient** is slightly higher than on the previous section: 1.9 feet per mile.

For **water levels,** see Kaskaskia River 1.

Put in above the Moore Bridge, on the north bank; don't block access to the nearby farm field. After the put-in, the river is straight for half a mile, then curves right. About 75 feet wide, it is deeply forested, with steep 8-foot banks. The first bend is followed by a long south straightaway, ending at a right bend where there's a small cabin. After Jordan Creek enters on the left, more cabins appear on the right. Sharp right, then left turns lead to another straightaway, where the setting becomes quite wild, especially the deep, dense shoreline on the right. A long series of bends now begins, with frequent cutbanks and occasional open fields. Eventually, the curves end and the river straightens out toward the southwest, sometimes widening to 100 feet.

A long left bend follows the straightaway. Finally, after a couple of sharp turns, the modern bridge at County 1725E appears. The covered bridge is just downstream. **Take out** on the right, upstream, at the clay bank alongside the old bridge, adjacent to a small visitor parking lot.

Other trips. Three more bridges follow shortly (see the map), none of which provides a convenient access. Then, after Highway 128, bridges are quite sparse all the way to Vandalia, where there's a boat landing on the southeast side of town. Soon thereafter, the river begins to slow in its approach to Carlyle Lake.

Whether you paddle to Vandalia or not, don't miss seeing the old capitol building there. Vandalia was the state capital from 1819 to 1839, and the building is a charming reminder of that time. Vandalia was the western terminus of the famous Cumberland Trail that extended 591 miles from Maryland and served as a conduit for thousands of settlers on their westward trek.

Thompson Mill Covered Bridge near Cowden

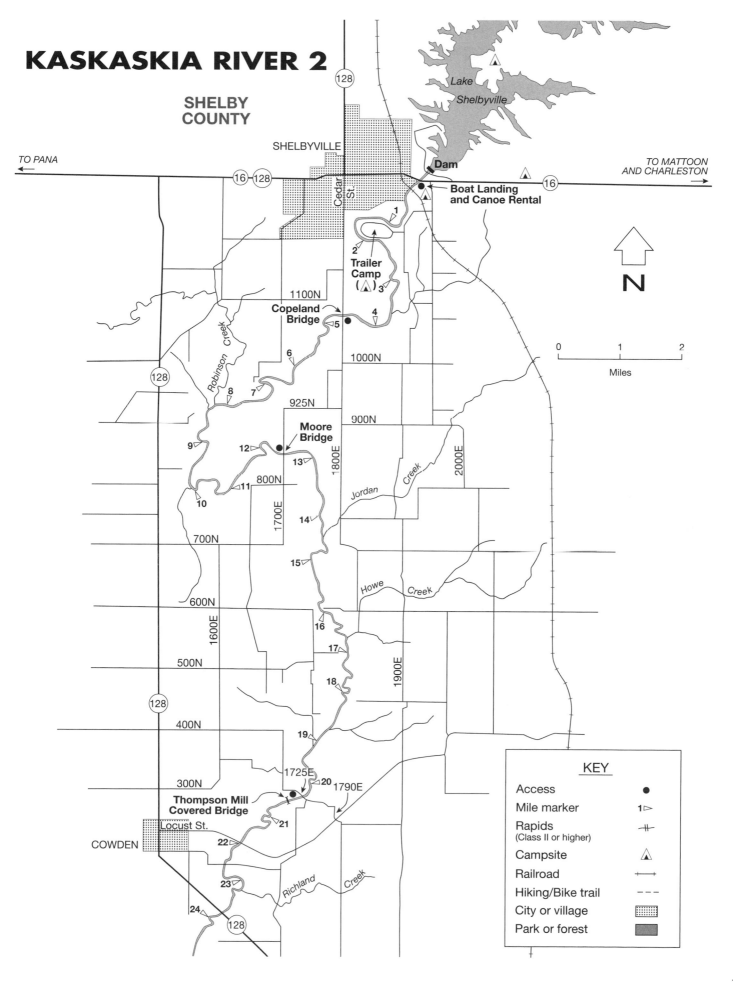

KASKASKIA RIVER 2

SHELBY COUNTY

TO PANA

TO MATTOON AND CHARLESTON

SHELBYVILLE

Lake Shelbyville

Dam

Boat Landing and Canoe Rental

Cedar St.

1100N

Copeland Bridge

Robinson Creek

1000N

925N

900N

Moore Bridge

800N

700N

Jordan Creek

1800E

2000E

600N

1600E

1700E

500N

Howe Creek

1900E

400N

1725E

300N

1790E

Thompson Mill Covered Bridge

Locust St.

COWDEN

Richland Creek

KEY

Access	●
Mile marker	1▷
Rapids (Class II or higher)	╫
Campsite	△
Railroad	┼┼┼
Hiking/Bike trail	---
City or village	▦
Park or forest	▩

KISHWAUKEE RIVER 1
Belvidere to Cherry Valley (7.2 Miles)

One of Illinois's canoeing jewels, the Kishwaukee can be paddled in many places, but its most popular section is the 15.7 miles from the city of Belvidere to Atwood Park near Rockford. Many splendid canoe landings provide convenient access, and make it easy to design trips of varying length. Woodlands are almost unbroken along the shoreline, partly because Boone and Winnebago counties have protected much of the river corridor with forest preserves and conservation areas. Moreover, the municipalities of Belvidere, Cherry Valley, and Rockford have created lovely riverside parks with excellent landings. You'll see almost no houses, cabins, or trailers along the whole stretch—just woods, wildlife, and natural scenery. The section from Belvidere to Cherry Valley is narrower, steeper, and more winding than the next stretch. Because there are occasional obstructions and places that require boat maneuvering, especially in curves or tight channels, beginning canoeists should paddle elsewhere.

Appropriately, the name *Kishwaukee* comes from a Potawatomi word meaning "big tree" or "sycamore." Chief Black Hawk, who called the river the *Kishawacokee* in his autobiography, followed its shores during part of his ill-fated flight to Wisconsin in 1832.

Public **camping** is available north of Rockford at Rock Cut State Park and at the Hononegah Forest Preserve. At New Milford, camping is available along the river at Larsen's Landing, downstream-right from Highway 251, off New Milford School Road (see p.81). Several other private campgrounds are located on the river: Paradise Park Campground near Garden Prairie, Jellystone Park of Belvidere on Epworth Road, and Blackhawk Valley Campground near New Milford.

Canoe rentals and shuttles are available at Canoe the Kish at Larsen's Landing, near New Milford (815-544-1823 or www.canoethekish.com). Rentals without shuttle are available at Chicagoland Canoe Base in Chicago (773-777-1489 or www.chicagolandcanoebase.com).

The **shuttle route** (6.1 miles) goes south a short distance on Stone Quarry Road, west on Newburg Road, south on Mill Road, east on State Street into Cherry Valley, and south on Walnut Street to Baumann Park.

The **gradient** is a riffly 4.2 feet per mile.

For **water levels**, check the gauges at Belvidere (station #05438500) and Perryville (#05440000) on the USGS Web site listed in the introduction.

Before or after your trip, be sure to visit Belvidere Park, just upstream from the put-in. Accessed on the west from Stone Quarry Road or on the south from Locust Street, this beautiful 105-acre park is popular with picnickers, bicyclists, hikers, fishermen, swimmers, and others. At the east end of the park is a V-shaped dam, below which the Kishwaukee continues on its way, together with a parallel millrace. The millrace flows through a delightful, rock-lined channel with charming footbridges and little waterfalls, past the scenic Baltic Mill (built in 1845). The park is a model of what can be done with riverfront development.

Put in at the Belvidere Park District canoe landing (one of the best you'll see anywhere) at the Appleton Road bridge, downstream-right. The river bends left past a wastewater-treatment facility, then back to the right where the millrace rejoins the main channel. The 45-foot-wide river flows over a gravel-and-sand bottom between 4-foot banks covered with grass and trees. After Spencer Park on the right, a large island appears in a left bend, with good riffles on both sides. Gravel bars and riffly shoals begin appearing, and the surroundings grow increasingly wild, except for occasional power lines and shoreline riprap. Dead trees are found in some of the bends but are usually not difficult to get around.

In a big right bend, near some concrete riprap, is a mobile home park on the left; however, only the metal service building can be seen easily from the river. One pleasant riffle after another is encountered as shoals, islands, and sandbars continue. Just downstream-right from a set of power lines and the biggest island of the trip is the canoe landing at the end of Distillery Road, a sandy beach with huge boulders on both sides. After Distillery Road, the river becomes quite narrow (as little as 30 feet), intimate, and winding. Deadfall is more frequent, requiring maneuvering.

After some old abutments, Newburg Road passes overhead. The bridge can be accessed downstream-left, where there's room for a number of cars. In the wide straightaway that follows, you can see traffic whizzing by on the Interstate 90 bridges downstream. Several islands precede I-90. Then, in the approach to Highway 20, the river is not only straight and wide but also shallow, open, and often breezy. Be on the lookout for wire or fencing across the river in the vicinity of the I-90 and Highway 20 bridges.

Immediately after Highway 20, the houses of Cherry Valley begin on the left. After paddling under the State Street bridge and a railroad bridge, take out at the sand-and-gravel landing on the left at Baumann Park. A large parking area is located nearby. The park stretches along the southeast bank of the Kishwaukee and features a 15-acre lake surrounded by a biking/hiking path. Cherry Valley itself is an attractive little town whose main street is paved with brick.

Other trips. Much of the South Branch (in De Kalb and Winnebago Counties) is paddleable from the Sycamore area to the main branch. Occasionally paddled by locals is the section on the main branch upstream from Belvidere (from County Line Road or Garden Prairie to the public boat ramp in Belvidere), but there is a 2-foot dam to portage just downstream from Epworth Road.

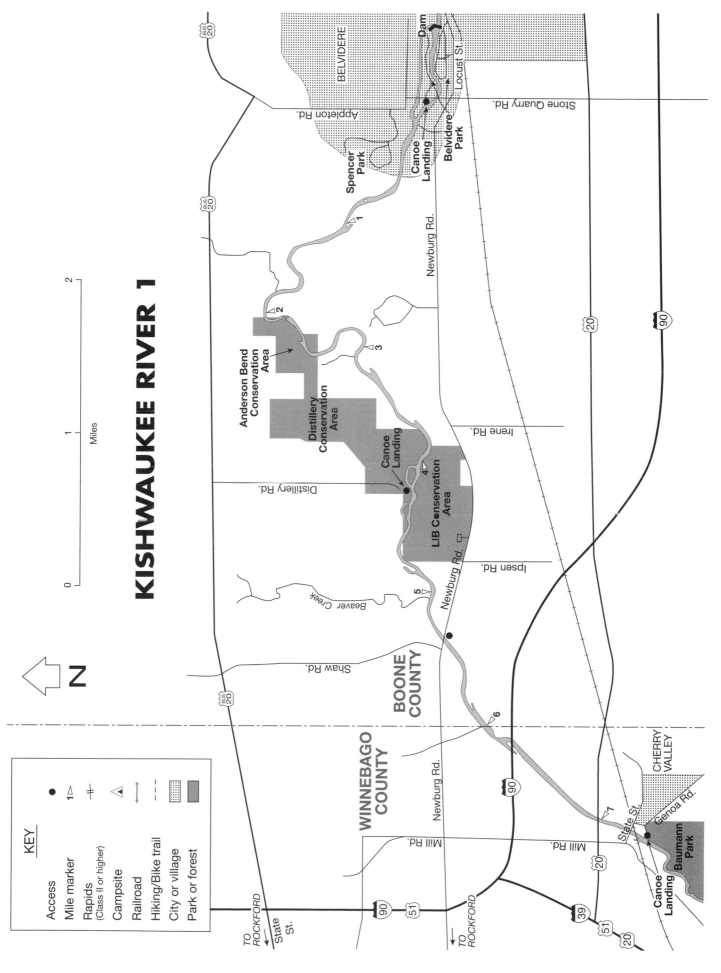

KISHWAUKEE RIVER 1

KISHWAUKEE RIVER 2
Cherry Valley to Atwood Park (8.5 Miles)

One of the most canoeing-friendly sections of river in Illinois, the Kishwaukee downstream from Cherry Valley is always a delight. Thanks to the foresight of the village of Cherry Valley, the Winnebago County Forest District, and the Rockford Park District, most of the river corridor here is publicly owned. As a result, paddlers enjoy not only first-rate accesses but also scenic, unspoiled surroundings, with a number of convenient places to stop and relax along the way. Bigger than the upstream stretch, the river is nevertheless seldom more than 100 feet wide here and consists mostly of big, sweeping curves. Heavily wooded, the Kishwaukee is especially beautiful in the spring, when wildflowers are resplendent, and in the midst of fall's colors. A highlight is the deep gorge near the end of the trip—which can be previewed from the high Interstate 39/51 bridge. This is a good section for beginners, but offers consistently good paddling for everyone.

For **camping** and **canoe rentals**, see the description of Kishwaukee River 1.

The **shuttle route** from Cherry Valley goes west on State Street, southwest on Mill Road, south on Perryville Road, west on Blackhawk Road, south on Highway 251, east on Rydberg Road, and east into Atwood Park to the boat landing.

The **gradient** is 2.3 feet per mile.

For **water levels**, check the Perryville gauge (station #05440000) on the USGS Web site listed in the introduction.

Put in from Baumann Park in Cherry Valley. From State Street, turn onto Walnut, which leads to the park entrance. The landing is downstream from a railroad bridge, with plentiful parking. Baumann Park, located along the river, offers playgrounds, a lake, trails, and picnic and athletic facilities.

The river here is fairly narrow, about 60 feet, and flows over a

The beautiful gorge of the Kishwaukee

sand-and-gravel bed. On the left, the park continues for awhile, followed by a few houses in a sharp left turn. Sandbars begin appearing soon. More houses are seen on the right near a creek mouth, then thin out. Before long, within sight of some power lines, McKiski Forest Preserve begins on the left and the river widens. Then, after a right bend and an island, more power lines and a railroad bridge come into view. Downstream, where the river turns sharply to the right, then left, there's an excellent

landing at Espenscheid Memorial Forest Preserve, cut back into the bank and made of wooden timbers. Shortly after the landing, the river quickly turns right again at a big wooded island. Be careful of the swirling current and potential deadfall in the S curve at Espenscheid. A big left curve follows, with a large grassy island.

Downstream from Perryville Road and an old concrete bridge, the South Branch enters on the left; at its mouth is a rock outcropping. (You'll see a couple of additional small outcrops downstream.) The river now bends through Blackhawk Springs Forest Preserve, widening to 100 feet. In a left bend, wooden steps lead up the hill to the right. Finally, at the end of a right arc with very high wooded banks, the Blackhawk Road bridge appears. Forest preserve roads now parallel the river for some distance, and there are many places on the shore to land your boat; this area makes an excellent access for a short trip. You'll see many hikers, fishermen, and picnickers along the river here. Just downstream from a big island is a beautiful stand of pines on the left shore. Then, private property is found on both sides until the river turns right and begins its westward course.

After passing through the Rockford Rotary Forest Preserve, the river soon approaches the beautiful Kishwaukee Gorge. High bluffs begin, and the area is wild and serene. In a long right bend, a large wooded island and several smaller gravelly islands are passed; then the tall, graceful spans of I-39/51 loom ahead. The high bluffs are close to the river here, making the gorge a very impressive experience.

After the bridges, the river gently arcs left, then right, passing a couple of houses where the shoreline is private. After a straightaway, a long line of recreational trailers on the right shoreline mark the location of the Blackhawk Valley Campground, where there's a landing for canoe renters. The river now bends gently to the left, and soon a white suspension footbridge can be seen in the distance. This bridge connects the north and south segments of Atwood Park—a beautiful 334-acre tract that was once an artillery firing range for nearby Camp Grant during World War I, and was donated later to the Rockford Park District by a philanthropist.

Take out at Larry's Landing, downstream-left from the pedestrian bridge. If you're renting a canoe from Canoe-the-Kish at Larsen's Landing or are camping there, you can **take out** at the Landing downstream-right from Highway 251.

Other trips. After Atwood Park, the river continues westward, under Highway 251 and Beltline Road, toward the Rock River. At one point, upstream from the mouth of Kilbuck Creek, the river splits into two channels. If you take the left channel (into which Kilbuck Creek flows), the distance from Atwood Park to the Rock is 5.4 miles. Take out at Hinchliff Forest Preserve at the Kishwaukee Road bridge, upstream-left.

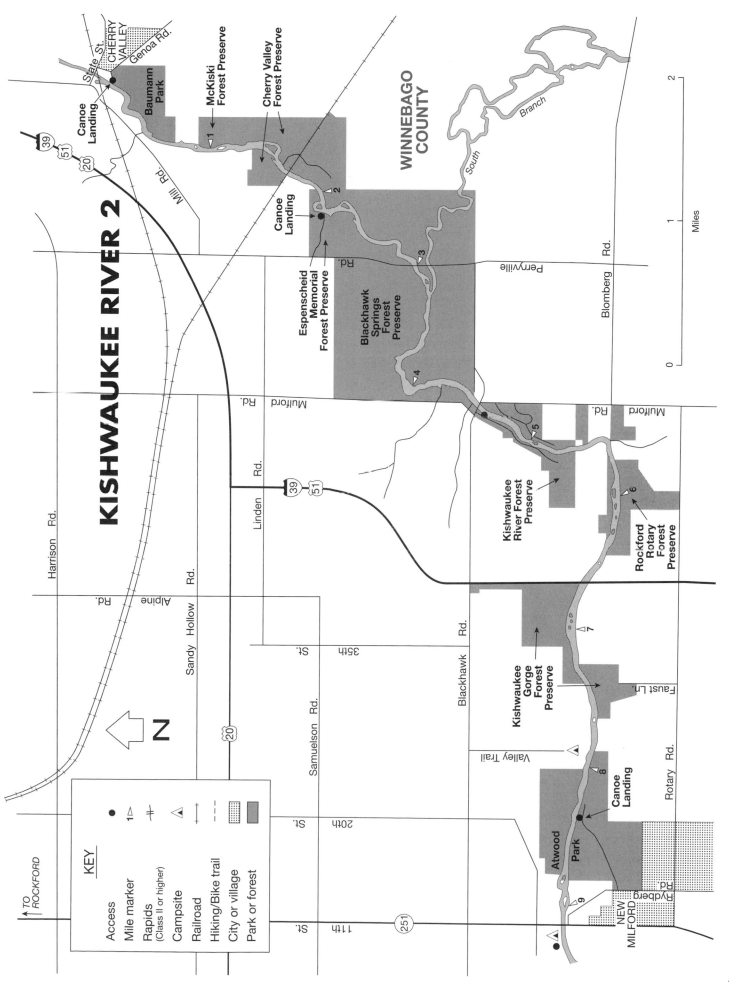

KISHWAUKEE RIVER 2

LITTLE VERMILION RIVER 1
Troy Grove to County Road N3179 (9 Miles)

Famous Illinois Gunfighters

Before or after your trip, drive into the nearby community of Troy Grove, the hometown of Wild Bill Hickock, where a plaque on a large rock memorializes this favorite son. Born in 1837, Hickock spent his first eighteen years in Troy Grove, then moved to Kansas. A scout for the Union in the Civil War, he became a legendary U.S. marshal in several western towns before being shot in the back by Jack McCall in Deadwood, South Dakota, while playing poker. He was only thirty-nine at the time.

Hickock was by no means the only famous gunslinger to hail from Illinois. Wyatt Earp (of OK Corral fame) was born near Monmouth in 1848, and had an even more colorful career before dying peacefully at eighty-one. Another famous scout, gambler, and law officer was Bat Masterson, born in 1853 near Golden Gate in Wayne County. As if that weren't enough, Decatur lays claim to being the hometown of the famous bandit and poet Black Bart, who headed to California in the 1860s to waylay stagecoaches.

Originating in the Mendota area, the Little Vermilion is not a long river, but in its short course it helps dispel the stereotype of Illinois rivers as plodding prairie streams. Narrow, winding, and intimate, it has one of the highest gradients in the state, resulting in a long succession of riffles and rapids, and it passes many breathtaking cliffs. For experienced paddlers only, it requires a great deal of river-reading skill and maneuvering ability. Some obstructions are likely, especially in tight, twisting wooded areas. The window of paddleability is rather small: too little water means interminable scraping, while too much spells danger. The scenery is gorgeous, and the rapids are exciting, but paddlers also must anticipate some negative aspects. On the upper stretch, for example, there are four small earthen dams to portage and several strands of wire to squeeze under. Incidentally, there are two Little Vermilion rivers in Illinois; this one is found entirely in La Salle County, while the other originates to the south in Vermilion County before flowing into Indiana.

Most of the upper section of the river is creeklike; sometimes as narrow as 10 feet, it averages only 35 feet in width, flowing by rocky cliffs, wooded banks, and pastures, with only a few houses. Accesses are mediocre but doable. The entire section is on private property, so you must do everything possible to respect the rights of landowners. Stay off the banks, and don't disturb fences and cattle.

Public **camping** is located nearby at Starved Rock State Park, just east of Oglesby. There is also a KOA campground a few miles north of Utica.

The **shuttle route** (7.7 miles) goes west on Highway 52 to Troy Grove, south on Vermilion Street (County E500), west on N3300, south on E300, and east on N3179.

The **gradient** is 7.7 feet per mile, resulting in a steady succession of riffles and rapids.

Water levels. To determine whether there's enough water to paddle comfortably, check the gauge painted on the center pier under the N3000 bridge (just south of Interstate 80); the gauge should read at least 1. (You can read the gauge from the bridge.) The river becomes quite pushy when high (i.e., 3 or higher on the gauge).

Put in at the Highway 52 bridge just east of Troy Grove, downstream-left. Between the put-in and County

N3500, much of the property is owned by a silica sand company. Canopied with trees, the river is only 25 feet wide at the beginning—it will seldom be wider—and is winding, narrow, and riffly all the way to the E500 bridge (where some paddlers put in). Just downstream-right from E500, you get a glimpse of the large plant that produces silica sand for various industrial applications.

After an overhead pipeline that conveys sand and water, the river approaches a river-wide earthen dam. Pipelines again pass overhead, a road crosses the dam, and the river flows through two big culverts on the right. The culverts usually are partially blocked with debris, so you MUST take out to the left and portage your boat over the dam. Three more dams of this kind block the river between here and N3500; portaging them isn't difficult but takes time. Between dams, the river is curvy, tight, and riffly, with many lovely cliffs. Between the second and third dams, grassy hillsides mark a land-restoration area. After the fourth dam, the river passes through the most wooded, quiet, and isolated area so far, encountering one gorgeous cliff after another, all the way to the N3500 bridge.

Pastureland begins below N3500, together with several cattle chains hanging over the river (potentially electrified!) and a couple of low concrete slabs in the streambed. Dense forest and open pastureland now alternate, with a twisting river-course and many impressive cliffs, all the way to the N3300 bridge. Be on the lookout for deadfall in the turns, and for barbed wire in the vicinity of the bridge.

The river is somewhat wider, straighter, and less prone to deadfall after N3300, and the trip's highest and most beautiful cliffs and best riffles occur alongside a home with a white picket fence. Several homes in quick succession signal the approach of the N3179 bridge. **Take out** upstream on the left. The bridge is on a narrow, curving road with little room to park; don't block driveways.

Upstream from N3179, the Little Vermilion is riffly and lined with cliffs.

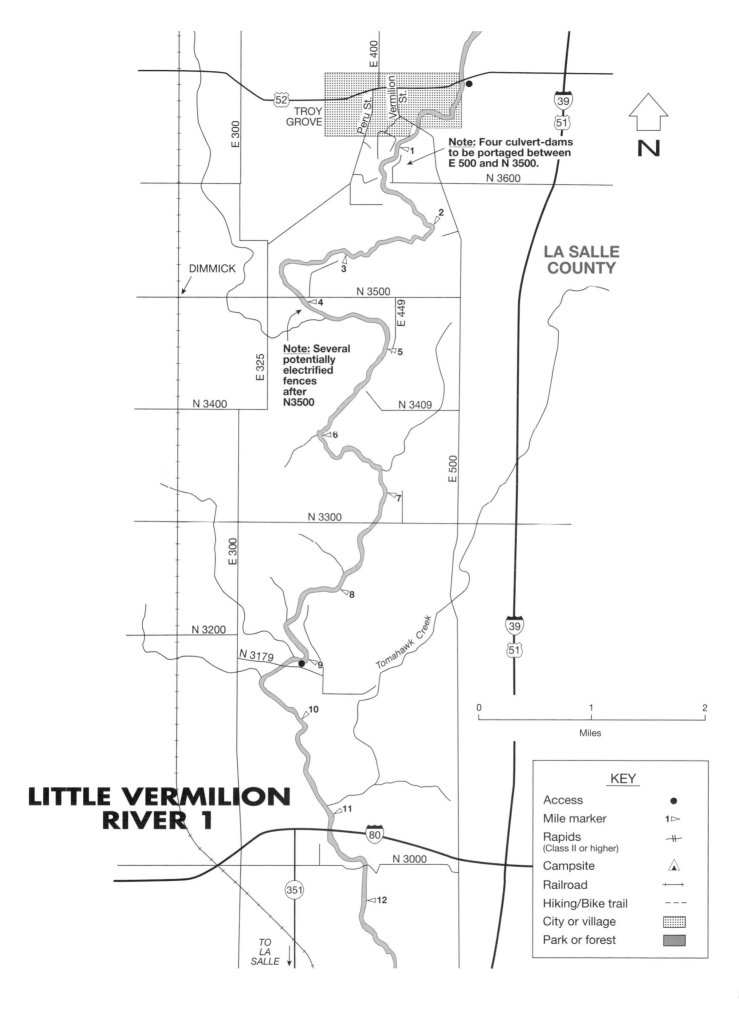

LITTLE VERMILION RIVER 1

TROY GROVE

Note: Four culvert-dams to be portaged between E 500 and N 3500.

LA SALLE COUNTY

DIMMICK

Note: Several potentially electrified fences after N3500

Tomahawk Creek

TO LA SALLE

KEY

Access	●
Mile marker	1▷
Rapids (Class II or higher)	─#─
Campsite	△
Railroad	─┼─
Hiking/Bike trail	─ ─ ─
City or village	▦
Park or forest	▩

LITTLE VERMILION RIVER 2
County Road N3179 to La Salle (6.8 Miles)

Up a side canyon of the Little Vermilion

Offering the best rapids in Illinois, this part of the Little Vermilion is definitely **appropriate only for expert whitewater boaters**. With a couple of exceptions, it doesn't have the beautiful cliffs of the upstream section, but it has a turbulent beauty of its own. Its average gradient of 14.7 feet per mile is one of the highest in the state (twice that of the better-known Lowell section of the North Vermilion), and the result is a multitude of riffles and Class I–II rapids, together with a magnificent steep-walled canyon that begins and ends with Class III drops. Never more than 45 feet wide, and sometimes as narrow as 20 feet, it has brisk current and lots of rocks to dodge; moreover, its narrowness makes potential deadfall quite hazardous, especially in tight, blind curves.

For **camping** in the area, see Little Vermilion River 1.

The **shuttle route** (5.6 miles) from the put-in goes west on County N3179, south on E300 (which becomes Chartres Street in La Salle), east on 11th Street, south on Highway 351 (Joliet Street) across the canal, then northwest on the Lock 14 access road.

Water levels. Because of its steepness and small watershed, the Little Vermilion is difficult to catch with enough water for pleasurable paddling. There is no USGS gauge, but a rough gauge is painted on the center pier beneath the County N3000 bridge—you can see it from the bridge—that should read at least 1; otherwise, you'll be walking much of the day. On the other hand, when the gauge reads 3 or higher, the river is quite pushy and dangerous, especially in Canyon Rapids, and response time drops significantly.

Put in upstream-left at the N3179 bridge, where there's room only for temporary parking of a couple of cars alongside the road. Don't block the nearby gate or driveways, and be careful of vehicular traffic on the blind curve at the bridge. About 35 feet wide at the beginning, the river winds around through one riffle after another, past a couple of small shale-and-sandstone cliffs. A couple of Class I+ rapids require maneuvering. Just upstream from I-80, a large wooded island precedes the mouth of Tomahawk Creek (on the left), a major tributary. A quarter-mile up the creek is a lovely cascade. Immediately upstream from the same island, a small creek enters on the right. A short distance upstream is a box canyon and an 8-foot waterfall.

After I-80, the river levels out for awhile, but riffles resume as you approach N3000, where lovely sandstone cliffs precede and follow the bridge. After a few houses in the vicinity of the bridge, the river is placid again and widens to 45 feet, with silt cutbanks appearing for the first time, then some piles of mining spoil atop the high banks. After a small concrete bridge, then a home on the right bank near a rock outcropping, the river veers left into Canyon Rapids. The distinct horizon line, steep gradient, and sheer 25-foot rock walls of the 100-yard-long canyon are quite striking. Be sure to get out of your boat and scout the whole canyon from the well-established trail on the right, along the canyon wall. Huge limestone blocks have fallen into the water near the beginning and end, forming complex drops of 3–4 feet, with swift, boulder-laden water in between. Big holes appear in the canyon when the gauge reads 3 or higher, but the run is **dangerous at any level** (normally Class III, but Class IV at medium to high water levels). Potentially lethal deadfall is often found within the canyon. Portage if you're uncertain about your ability to handle the canyon.

After the canyon, the river quickly turns left around a small island. The main channel (on the right) also should be scouted because of the Class II boulder garden found there and the possibility of hidden deadfall. Rapids continue downstream for awhile, then end at a pool that signals a **dangerous, 4-foot low-head dam** downstream; portage on the right (do NOT attempt to run the dam). After the dam, the river continues to be calm, winding around through a very natural-looking area. Riffles and rapids resume when you get closer to Highway 6. Big cinders from an old mining operation begin appearing on the right bank, and at one point there's an exciting Class I–II rapid where numerous cinders have washed into the streambed.

Pleasant riffles continue downstream from Highway 6, past a cement company plant on the left. Before long, you pass under three overhead structures in quick succession: the Canal Street bridge, the railroad bridge, and the Illinois and Michigan Canal aqueduct. The easiest **take-out** is at the La Salle Waterworks building, upstream-right from Canal Street. Or you can get out downstream-right from the aqueduct, carry your boat up to the canal, then paddle half a mile west to the end of the canal at Lock 14 in La Salle (**take out** on the left, next to the parking lot). Caution: if the water is high, there may be insufficient clearance beneath the aqueduct.

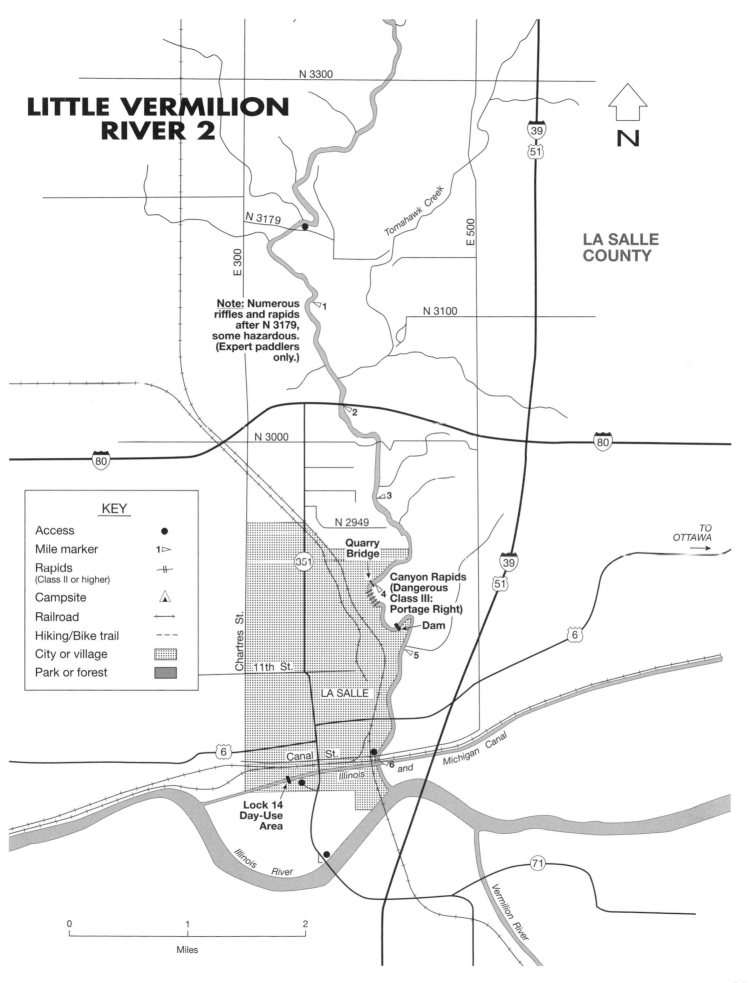

LITTLE VERMILION
RIVER 2

N 3300

Tomahawk Creek

N 3179

LA SALLE
COUNTY

E 300

E 500

Note: Numerous
riffles and rapids
after N 3179,
some hazardous.
(Expert paddlers
only.)

N 3100

▽1

▽2

N 3000

80

80

▽3

N 2949

KEY

Access	●
Mile marker	1▷
Rapids (Class II or higher)	─╫─
Campsite	◮
Railroad	─┼─
Hiking/Bike trail	─ ─ ─
City or village	▦
Park or forest	▨

**Quarry
Bridge**

**Canyon Rapids
(Dangerous
Class III:
Portage Right)**

4

Dam

051

▽5

*TO
OTTAWA*
→

39

51

6

Chartres St.

11th St.

LA SALLE

Michigan Canal

6

Canal St.

▽6 *and*

Illinois

**Lock 14
Day-Use
Area**

Illinois River

71

Vermilion River

0   1   2

Miles

LITTLE WABASH RIVER
Carmi to New Haven (29.5 Miles)

Daniel Boone's Kid Brother

If you're into charming old homes, a drive around Carmi is a good idea. Named after a biblical character, the city has a number of residences on the National Register of Historic Places. Oil was discovered in the area in the 1940s, and has been a significant local industry ever since. As you drive the shuttle route, you'll see many operating oil wells. The small community at the take-out, New Haven, is also historically interesting. Jonathan Boone, the younger brother of the famous frontiersman Daniel, built a mill here in the early 1800s. The mill is gone, but you can still view the site.

Originating near the city of Mattoon in Coles County, the Little Wabash is a rather long river that flows southward past Effingham, Flora, Olney, Fairfield, and Carmi before merging with the Wabash River near New Haven. Muddy banked and silt bottomed through most of its course, it is considered paddleable from the Fairfield area to the Wabash, but the most frequently canoed section begins at Carmi. This stretch is wooded all the way, and almost completely devoid of houses and cabins. When the river is low, there are a number of riffly shoals with long pools in between. Logjams are seldom a problem because the stretch is never less than 125 feet wide. Fishing is said to be good for catfish, crappie, white perch, smallmouth and largemouth bass, stripers, and buffalo. Wild turkey, deer, herons, and other wildlife are common, and poisonous snakes are plentiful enough to warrant caution.

The big disadvantage is the length of the trip—29.5 miles, with no convenient intermediate accesses. Thus, you're more likely to see an occasional fisherman than other canoeists. Unless you have permission from a landowner to camp somewhere along the way, or to take out on the muddy bank at the Emma bridge (County 600N), your only option is to make a very long day of it and paddle all the way to New Haven. The trip begins and ends with excellent concrete ramps, but the steep banks make it difficult to land canoes most of the way—particularly when the river has been high and mud is everywhere.

Several public **campgrounds** are found to the south within 35 miles of New Haven (e.g., the Saline County Conservation Area, Garden of the Gods, and Pound Hollow—all south of Equality), and to the west at Hamilton County Conservation Area off Highway 14. Burrell Park Campground (private) is located on the western edge of Carmi.

The **shuttle route** (16.8 miles) goes northeast for a short distance on Highway 1 (Main Street), southeast on Epworth Road to the grain elevator at Epworth, south on County 1450 E, and west on Highway 141 across the bridge to New Haven. Proceed on Vine Street (the main street), turn left on Hickory, then right on Front Street, which leads to the public boat ramp.

The **gradient** on this section of the Little Wabash is negligible (less than a foot per mile).

For **water levels**, check the Carmi Main Street gauge (station #03381495) on the USGS Web site listed in the introduction.

Put in at the concrete boat ramp downstream-left from the Highway 1 bridge on the east side of Carmi. To get to the landing, turn off Highway 1 onto First Street, then south onto Hays Street. The landing is on private property, but the owner allows its use as long as boaters don't abuse the privilege. Upstream from the bridge a short distance is a dangerous low-head dam.

From the beginning, the mud banks are steep and heavily wooded, and the river is never straight for long, curving back and forth in gentle bends. Deadfall piles up periodically along the banks or even in the middle, but the river's wideness usually makes it easy to get around. Several rocky shoals tend to discourage motorboaters when water levels are normal or low. After the Possum Road bridge, the river continues in a series of long, gentle bends, finally making a sharp S curve near the mouth of Grindstone Creek and passing a modest rock outcropping on the left. A long left bend then leads to Lick Creek, which is preceded by power lines and a fishing camp on the right.

After Lick Creek, the river goes into a long right bend that leads to several tight loops ("cutbacks"). Eventually, oil tanks appear on the right shoreline opposite the tiny community of Emma, and the bridge at 600N soon follows. The homeowner at the bridge, upstream-left, will allow canoeists to take out here, with permission in advance, but the bank must be dry to make this possible.

Tight loops resume after the bridge. In the last couple of miles before New Haven the river widens to 175–200 feet and straightens. Several trailers precede the Highway 141 bridge, and the community of New Haven begins on the right immediately afterward. After another rocky shoal, **take out** at the public boat ramp on the right, at a pleasant village park with a sizable parking area.

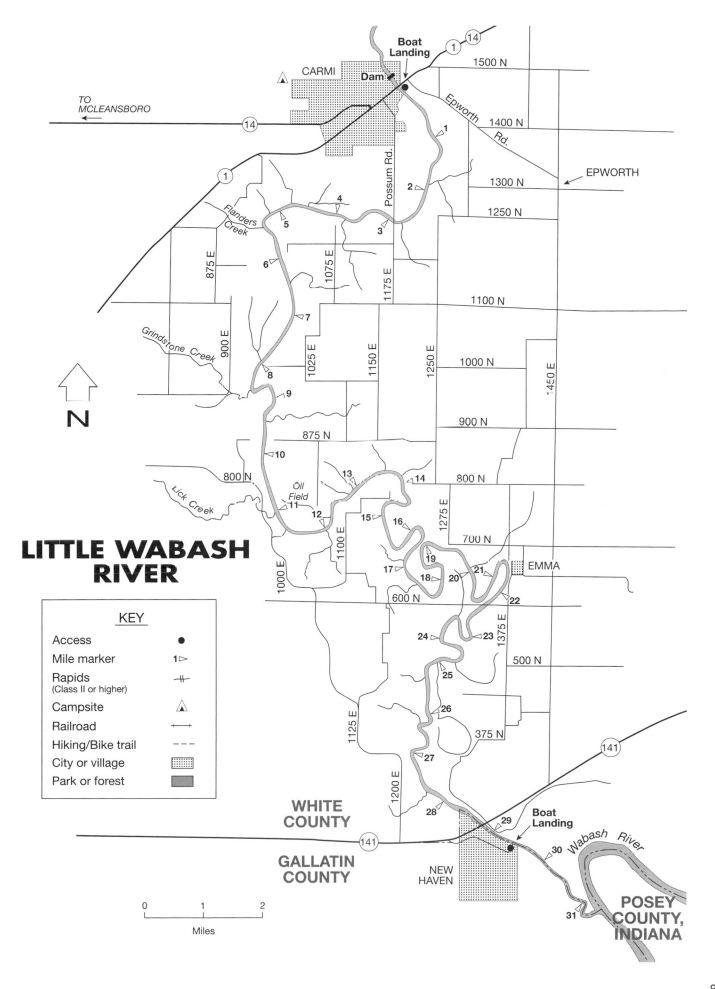

LITTLE WABASH RIVER

KEY

Access	●
Mile marker	1▷
Rapids (Class II or higher)	─╫─
Campsite	△
Railroad	─┼─
Hiking/Bike trail	– – –
City or village	▦
Park or forest	▤

CARMI

TO MCLEANSBORO

Boat Landing

Dam

EPWORTH

Flanders Creek

Grindstone Creek

Lick Creek

Oil Field

EMMA

WHITE COUNTY

GALLATIN COUNTY

NEW HAVEN

POSEY COUNTY, INDIANA

Wabash River

Boat Landing

Possum Rd.
Epworth Rd.

1500 N
1400 N
1300 N
1250 N
1100 N
1000 N
900 N
875 N
800 N
700 N
600 N
500 N
375 N

875 E
900 E
1075 E
1175 E
1025 E
1150 E
1250 E
1450 E
1275 E
1100 E
1000 E
1375 E
1125 E
1200 E

0   1   2
Miles

LUSK CREEK
Eddyville Road to Forest Road 452 (7 Miles)

Lusk Who?

Lusk Creek was named after Major James Lusk, a Revolutionary War figure who established an Ohio River ferry in 1797 near what is now Golconda. When he died, his wife, Sarah, took over the ferry, carrying a firearm for protection against river pirates. Lasting until 1957, the ferry transported thousands of Southern settlers into Illinois, and played a role in the infamous Trail of Tears in 1838–39. Almost 2,000 Cherokee died in winter camps in southern Illinois while being force-marched from their homes in Georgia to Oklahoma.

One of the prettiest canoeing streams in Illinois, Lusk Creek isn't easy to access, but it's worth the extra effort. Flowing alternately through national forest land and private property, it is a small, remote creek that is best in the spring when water volume is adequate and the bankside wildflowers and dogwood are at their peak. Not for beginners, it is fairly steep, falling through countless riffles and small rapids, with occasional fallen trees that must be maneuvered around or portaged.

Heavily wooded from beginning to end, the creek is only 30 to 40 feet wide, flowing over a sand-and-gravel bottom and passing many beautiful outcroppings of limestone. Wildlife is abundant. You probably won't see any venomous snakes, especially if you paddle early in the spring, but they are found in the area and warrant caution. Fishermen catch smallmouth and largemouth bass, catfish, and panfish. The water quality is what you'd expect of an Ozark-like stream in the Shawnee Hills—clear, with a greenish tint. No houses whatsoever are seen, and the setting is completely wild and pristine. Dangerous when high, Lusk Creek is a canoeing gem at medium water levels. When low, however, it involves a lot of scraping and walking through shallows.

Excellent public **camping** is located nearby—to the west at Dixon Springs State Park and Lake Glendale Recreation Area. In the early 1900s there was a popular hotel and spa at Dixon Springs where visitors sought the curative powers of the abundant mineral water there. Many picturesque rock formations and trails are found in the park, which sits on a geologic fault line. Camping is also available to the northwest at Bell Smith Springs, where you can see a beautiful gorge, a natural bridge of stone, and other scenic places.

The **shuttle route** goes southeast on Eddyville Road, west on Reddick Hollow Road, and south on FR 452. Park your shuttle vehicle(s) at the end of the road, within a short walking distance of the creek. Because you'll never recognize the take-out location otherwise, you should walk down to the bank and fix its appearance in your memory, perhaps hanging a piece of surveyor's tape or a bright bandanna from a limb to make sure you don't continue paddling downstream.

The **gradient** is a riffle-producing 8.6 feet per mile.

For **water levels,** check the Eddyville gauge (station #03384450) on the USGS Web site listed in the introduction.

Put in at the old metal bridge on Eddyville Road, downstream-left. From the beginning, beautiful rock formations, riffles, Class I rapids, and twisting turns are frequent. Small drops add to the excitement. The only sound comes from the rushing of water and the music of birdcalls. In the middle of a southerly stretch, a couple of small tributaries on the left indicate the location of Manson's Ford. There are some pleasant riffles here and a difficult, easy-to-miss access on the right bank. A rough road comes within a few yards of the no-longer-used ford, which lies within the Shawnee National Forest.

Downstream, Quarrel Creek enters on the right in a tight left turn. Pools and riffles continue to alternate. After Beatty Branch enters on the left, a 15-foot rocky cliff appears on the left, with a huge rock in the creek: this is known as Porter Springs. A trail was once located nearby where mail riders crossed on horseback. Immediately downstream-right is a private hunting club, reached from Waltersburg Road. Riffles continue for about a mile below Porter Springs, then diminish and eventually disappear as the creek slows and heads toward the "pool" of the Ohio River.

Take out on the left shore and carry or drag your boats up to FR 452, on national forest land. Farther downstream the creek flows almost entirely through private land, and there is no public take-out until the boat ramp in Golconda upstream from the Highway 146 bridge, on the left. This part of the creek is not recommended because of the relatively unattractive cutbanks, sluggish current, logjams, and (in the approach to Golconda) motorboat traffic.

Clean, riffly, and intimate, Lusk Creek is a great springtime run.

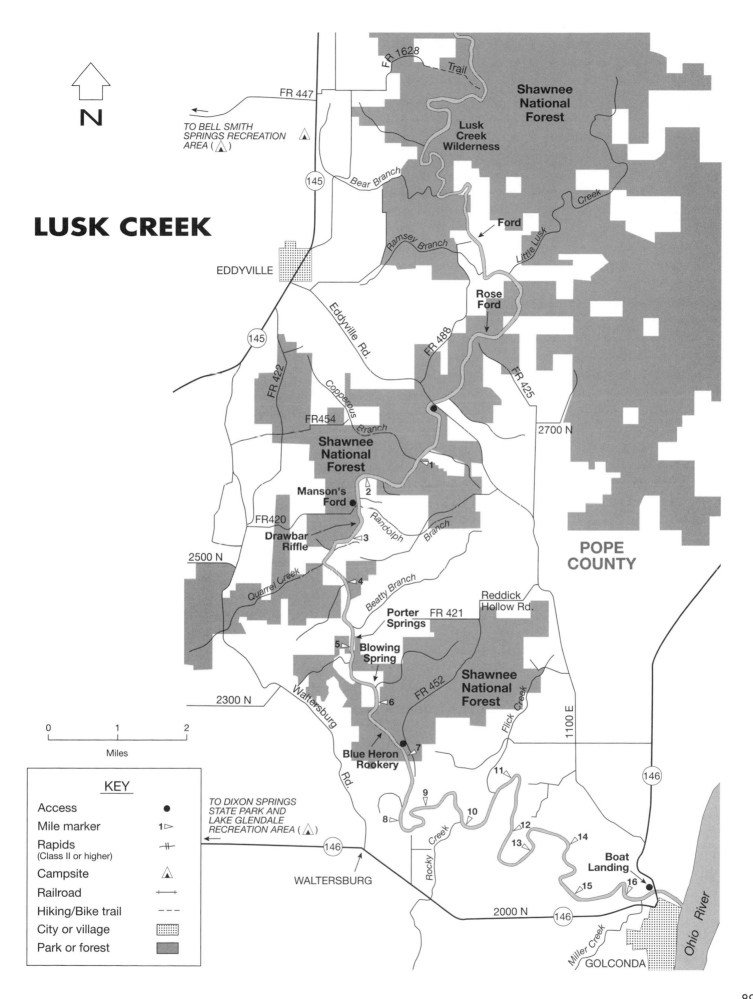

LUSK CREEK

N

TO BELL SMITH
SPRINGS RECREATION
AREA (⛺)

FR 447

FR 1628

Trail

Shawnee
National
Forest

Lusk
Creek
Wilderness

Bear Branch

Ford

EDDYVILLE

145

Ramsey Branch

Little Lusk Creek

Rose
Ford

145

FR 488

FR 425

FR 422

Eddyville Rd.

2700 N

FR454

Copperous Branch

Shawnee
National
Forest

1

2

Manson's
Ford

Randolph Branch

POPE
COUNTY

FR420

Drawbar
Riffle

3

2500 N

Quarrel Creek

4

Beatty Branch

Reddick
Hollow Rd.

Porter
Springs

FR 421

5

Blowing
Spring

FR 452

Shawnee
National
Forest

2300 N

Waltersburg Rd.

6

Flick Creek

1100 E

Blue Heron
Rookery

7

11

0   1   2
Miles

TO DIXON SPRINGS
STATE PARK AND
LAKE GLENDALE
RECREATION AREA (⛺)

9

8

10

146

12

14

13

Boat
Landing

KEY

Access	●
Mile marker	1▷
Rapids (Class II or higher)	—╫—
Campsite	⛺
Railroad	—╂—
Hiking/Bike trail	- - -
City or village	▦
Park or forest	▉

146

WALTERSBURG

Rocky Creek

15

16

2000 N

146

Miller Creek

GOLCONDA

Ohio River

MACKINAW RIVER 1
Sparks Bridge to Highway 150 (15 Miles)

Only forty-two American rivers that are at least 125 miles long are undammed—and the Mackinaw is one of them. Fortunately, dam-building efforts were thwarted in the 1960s and 1980s, and this classic prairie stream still flows freely through central Illinois. Beginning modestly on treeless flatland near Sibley in Ford County, the Mackinaw has been straightened and channelized for its first 11 miles. Near Colfax, however, its narrow channel begins winding through a lovely, tree-lined corridor. On its westward course it parallels one glacial moraine, then flows through three more, giving canoeists a pleasant panorama of wooded bluffs. In its final miles before joining the Illinois River just south of Pekin, silt-and-clay banks give way to sand as the surroundings flatten out.

The Mackinaw is not without problems, the biggest of which are flooding and excessive sedimentation. Beginning in the mid-1990s, however, an impressive cooperative effort by landowners, the Nature Conservancy, DNR, and other individuals and groups began to work on such long-term solutions as restoration of wetlands and forests. It is hoped their work will result in the preservation of this remarkably unspoiled river.

In its 125 miles, the Mackinaw falls an average of 3.3 feet per mile, creating frequent riffles that suggest smallmouth bass habitat. Indeed, smallmouth are often caught by fishermen, together with catfish, white bass, and rock bass. You'll also see a lot of mussel shells in the water. River otters were reintroduced in the area in 1996, joining the commonly seen deer, raccoons, wild turkey, herons, owls, hawks, turtles, and other wildlife. The name *Mackinaw*, incidentally, comes from the Ojibwa word for "turtle." Tranquil throughout its four-county journey, the Mackinaw passes through no cities or towns and is a perfect place for a quiet float trip.

There are several beautiful sections downstream from Colfax, but the first stretch where you can paddle with a reasonable expectation of encountering no significant obstructions is the one starting at Sparks Bridge. From this point downstream, the river is a bit wider, and fallen trees generally do not block the channel.

For **camping**, Yogi Bear Jellystone Campground is located nearby, just north of Goodfield. The nearest public camping is Moraine View State Park, east of Bloomington and north of LeRoy.

The **shuttle route** goes south from Sparks Bridge on County 2275E, west on 375N, south on 2225E, west on 2225N, then west on Highway 150 through Congerville to the Mackinaw River bridge.

The **gradient** is only 1.3 feet per mile.

For **water levels,** check the Congerville gauge (station #05567500) on the USGS Web site listed in the introduction.

Put in on the south bank, upstream from Sparks Bridge; carry boats down the concrete flue to the bank. The river begins about 45 feet wide, with 8- to 10-foot banks and a gravel bottom. Cultivated fields aren't far away, but are almost always hidden by woods. Often canopied by overhanging trees, the river winds through a series of turns, occasionally narrowing. Gravel bars begin appearing soon, with periodic riffles and big rocks along the shoreline. At one point, signs on both sides indicate the location of a 663-acre tract owned by the Nature Conservancy. There are no houses, power lines, or noise. For awhile, high bluffs rise over the river on the right.

Near the mouth of Denman Creek on the left, the river widens to about 80 feet and open pasture is seen briefly. Shortly thereafter, cabins and trailers appear at Wyatt's Ford, where the river swings sharply right, then left, with good riffles. There's an attractive gravel beach here, but be wary of deadfall that collects in the S curve.

The river now narrows again and winds through another lovely stretch overhung with trees. High wooded bluffs resume on the left, and gravel bars become more frequent. Sheer cutbanks are found where farm fields come close to the river. After the mouth of Panther Creek (a major tributary) on the right, the Robinstein Bridge appears. The homeowner at the downstream-right corner of the bridge will allow canoeists to take out or put in here if they ask permission in advance; access is through a fenced and gated lane.

Near Robinstein Bridge the Mackinaw encounters the Eureka Moraine, which the river has penetrated since the retreat of the Wisconsin Glacier 10,000 to 15,000 years ago. Thus, you'll pass more bluffs, including some 75-foot-high clifflike exposed hillsides. Eventually an attractive, old inverted-truss railroad bridge comes into view downstream; pleasant riffles are found under it. Back in the 1920s a dance hall called the Mackinaw Dells was located in this area on the right. The building is now gone, but the name persists, leading many canoeists to erroneously expect stone formations.

Take out at the Highway 150 bridge, downstream-right, where a dirt access road leads down to the river, with room to park several cars.

Other trips: Narrow, heavily forested, and wild, the upper Mackinaw is a wonderful experience for small-stream enthusiasts. If you don't mind occasional obstructions, the following sections are worth considering: (1) County 3075E west of Colfax to Old Route 66 at Lexington (11 miles); (2) Old Route 66 to Coonsford Bridge east of Kappa on County 1725E near 2700N (10 miles); and (3) Coonsford Bridge to Sparks Bridge (11 miles).

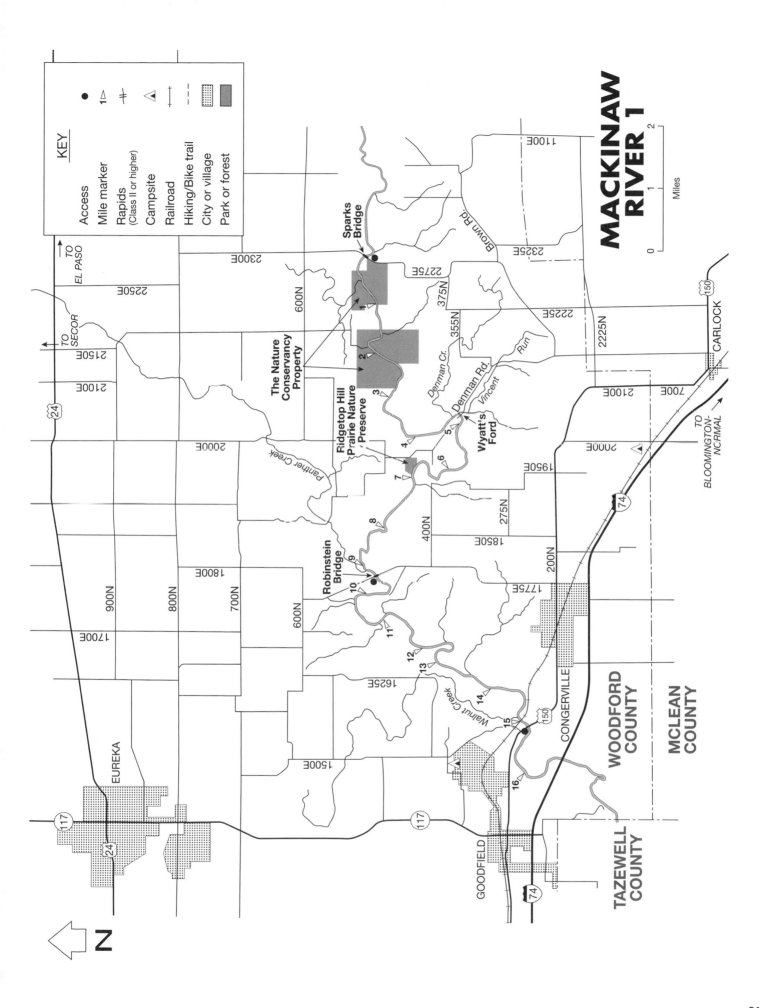

MACKINAW RIVER 1

KEY

- Access •
- Mile marker 1△
- Rapids (Class II or higher) ⊬
- Campsite ◁
- Railroad ╫
- Hiking/Bike trail ┊┊┊
- City or village ▦
- Park or forest ▨

Miles
0   1   2

Sparks Bridge

The Nature Conservancy Property

Ridgetop Hill Prairie Nature Preserve

Wyatt's Ford

Robinstein Bridge

Denman Cr.

Denman Rd.

Vincent Run

Panther Creek

Walnut Creek

TO EL PASO
TO SECOR

EUREKA

GOODFIELD

CONGERVILLE

CARLOCK

TO BLOOMINGTON-NORMAL

WOODFORD COUNTY
MCLEAN COUNTY
TAZEWELL COUNTY

2300E
2275E
2250E
2225E
2235E
2215E
2100E
2000E
1950E
1850E
1800E
1775E
1725E
1700E
1625E
1500E
1100E
700E

600N
375N
355N
275N
200N
400N
600N
700N
800N
900N

2225N

N

91

MACKINAW RIVER 2
Highway 150 to DNR Canoe Landing (8.7 Miles)

Over 90 percent of the 728,000 acres in the Mackinaw River basin is classified as agricultural (principally corn and soybean cultivation), with only 6 percent still forested. Fortunately, most of the remaining woodland is concentrated along the river, insulating it from farm fields and lending a wild character to the shoreline environment. Adding to the variety and beauty of the Mackinaw's surroundings are the glacial moraines that it has breached in its westward path. On this section, for example, it cuts through the sizable Bloomington Moraine, which presents lovely rolling terrain much like the foothills of New England or the Ozarks. Another legacy of the glaciers is a thick deposit of rich soil ("loess") that makes Illinois so agriculturally productive. Canoeists see several feet of this soil along the banks, overlying clay, sand, silt, and gravel. Unfortunately, this soil is quite subject to erosion, so you'll paddle by many sheer cutbanks, especially where crops are cultivated to the very edge.

A tight squeeze

Downstream from Highway 150, the river averages 70 feet wide. Deadfall occasionally must be avoided or portaged but is seldom a big problem. Gravel bars become increasingly common and provide numerous stopping places. On this section there is an often-repeated structural pattern in bends, particularly the sharp ones: on the faster outside part of the bend, the river erodes the shoreline and creates a steep cutbank, while the slower current on the inside of the bend deposits sand and gravel to form gravel bars (often quite large). Frequent layers of assorted rocks make this a good trip for rock hounds, and such fossils as trilobites and coral are often found. At normal summer and fall water levels, the water is fairly clear, and shells can be seen on the gravel bottom. There are a couple of open areas along the shoreline, but woods prevail most of the time, with no houses.

For **camping** and **water levels**, see Mackinaw River 1.

The **shuttle route** (8.2 miles) is rather complicated but pleasant, winding through attractive hill country. From the put-in, go west on Highway 150 to the intersection with Highway 117 in Goodfield, then south across Interstate 74 to a T, west on Martin Drive, south on County 3400E, south on Zimmerman Road, west on Ragar Road, south on Wiegand Road, and southwest on Schlappi Road to the DNR access road.

The **gradient** is 2.3 feet per mile.

Put in at the Highway 150 bridge, downstream-right, where you can park several cars. This is a popular area with fishermen. Gravel bars and cutbanks begin in the first bends, and a high bluff soon appears on the right. After a couple of huge boulders on the right shore, the I-74 bridges come into view. A straight stretch follows, then another series of bends. Along the way, gravel bars sometimes show signs of having been used by fishermen and campers. It's never a bad idea to stop and pick up cans and other mementos left behind by inconsiderate river users. Densely wooded, the stretch after I-74 becomes increasingly remote, although noise can sometimes be heard from nearby gravel pit operations.

After a sharp left turn and some concrete riprap, Zimmerman Road pulls alongside the river on the right. The steep but short bank alongside the culvert here can be used as a rough access. Then, as the river bends right, there's an interesting 25-foot cutbank on the left, with a huge pile of rocks at its base and a plentiful layer of gravel. Rocky Ford Bridge soon appears downstream. About 100 yards upstream from the bridge on the left is a gravel bar that is popular with fishermen. This makes a good access (through the woods to nearby River Road), but is on private land.

Arcing right, the river soon splits around a big gravel bar in a short, sharp S curve. There are excellent riffles here, but you must be careful of deadfall, especially in the left channel alongside a cutbank. After a quarter mile of open fields on the left, woods resume. Gravel bars often constrict the channel, speeding up the current and creating pleasant riffles. Later, in a long left bend, there's a twisty S curve where a big gravel bar comes out from the right shore; a limb or tree often blocks the narrow channel, but it's easy to get out on the gravel bar and carry your boat a few steps past the obstruction. Near the end of the long left bend, the river is deflected by a 70-foot clay-and-sand cliff, alongside a creek. The river now swings to the right, past the densely wooded bluffs of the 1,428-acre Mackinaw River State Fish and Wildlife Area.

Passing between steep mud banks, the river turns left past some farm buildings on the right—the first of the trip. As the left bend continues, look for a bare patch on the right: this fairly steep clay-and-gravel landing leads up to the DNR canoe-access area, an excellent **take-out** (or put-in), with ample parking nearby.

Other trips: Between the DNR landing and Highway 155, there are two pleasant day trips, shown on the maps for Mackinaw River 2 and 3: (1) from the DNR landing to White Oak Grove Road (12.3 miles), with an intermediate access about 100 feet upstream on the left from the Dee-Mack Bridge; and (2) from White Oak Grove Road to the old Highway 121 bridge (7 miles).

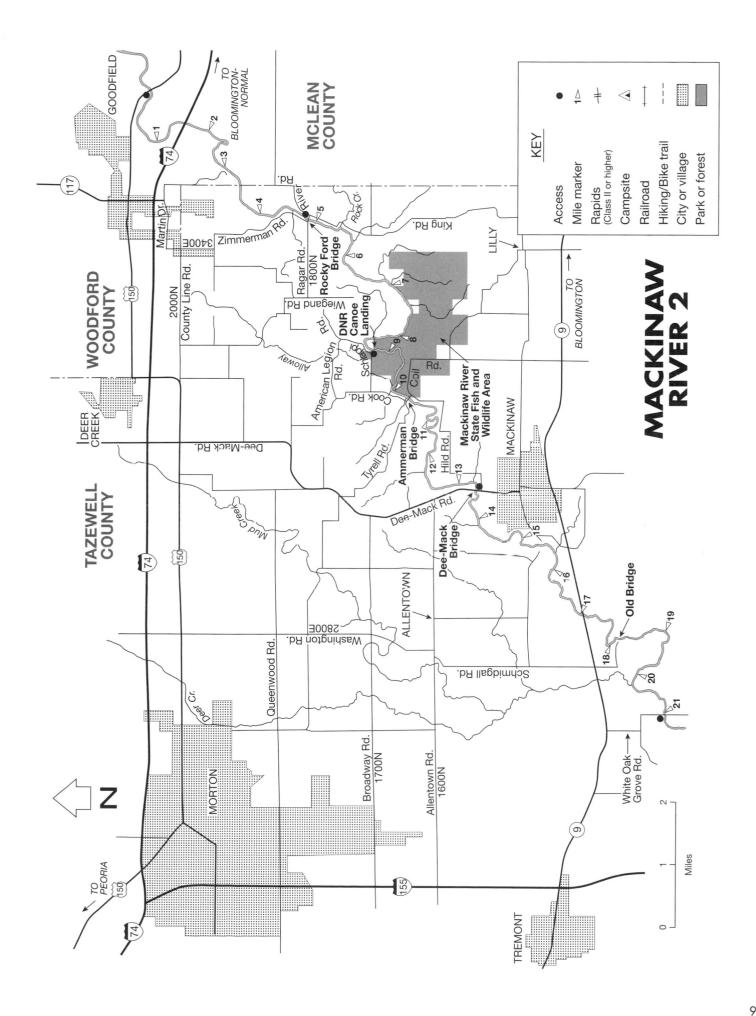

MACKINAW RIVER 2

MACKINAW RIVER 3
Highway 155 to Towerline Road (12 Miles)

In this stretch, the Mackinaw has not yet reached the low sandy plain through which its final miles pass. In fact, the 12 miles of Mackinaw River 3 still have a healthy **gradient** of 3.3 feet per mile. But sand is much more abundant here than upstream, especially in the huge and frequent sand-and-gravel bars and in the many steep cutbanks where the river has eaten away at the shoreline in curves. The Mackinaw here forces its way through two more end-moraines, the LeRoy and Shelbyville, which represent the southernmost advance of the last glacier.

This is a very relaxing part of the river, with little sign of habitation, several dramatic cliffs, and many places to stop for lunch and rest breaks. Occasional erosion-retardant riprap along the shoreline and brief open spaces take a little away from the naturalness.

In addition to the **campgrounds** listed for Mackinaw River 1 and 2, there is public camping available to the south (near Manito) at Sand Ridge State Forest and Spring Lake State Fish and Wildlife Area.

The **shuttle route** is 14.2 miles. From the put-in, drive north along the Old 121 frontage road to Highway 155, then north to Townline Road (County 1100N), west to Towerline Road (County 1700E), and south to the bridge. Shuttling to the south via Prairie Road and Toboggan Road is about a mile shorter.

For **water levels,** check the Green Valley gauge (station #05568000) on the USGS Web site listed in the introduction.

Put in at the Old 121 bridge, downstream-left. To get to the put-in, turn off Highway 155 at Exit 19 (Highway 122); turn west for a short distance, then north onto Old 121. A short gravel road leads from Old 121 to the river, where a gravel bar provides easy access. About 55 feet wide at the put-in, the river begins with several short bends, then a westward straightaway. The silt-and-sand banks are wooded, but farm fields usually aren't far behind the trees and occasionally come to the edge of the bank. After a series of sharp turns, an old iron truss bridge appears, with a house just upstream.

Another series of rather sharp turns follows, with characteristic cutbanks and gravel bars, and the river widens at times to as much as 100 feet. Dead trees accumulate in some of the bends, requiring attentiveness. Boaters also must be aware of the often tricky eddies and currents in many of the bends. At one point, after a sharp left turn, the river passes a 70-foot exposed bluff on the left that locals call "The Cliff." Downstream are a huge gravel bar and the ruins of an old cabin. More twists and turns lead to the Springfield Road bridge (south of the small community of Dillon), where access is possible upstream-right.

Long, gentle bends follow, one of which ends at another dramatic cliff of clay, sand, and rock. Sand becomes increasingly conspicuous along the shoreline, and occasional riffles continue. After another tall, exposed bluff (not as impressive as the previous two), the river bends to another old truss bridge. After the bridge, the river is wider and less curvy. Two more exposed bluffs appear, neither as sheer as the first two. Soon after a small cabin on the left shore, in a sharp right turn, the Towerline Road bridge can be seen. **Take out** downstream-left at a big gravel bar. Be sure not to block the farmer's field access with your vehicle(s).

Other trips: Another day trip begins at Towerline Road and takes out at Townline Road (1100N). This 10.5-mile section is wider, flatter, more open, and less attractive. There are no good take-outs near the mouth of the Mackinaw, so a canoe trip from Townline Road necessitates continuing downstream on the Illinois River to Kingston Mines, where there is presently no suitable access.

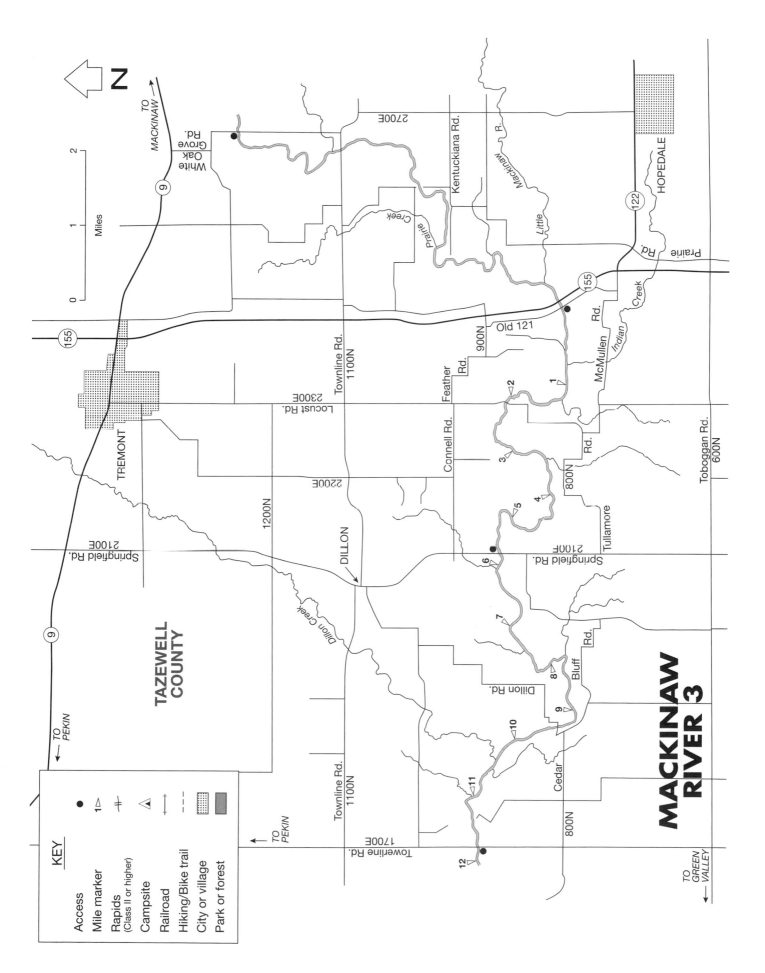

MACKINAW RIVER 3

KEY

- Access
- Mile marker
- Rapids (Class II or higher)
- Campsite
- Railroad
- Hiking/Bike trail
- City or village
- Park or forest

TAZEWELL COUNTY

TREMONT

DILLON

HOPEDALE

N

Miles
0   1   2

TO MACKINAW

TO PEKIN

TO PEKIN

TO GREEN VALLEY

White Oak Grove Rd.

Townline Rd. 1100N

Locust Rd. 2300E

Connell Rd. 2200E

Feather Rd.

900N

Old 121

McMullen Rd.

Kentuckiana Rd.

Mackinaw R.

Little

Prairie Creek

Indian Creek

Prairie Rd.

Springfield Rd. 2100E

Springfield Rd. 2100E

Toboggan Rd. 600N

Tullamore

800N

1200N

Dillon Creek

Dillon Rd.

Bluff Rd.

Cedar

800N

Towerline Rd. 1700E

Townline Rd. 1100N

MAZON RIVER
Highway 113 to Pine Bluff Road (9.6 Miles)

Attention, All Fossil-Hunters!

Although the Mazon is a popular canoeing stream in the springtime, it is world-famous for something altogether different. For many years, scientists and amateur fossil hunters have flocked to the area in pursuit of "Mazon Creek biota"—plants and animals that were fossilized 300 million years ago during the Pennsylvanian Period. The lush tropical growth of that geological era produced not only coal deposits but also ironstone concretions that often bear excellent fossils of plants, insects, fish, and other animals. Coal in the area has been extensively strip-mined, exposing the heavy, ovular nodules prized by fossil hunters. As you paddle alongside the banks of the river, be on the lookout for these dark, egg-shaped rocks; a rap with a hammer will frequently reveal a fossil inside. Incidentally, there is a fascinating collection of Mazon fossils nearby at the Goose Lake Prairie visitor center, only a few miles east of the take-out.

For a brief introduction to the coal and fossil history of the Mazon area, see chapter 6 ("Age of the Coal Forests") in Christopher Schuberth's *A View of the Past: An Introduction to Illinois Geology* (Springfield: Illinois State Museum, 1986). The Illinois State Museum also has an excellent Internet exhibit on the "Mazon Creek Fossils," with text and photos: <www.museum.state.il.us/exhibits/mazon_creek>.

Not really a whitewater river, the Mazon nevertheless has a steep enough **gradient** (4.7 feet per mile in this stretch) to offer many enjoyable riffles and minor rapids, some laced with rocks that require dodging. Thus, the river is recommended for experienced paddlers. Frequent stone formations, cliffs, and bluffs make the Mazon a very attractive canoeing river. Deadfall is usually not a problem on this section because of the average width of 90 feet. Bankside dwellings are minimal, and most of the stretch is wooded. Like many Illinois rivers, the Mazon was named by the Native Americans who once inhabited the area; *Mazon* is from an Algonquin word for a type of nettle used to make cord.

Public **camping** is located to the east at the Des Plaines Conservation Area and Channahon State Park, and to the west at Gebhard Woods State Park (at Morris).

The **shuttle route** goes west on Highway 113, north on Higgins Road, west on Southmor Road, north to Old Pine Bluff Road, then east to the access on the right just before Pine Bluff Road.

Water levels. Because of its steepness, the Mazon is normally a springtime run. Check the Coal City gauge (station #05542000) on the USGS Web site listed in the introduction.

The **put-in** is not easy. Park carefully along the narrow shoulder on the upstream side of the Highway 113 bridge and carry boat(s) down to the river's east bank. If you'd like to lengthen the trip by a few miles, you can put in farther upstream at Reed Road (County S2000) or Gorman Road (E4000).

A couple of homes, some power lines, and another bridge soon appear after the put-in. A thin, forested corridor lies along the grassy banks. As the river curves left after McCardle Road, there are some pleasant riffles, together with limestone outcroppings on the right. At one point, the river turns abruptly left, then right, around an island. Houses continue on the left side for awhile.

After a straightaway, the river curves right again, with several huge boulders lying in the river in the midst of the curve. At the end of the bend, there's an island where the main channel flows to the right. At some water levels, a Class I rapid is located here, with a "Yahoo!"-type wave train of about 50 yards and some rocks to avoid. The limestone-littered beach just below the rapid, on the left, is a good place to look for fossils. In the half-mile straightaway that follows, there are some trailers on the left and high banks on the right. Then, immediately after a short left turn, the river drops about a foot where a line of boulders crosses the river.

Downstream from the next bridge are a small island, houses on the right, and a rocky, riverwide ledge about 2 feet high—the biggest drop on the river. To run the ledge, pick a tongue of water, usually near the center. A riffly S curve follows, then a sandstone-and-shale cliff where the river bends back to the right.

After a high bluff on the left and a house on the right, the river curves left past shale cliffs, in the middle of which Claypool Ditch dramatically cascades into the river. Long, fast riffles follow, then a large island where the river bends right. Farther downstream, in a left turn, a concrete retaining structure on the right prevents erosion between the river and the former strip mine area that is now a Boy Scout camp.

For the rest of the trip, the river curves back and forth, with frequent riffles and intermittent bluffs, cliffs, and rock outcroppings. Finally, about a mile from the end, houses begin appearing on the left and the current slackens because of proximity to the Illinois River. **Take out** on the often muddy bank on river-left upstream from the Pine Bluff Road bridge. Carry boats a couple hundred feet on a dirt access road that leads to Old Pine Bluff Road, near its intersection with Pine Bluff Road. Park on the grass alongside the access road.

Enjoying the many riffles of the Mazon

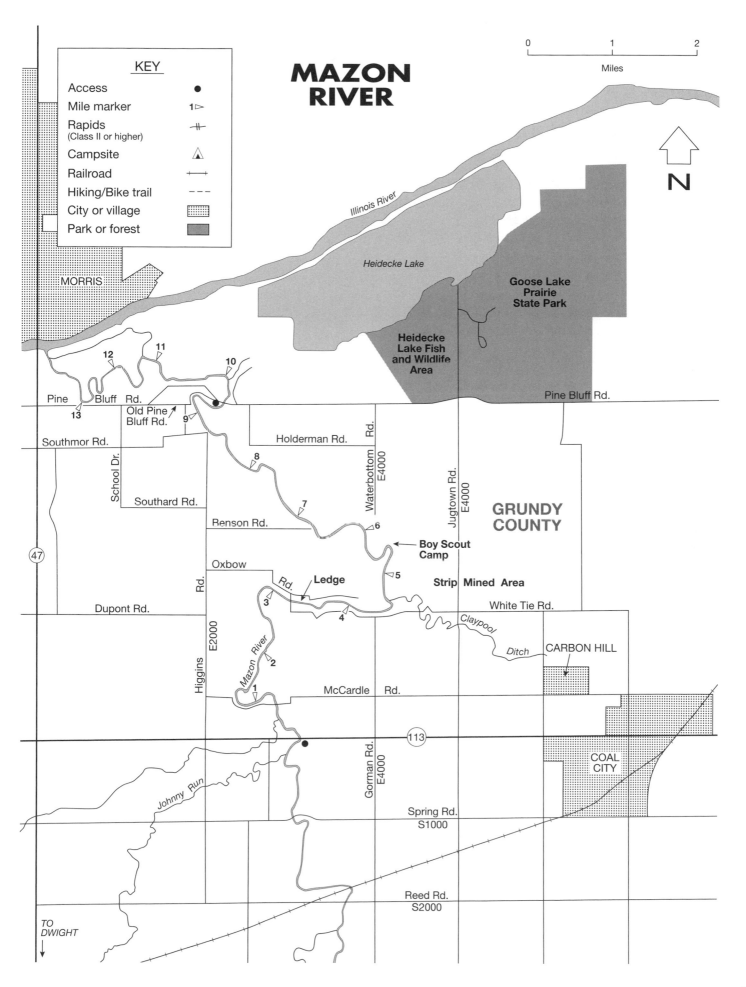

MAZON RIVER

KEY

Access	●
Mile marker	1▷
Rapids (Class II or higher)	╫
Campsite	▲
Railroad	┼┼┼
Hiking/Bike trail	---
City or village	▦
Park or forest	▨

0   1   2
Miles

N

Illinois River

Heidecke Lake

Goose Lake Prairie State Park

Heidecke Lake Fish and Wildlife Area

MORRIS

12
11
10
Pine   Bluff   Rd.
13
Old Pine Bluff Rd.
9
Pine Bluff Rd.

Southmor Rd.
Holderman Rd.
School Dr.
8
Waterbottom Rd. E4000
Jugtown Rd. E4000

Southard Rd.
7
GRUNDY COUNTY

Benson Rd.
6
Boy Scout Camp

Oxbow
5
Strip Mined Area

Ledge
Rd.
3
4
White Tie Rd.
Claypool
Ditch
CARBON HILL

Dupont Rd.
Higgins   Rd.   E2000

Mazon River
2

47

1
McCardle   Rd.
Gorman Rd. E4000

113

COAL CITY

Johnny Run

Spring Rd.
S1000

Reed Rd.
S2000

TO DWIGHT

MIDDLE FORK OF THE SOUTH VERMILION RIVER

Kinney's Ford to Kickapoo State Park (12 Miles)

Oops!

A remarkable success story, the Middle Fork has twice approached ruination, eventually emerging as a permanently protected canoeing jewel. For almost a century, strip-mining scarred much of the landscape, leaving thousands of acres of ugly spoil piles and mine ponds. Today, however, thanks to wise land acquisitions and reclamation efforts, nature has gradually recovered, and many canoeists are unaware of the area's mining history as they paddle down the river. Another threat to the Middle Fork was a plan in the 1960s and 1970s to dam the river to form a reservoir—an effort that was abandoned in 1978. Then, in 1989, came the welcome news that the U.S. Department of Interior had added it to the National Wild and Scenic River system.

Beginning near Paxton, the Middle Fork flows southward for 83 miles to the Danville area before joining the Salt Fork to form the South Vermilion. Deadfall tends to be a problem in the upper section, but paddling is good south of Potomac. The first public landing is at Kinney's Ford; the stretch from there to Kickapoo State Park is deservedly one of the most popular in the state. Often paddled by advanced beginners, it nevertheless has numerous tight turns to negotiate and occasional limbs to avoid. The average **gradient** of 5 feet per mile is reflected in a steady succession of delightful riffles, and the setting is enhanced by lovely bluffs and cliffs. Canoe landings are easy and convenient, and make it possible to design trips of various lengths. Multiday trips are facilitated by the bankside presence of Kickapoo State Park—one of the most attractive parks in the state.

Public **camping** is available near the river at the Middle Fork State Fish and Wildlife Area Kennekuk County Park, and Kickapoo State Park.

Canoe rental and shuttle service are available at Kickapoo Landing in Kickapoo Park (217-446-8399).

The **shuttle route** (9.2 miles) from Kinney's Ford goes east on County 2600N, south on 900E, and east on Glenburn Creek Road into the park.

Water levels. During dry periods the river is some-times too low for comfortable paddling. Check the Middle Fork gauge (station #03336645) on the USGS Web site listed in the introduction.

After the **put-in** at Kinney's Ford, the river curves to the right past tree-topped cliffs. Several sharp turns lead to the Higginville Bridge, where there's a convenient access. Many riffles and gravel bars are found in the bends after the bridge, together with more bluffs and cliffs. At normal levels, the water is clear and clean—good smallmouth, crappie, and catfish habitat—as the river alternates between riffles and pools. The setting is heavily wooded, remote, and wonderfully peaceful. A right bend downstream from the mouth of Gimlet Branch leads to the sandy, river-right access at Bunker Hill, an excellent put-in for a short trip to the state park.

After a straight southerly stretch, the area along the banks is fairly open for awhile. In a sharp right turn, the river veers past two more cliffs. Then, after a wooded island, the Illinois Power Company plant looms on the right, alongside a big grassy berm; this is the only building on the trip.

For a short time, the river widens and becomes shallower, and the largest riffle of the day comes in an S curve just upstream from the old Coal Shaft Bridge (no longer in use). A high shale formation follows. When the river swings sharply to the right, sheer 20-foot banks on the left are composed of strip-mined material. In the left bend that follows, large ironstone nodules (like squat loaves of bread) can be seen in the right bank and in the shale wall farther downstream; these nodules often bear 300-million-year-old fossils.

A marvelously peaceful stretch follows, leading to Johnson Hill Bridge, which is crossed by a foot trail. A long, pleasant riffle in an S curve precedes the bridge. From this point downstream, the river is mostly placid, and at one point a long 25-foot shale wall runs alongside on the right. Finally, a series of gentle, riffly curves brings you to the Kickapoo State Park bridge. **Take out** on the left at the upstream gravel landing; a paved parking lot is located nearby.

Other trips. (1) There are no suitable accesses near Potomac, but Gray Ford (off County 2900N) is a good put-in for the 4-mile stretch down to Kinney's Ford. The access is on river-right just downstream from a small, breached rock dam, on private land. This section is quite curvy, with a brisk gradient of 7.1 feet per mile. (2) After the take-out at Kickapoo State Park, the river continues for 3.5 miles, under Interstate 74 and Highway 150, to its confluence with the Salt Fork. Canoeists can take out soon thereafter upstream from the Anderson Hill Bridge, on the right, or can continue downstream to the mouth of the North Fork, then paddle half a mile up the North Fork to the boat landing at Ellsworth Park. (See the map for Salt Fork of the South Vermilion 2.) Please note the presence of a **very dangerous dam** on the South Vermilion downstream from the mouth of the North Fork.

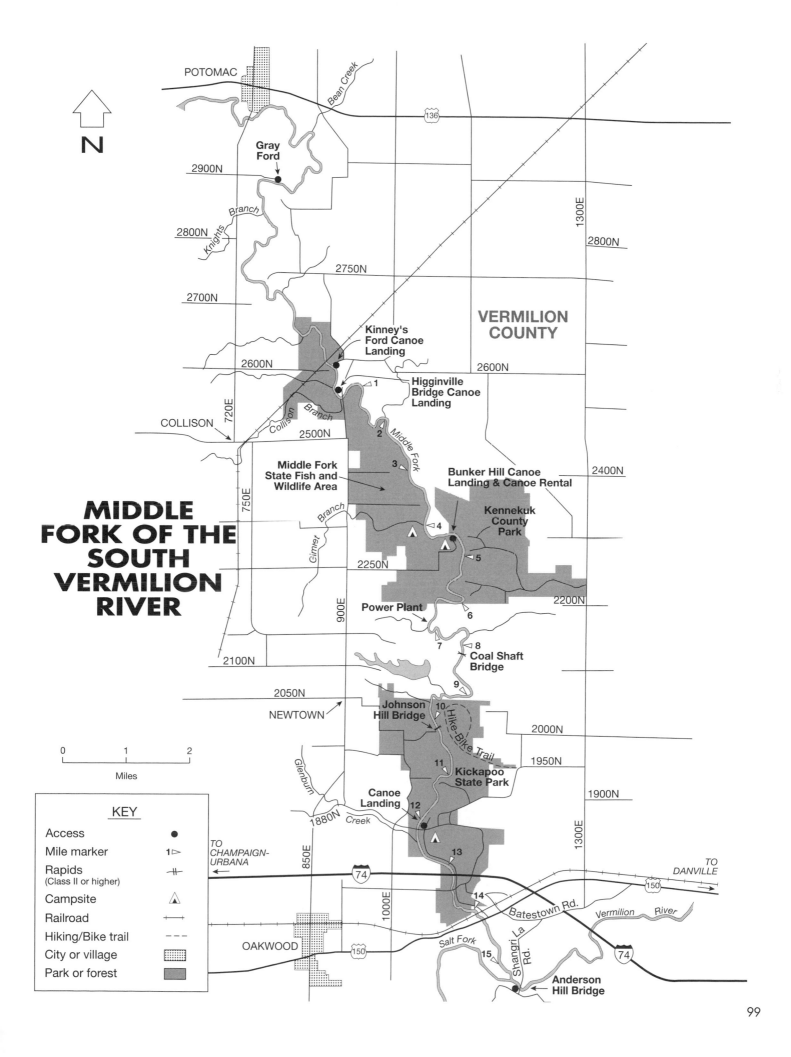

MIDDLE FORK OF THE SOUTH VERMILION RIVER

N

POTOMAC

Gray Ford

2900N

2800N

Knights Branch

2750N

2700N

2600N

Kinney's Ford Canoe Landing

Higginville Bridge Canoe Landing

COLLISON

720E

750E

Collison Branch

Middle Fork

2500N

Middle Fork State Fish and Wildlife Area

2250N

Gimlet Branch

900E

Power Plant

Bunker Hill Canoe Landing & Canoe Rental

Kennekuk County Park

VERMILION COUNTY

Bean Creek

136

1300E

2800N

2600N

2400N

2200N

Coal Shaft Bridge

2100N

2050N

NEWTOWN

Johnson Hill Bridge

Hike-Bike Trail

2000N

1950N

Kickapoo State Park

1900N

Canoe Landing

1880N

Glenburn

Creek

850E

TO CHAMPAIGN-URBANA

74

1000E

OAKWOOD

150

TO DANVILLE

150

Batestown Rd.

Vermilion River

1300E

Salt Fork

Shangri La Rd.

Anderson Hill Bridge

74

KEY

Access	●
Mile marker	1▷
Rapids (Class II or higher)	╫
Campsite	⛺
Railroad	┼┼
Hiking/Bike trail	- - -
City or village	▦
Park or forest	▉

0   1   2
Miles

NIPPERSINK CREEK
Glacial Park to Nippersink Canoe Base (12.5 Miles)

A Glacial Showcase

Don't miss the opportunity to visit Glacial Park: it offers a unique, close-up experience of such glacial features as kettles and kames. Trails lead to many of these landforms (including a walk to the top of the Camelback Kame, where the view is gorgeous), and a boardwalk takes you over a bog. Oak savannas and remnant prairie also can be seen up close. Running through the park (north-south) is a 7-mile biking and hiking trail. It's easy to see why Glacial Park is so popular with canoeists, birdwatchers, hikers, bicyclists, horseback riders, and snowmobilers. Start your walking tour of the park from the parking area near the intersection of Keystone Road and Barnard Mill Road.

Just a few miles to the south (near McHenry) is another fascinating reminder of Illinois's glacial past—1,690-acre Moraine Hills State Park. As the Wisconsin Glacier retreated, it left behind a series of gravelly kames that make up the park's wooded ridges. Lake Defiance, a 48-acre kettle lake in the park, was formed when a gigantic piece of the glacier broke off in the ground and gradually melted. Elsewhere in the park is a huge bog with a floating mat of sphagnum moss, and a fen that is home to many rare plants.

Like many Illinois rivers and streams, the Nippersink flows between the higher elevation of two end-moraines as it flows east to the Fox Chain O' Lakes. At the beginning of this popular canoeing stretch, it passes through a fascinating park that exhibits many landforms left behind by the Wisconsin Glacier. Mostly winding and narrow (35–60 feet), the creek runs through woods, marshy lowland, grassy hills, pastures, and even a short urban area. Appropriately, the Nippersink's name is from a Potawatomi word meaning "little water" (i.e., creek). Sometimes too low to paddle in the summer, it is generally intimate and secluded. Some canoeing experience is recommended because there are occasional obstructions that must be maneuvered around. Accesses are first-rate and allow shorter trips, if desired. The Nippersink is a delightful little stream that many canoeists return to again and again.

Public **camping** is plentiful in the area. A few miles to the east, Chain O' Lakes State Park offers 237 campsites in a huge tract. McHenry County also provides camping facilities at a number of nearby conservation areas, including Glacial Park and Harrison Benwell. Two private campgrounds are located nearby: Lazy K Camping north of Spring Grove, and Fox River Recreation west of Antioch.

Canoe rental is available at Chicagoland Canoe Base in Chicago (773-777-1489) and TipACanoe Canoe Rental in Burlington, Wisconsin (262-537-3227).

The **shuttle route** (9.7 miles) from the put-in goes north on Keystone Road, east on Tryon Grove Road, and east on Highway 12 to Nippersink Canoe Base.

The **gradient** is 3.3 feet per mile, usually producing steady current and some riffles.

For **water levels,** check the Spring Grove gauge (station #05548280) on the USGS Web site listed in the introduction.

Put in at the Keystone Road landing (near the road's intersection with Barnard Mill Road) in Glacial Park, an excellent access with nearby parking, toilets, and picnic facilities. The setting is relatively open at the beginning, and a wooden footbridge soon passes overhead. Off to the right stands the Camelback Kame, produced by the retreating glacier about 15,000 years ago. Hikers

can usually be seen on the trail paralleling the creek, and fishermen along the bank are common.

For many years, paddlers now entered a long, straight, channelized section. In a remarkable project, the McHenry County Conservation District has restored the original, winding channel—designated "Restored Channel" on the map.

Heading east, the creek flows through a long, meandering stretch in a marshy area, with tight loops. After the old railroad bridge that now carries the McHenry County Prairie Trail, the creek becomes quite intimate, with overhanging trees. Highway 31 and Pioneer Road follow. On the right, upstream from Pioneer Road, there's an excellent access, with parking, toilets, and picnic tables. Downstream the creek continues to be heavily wooded and winding.

Upstream from Highway 12 there are few houses, but downstream they begin appearing occasionally. At one point, there's a golf course on both sides, with a rickety wooden bridge. Downstream, a foundry on the right and some power lines precede Spring Grove Road. Then, in Spring Grove, the creek passes under the Blivin Street bridge, where Lyle C. Thomas Memorial Park offers another splendid landing, with toilets, parking, and picnic facilities (downstream-left). Homes and cabins continue after the park. A short distance downstream from the Wilmot Road bridge, a very low, private suspension bridge offers little clearance—a potential problem at higher water levels. Also be alert for wire that might be strung over the creek in this area. After the low bridge the creek is quite wide and winds back and forth through open pastureland in a floodplain environment.

After a long lowland stretch, some 20-foot banks appear on the left, followed by an old railroad bridge. Then, after some homes on the left in a right bend, **take out** at the Nippersink Canoe Base landing on river-right. This is another good access, with parking and toilets.

A day on the popular Nippersink

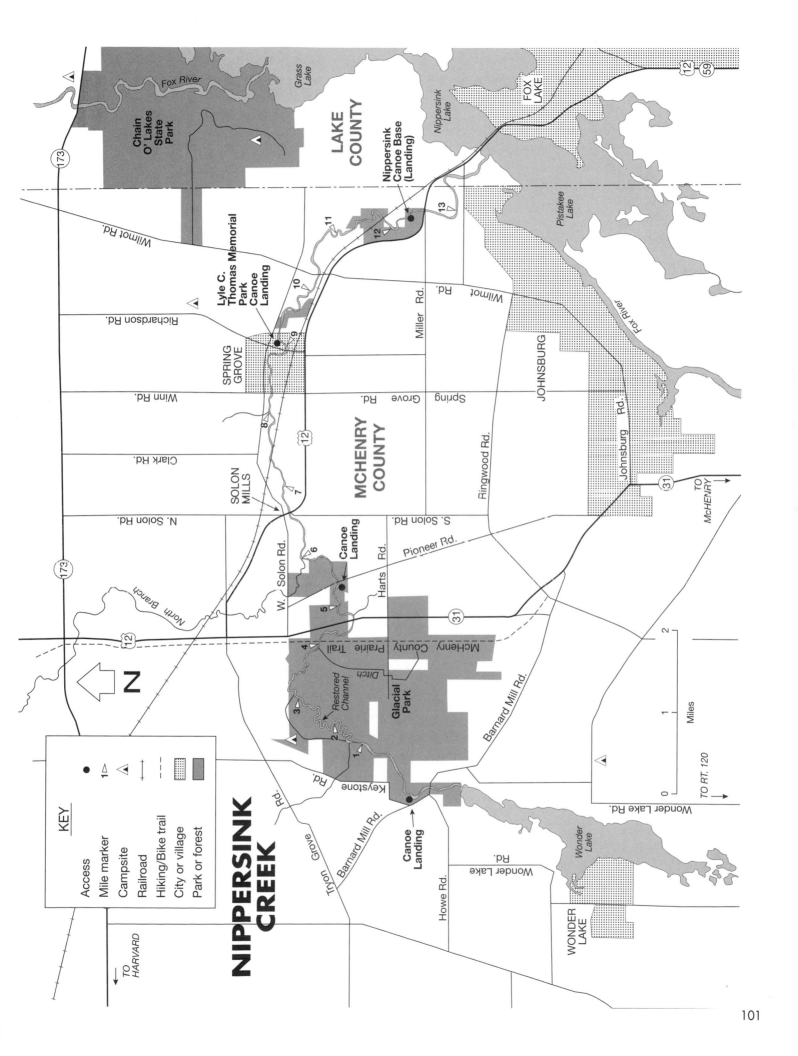

NIPPERSINK CREEK

KEY

•	Access
1△	Mile marker
◁	Campsite
┼┼	Railroad
─ ─	Hiking/Bike trail
▦	City or village
▨	Park or forest

N

TO HARVARD

Chain O' Lakes State Park

Fox River

Grass Lake

LAKE COUNTY

Nippersink Lake

FOX LAKE

Pistakee Lake

Fox River

Nippersink Canoe Base (Landing)

Lyle C. Thomas Memorial Park Canoe Landing

Wilmot Rd.

Richardson Rd.

SPRING GROVE

Winn Rd.

Clark Rd.

Miller Rd.

Wilmot Rd.

Spring Grove Rd.

JOHNSBURG

Johnsburg Rd.

SOLON MILLS

N. Solon Rd.

S. Solon Rd.

Ringwood Rd.

TO McHENRY

Canoe Landing

Harts Rd.

Pioneer Rd.

W. Solon Rd.

North Branch

Restored Channel

Ditch

McHenry County Prairie Trail

Glacial Park

Barnard Mill Rd.

Tryon Grove Rd.

Barnard Mill Rd.

Keystone Rd.

Canoe Landing

Howe Rd.

Wonder Lake Rd.

WONDER LAKE

Wonder Lake

TO RT. 120

Wonder Lake Rd.

MCHENRY COUNTY

Miles

0 1 2

101

NORTH VERMILION RIVER 1
Pontiac to Cornell (10.8 Miles)

The Great Chief Pontiac

The city of Pontiac takes its name from the famous Ottawa chief who led a widespread rebellion against the British. After a series of initial successes, he failed to capture Detroit and Fort Pitt, then was unable to raise needed support from tribes in Illinois and had to admit defeat in 1763. When he was killed by an Illini near Cahokia in southern Illinois several years later, he is said to have been avenged by several tribes (principally the Ottawa, Potawatomi, and Winnebago) that later wiped out a band of Illini on Starved Rock. A plaque near the Pontiac courthouse tells the story of the city's namesake.

Formed by the union of two branches near Fairbury, the North Vermilion flows northwest past parallel ridges of glacial moraines. Dams slow its progress at Pontiac, Streator, and near Oglesby. The best paddling begins at Pontiac—ironically, in one of the flattest areas of the state. From there, the scenery grows increasingly attractive, and the river culminates in the state's most popular whitewater run.

The first section makes a good beginner's trip, consisting mostly of big, gentle bends, with sufficient width (60–90 feet) to make logjams unlikely. Occasional riffly shoals are found at the end of long pools, and several islands add to the variety. There are many gravel bars for relaxation breaks, together with low, rocky shoreline shelves, silt-and-sand banks, and dense woods. Only a half dozen houses interrupt the feeling of isolation. A lovely nature preserve in the middle of the trip makes an alternate landing and a perfect lunch stop. Fish caught in the North Vermilion include largemouth and smallmouth bass, bullheads, catfish, and panfish.

Public **camping** is located a few miles west of Pontiac at the 4-H Fairgrounds on 4-H Park Road, and farther to the north at Starved Rock State Park near Oglesby and Illini State Park near Marseilles. Bayou Bluffs Recreational Park, a private campground, is on Rooks Creek near its confluence with the Vermilion. Another private facility, the Pleasant Creek Campground, is located a few miles south of Starved Rock State Park.

Canoe rental is available at Bayou Bluffs Recreational Park on Rooks Creek, near the take-out (815-358-2537).

The **shuttle route** (14.8 miles) from the put-in goes east on 4-H Park Road, north and then west on Highway 23, then south on the first county road west of Cornell; this road turns west to the take-out bridge.

The **gradient** is 2.3 feet per mile.

For **water levels**, check the Pontiac gauge (station #05554500) on the USGS Web site listed in the introduction.

Put in on river-right at a small township park alongside 4-H Park Road, near the intersection with County 1330E. The put-in is a rocky shoreline reached by a short trail down the bank from a small parking area.

As the river loops to the right under a bridge, then back to the left, a low shelf of limestone appears along the shoreline. Gravel bars follow, then an unsightly retaining wall on the right. The river here is about 60 feet wide, and riffles are fairly frequent. The setting is very natural-looking, although there is some trash from the nearby road. In the left channel of the first island is a pleasant riffle, followed by a set of power lines. Farm fields are seldom far away, but there are never any open spaces; dense woods always top the gently sloping banks. Low rocky shelves continue periodically.

At the Rowe Road bridge, the Humiston Woods Nature Center begins—almost 400 acres of forest with hiking trails, picnic pavilions, restored prairie, and oak savanna. In a left bend after the bridge, there's a concrete canoe ramp on river-right. The nearby trail leads to a picnic area, toilets, and observation deck upstream, and a parking lot downstream. Between the bridge and the canoe landing, the first exposed clay-and-sand bluffs of the trip appear on the left; after the landing, there is an interesting rock formation on the right. Wolf Creek enters on the right as the river curves left.

Several homes appear on both sides as the next bridge approaches, and riffles are less frequent for awhile. The river now passes an island and becomes quite narrow, tree-canopied, and beautiful. Just below the island are some old bridge abutments, and a short distance downstream is the mouth of Rooks Creek.

After Baker Run enters on the right, the river goes into a series of gentle bends, with a lot of broken rock and boulders on the shoreline. **Take out** downstream-right at the County 2400N bridge.

The next bridge downstream is Highway 23—not a good access because of the steep banks, long carry, and busy road. Downstream, the river slows because of backup from the Streator dam (located just south of the city on Smith-Douglas Road).

Examining an ironstone nodule along a North Vermilion cliff

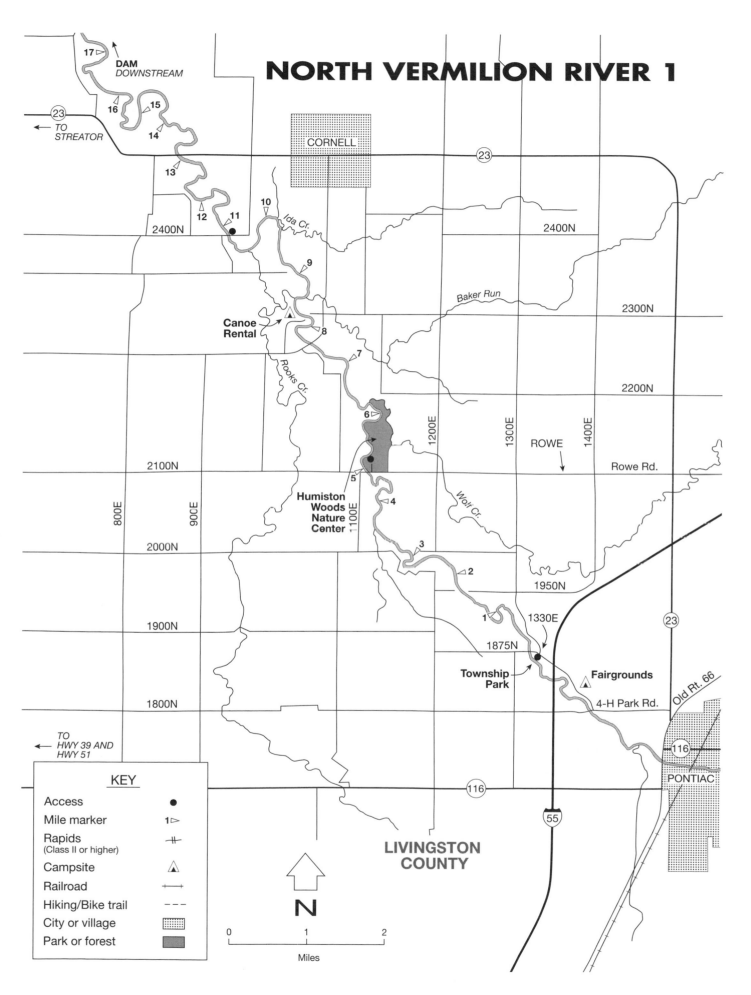

NORTH VERMILION RIVER 1

17
DAM
DOWNSTREAM
16
15
14
23
TO
STREATOR
13
CORNELL
23
2400N
10
Ida Cr.
2400N
9
Baker Run
2300N
Canoe
Rental
8
2200N
7
Rooks Cr.
6
1200E
1300E
1400E
ROWE
2100N
Rowe Rd.
800E
900E
5
Humiston
Woods
Nature
Center
1100E
4
Wolf Cr.
2000N
3
1950N
2
1900N
1
1330E
23
1875N
Township
Park
Fairgrounds
Old Rt. 66
1800N
4-H Park Rd.
TO
HWY 39 AND
HWY 51
116
PONTIAC
116

KEY

Access ●
Mile marker 1▷
Rapids ╫
(Class II or higher)
Campsite ⛺
Railroad ┼┼┼
Hiking/Bike trail - - -
City or village
Park or forest

N
0 1 2
Miles

**LIVINGSTON
COUNTY**

55

NORTH VERMILION RIVER 2

Streator to Sandy Ford (8 Miles)

But *Which* Vermilion?

Confusingly, there are four different rivers in Illinois that bear the name *Vermilion*—all of which are good canoeing streams. Two are located in the vicinity of Pontiac, Streator, and La Salle–Peru, while the other two are close to Danville. All derive their name from a red and yellow clay that was used by Native Americans as a pigment. In an attempt to lessen the confusion, mapmakers and writers have applied various names to the two principal rivers: Big Vermilion, Vermilion of the Illinois, Vermilion of the Wabash, etc. In this book, the river that flows into the Illinois near Oglesby is designated the North Vermilion, while the river that flows into the Wabash from the Danville area is called the South Vermilion. Near each of these is a Little Vermilion: the northern one flows south from the Troy Grove area to the Illinois River at La Salle, and the southern one runs eastward from the Georgetown area into the Wabash River.

For many paddlers, "the Vermilion" is synonymous with the whitewater section that begins at Lowell (see North Vermilion River 3). The river upstream certainly doesn't have the exciting rapids of the Lowell stretch, but does have much to recommend it. Starting at Streator, for instance, the North Vermilion presents canoeists with many beautiful stone cliffs, some of which are quite long and intricately shaped by wind and water. The shoreline is covered with dense woods, and there are almost no buildings. Flowing over a firm rock-and-sand bottom, the river has a steady **gradient** of 4.3 feet per mile between Streator and Sandy Ford and is filled with pleasant riffles. Consistently 100 feet wide, this section poses little prospect of deadfall obstructions. Broken rock frequently lies along the waterline—a good place for fossil hunters. Even some of the old bridge pilings from abandoned railroads are picturesque. Adding to the enjoyment of the trip are two excellent accesses at the beginning and end, thanks to the city of Streator and the DNR.

For **campgrounds** in the area, see North Vermilion River 1.

Canoe rental and shuttle services are available at Canoe the Vermillion, north of Streator (815-673-3218).

The **shuttle route** (8.5 miles) from the put-in goes west on Highway 18, north on County E1500, and west on N1800 (Sandy Ford Road).

For **water levels,** check the gauge near Leonore (station #05555300) on the USGS Web site listed in the introduction.

Put in at the Hopalong Cassidy Canoe Landing alongside Highway 18 West. A short path leads from a parking lot to the river-left landing, which is just downstream from an old, dismantled dam. The canoe landing is named in honor of Clarence Mulford, a Streator native who wrote the famous Hopalong Cassidy cowboy stories.

The abutments and piers of an old railroad bridge are soon passed, and layered sandstone formations begin on the left. Just upstream from another set of piers and

abutments is a big culvert from the Streator wastewater-treatment facility, opposite another attractive stone formation. The banks are varied and interesting, typically consisting of sharply pitched silt and sand, with frequent rock outcroppings.

Gravel bars begin appearing in the area of a beautiful 25-foot cliff, and a high railroad bridge crosses the river just downstream. Occasionally springs can be seen on the right, leaving red stains from the iron content. Unfortunately, a few unsightly old appliances have been dumped down the left shoreline. Downstream in a long left bend are 100 yards of exposed shale on the right, with a pronounced anticline (tilt). At the end of the left bend, a sharp right turn leads to the Oakley Avenue bridge; the river can be accessed here, downstream-right.

After Otter Creek enters on the right, impressive shale cliffs with a pronounced anticline appear on the right in a sweeping left curve. Look for fossil-bearing ironstone nodules protruding from the cliff face or lying in the talus slope at the base. More cliffs appear in the sharp right, then left turns that lead to the Klein Bridge north of Kangley (County E1500). Just upstream from the bridge, the river drops a little around a couple of small islands. About 100 yards downstream, there's a coal seam on the left. In the big left bend after the bridge, a lovely 40-foot cliff looms on the right for several hundred yards, often undercut. A very long right bend follows, with more cliffs on the left. Riffles continue, especially whenever small creeks have washed rocks out into the river.

Soon after the river swings back to the left, the only building of the trip (a small cabin) appears high up on the right bank as you approach the N1800 bridge. **Take out** at the wooden stair access upstream, river-right, next to a parking lot. Downstream-right from the bridge, a well-preserved old truss structure, is the Sandy Ford Nature Preserve.

Other trips. (1) Beyond Sandy Ford Bridge, a 2-mile-long left bend takes you to the Red White and Blue Bridge, where you can take out about 200 feet upstream, river-right, at the concrete remnant of an old bridge. A road parallels the river on this stretch, and several houses can be seen. Cliffs appear on the right for a while after N1800, but then disappear. (2) After Red White and Blue Bridge, 7 river-miles lead to Lowell Bridge. This stretch doesn't have as many riffles, woods, and cliffs as North Vermilion River 2, and has a very difficult, rocky take-out (downstream-right from the Lowell Bridge). Class II rapids begin upstream from the bridge and continue downstream; the take-out is located in the midst of the rapids and is quite hazardous for inexperienced canoeists.

An overhanging cliff on the North Vermilion below Streator

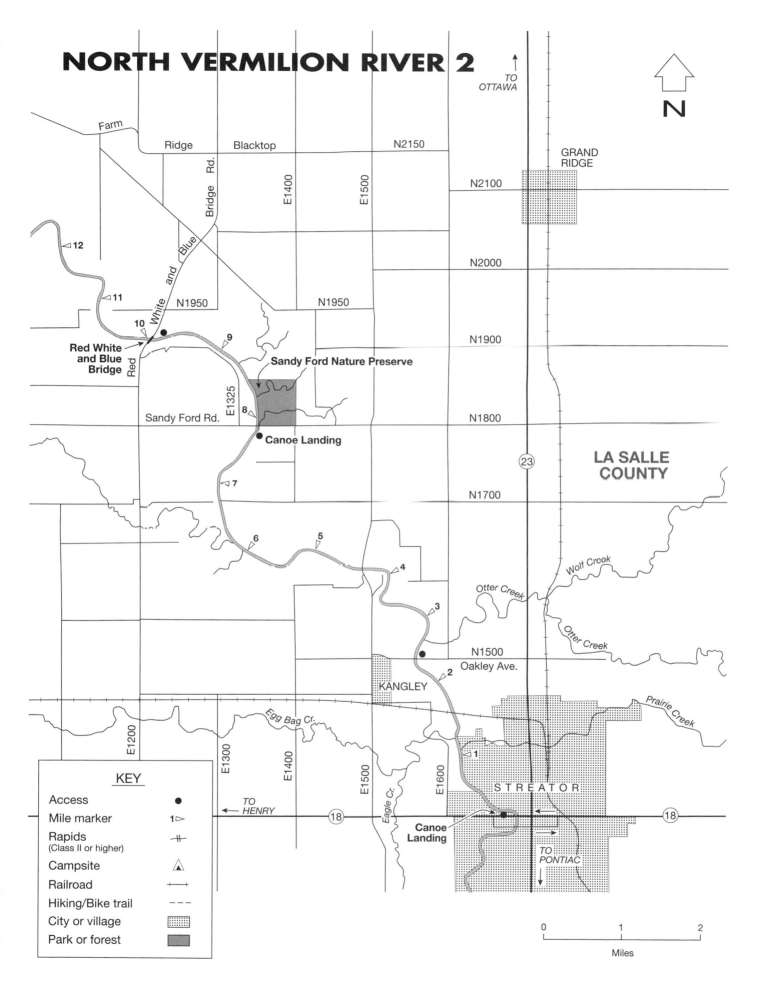

NORTH VERMILION RIVER 2

TO OTTAWA

N

Farm

Ridge   Blacktop   N2150

GRAND RIDGE

N2100

Bridge Rd.

E1400   E1500

N2000

◁12

White and Blue

N1950   N1950

N1900

◁11

Red

10 ◁ ●

Red White and Blue Bridge

9 ◁

Sandy Ford Nature Preserve

N1900

E1325

8 ◁

Sandy Ford Rd.   N1800

● Canoe Landing

(23)

LA SALLE COUNTY

◁7

N1700

6 ◁   5 ◁

Wolf Creek

4 ◁

Otter Creek

3 ◁

Otter Creek

N1500

●

Oakley Ave.

2 ◁

KANGLEY

Prairie Creek

Egg Bag Cr.

E1200   E1300   E1400   E1500   E1600

1 ◁

S T R E A T O R

(18)

TO HENRY

(18)

Eagle Cr.

Canoe Landing

(18)

TO PONTIAC

KEY

Access	●
Mile marker	1 ▷
Rapids (Class II or higher)	╫
Campsite	▲
Railroad	+—+—+
Hiking/Bike trail	- - -
City or village	▦
Park or forest	▨

0   1   2

Miles

NORTH VERMILION RIVER 3
Lowell to Oglesby Road (7.5 Miles)

Mecca for Illinois whitewater paddlers, the final section of the North Vermilion offers not only challenging rapids but also some beautiful scenery. Cliffs, fascinating geological formations, wooded bluffs, an intriguing side canyon, and numerous playspots make this short section a great destination for skilled whitewater paddlers. The only blot on the trip is a riverside cement plant, where a low-head dam has claimed the lives of several paddlers. Both the put-in and take-out are strenuous and steep. Always be prepared to portage around rapids that are beyond your skill level.

Public **camping** is available nearby at Starved Rock State Park, east of Oglesby.

The gorgeous dells of Matthiessen State Park—reachable from the North Vermilion

Raft rental is available from Vermilion River Rafting in Oglesby (815-667-5242) and from the Discovery Center in Chicago (773-348-8120 or www.discoverycenter.cc).

The **shuttle route** (5.2 miles) from the put-in goes north on Highway 178, west on Highway 71, and south on County E651.

The **gradient** of 6.7 feet per mile produces dramatic drops and many Class I–II rapids.

Water levels. Generally, canoeing and kayaking are best when the gauge painted on a pier of the Lowell Bridge reads 2 or higher; at 4+, Wildcat Rapids becomes squirrelly and the river in general is quite pushy. For current water levels and other information on this section, see the following excellent Web sites: (1) <www.rivers-end.org/vermilion/index.html> and (2) <http://wpr.pair.com/vermilion>. Or you can check the water gauge near Leonore (station #05555300) on the USGS Web site listed in the introduction.

Put in downstream-right from the graceful arches of the Lowell Bridge. At the end of a short road off Highway 178 (County N2249), a rocky path leads from the old bridge abutment down to the shoreline. Be respectful of the private property near the put-in. Class I–II rapids begin upstream from the bridge and continue downstream past the landing; big waves develop here when the water is high. If the river looks too ominous for you, don't go; it gets worse downstream.

Outcroppings of St. Peter sandstone appear immediately on the right after the put-in. Soon a shale cliff appears on the left as the river bends to the right; in the spring and after rainfall, a pretty little waterfall is found here. Sandstone cliffs rise on both sides, alternately, as the river bends left, then right. At the end of the right bend, the right channel of a large island is a popular playspot (called Hole-in-Rock). Several big boulders (one of which is severely undercut and thus **dangerous!**) form three chutes here.

After the island, the river gently arcs left again. Just before a sharp right turn, a gorgeous, undercut rock wall appears on the right, topped with white cedar trees. At the end of the right bend, another cliff on the right displays conspicuously pitched rock layers (an anticline). Now begins a long, sharp left bend, where riffles and cliffs continue. At one point, on top of the river-right bluffs, you can see a rail fence in Matthiessen State Park. Rock rubble becomes plentiful on the right as the river begins turning right, and soon a roaring noise and huge boulders on both sides indicate that Wildcat Rapids is near.

The Wildcat is an impressive 5-foot drop (Class II–III) where giant boulders are strewn across the river, with a clearly defined chute on the right. The drop dramatically changes character at different water levels, and always requires caution. Scouting is recommended. To portage, get out on the left shoreline upstream from the big boulders and carry your boat along the shoreline path.

A couple of straight stretches follow. Turning left, the river passes under a rusty old bridge preceded by a channel constriction and wave train. In the long right bend that follows, the current slows and the concrete towers of a cement plant suddenly loom ahead, signaling the impending danger of the dam. About 40 yards upstream from the dam, on the right, is a low shore where you can get out of your boat to scout the dam and—if you don't like what you see—pull your boat up the steep hillside past the dam. Sometimes the dam can be run in the tricky chute on the right, but only if the water level is safe and you're quite experienced. A portage is recommended. The water below the dam is fast and has a lot of hidden debris at the bottom (reinforcement bars, corrugated steel, etc.); a swim can be ugly. At certain levels, a lethal hydraulic "keeper" forms at the base of the dam.

After the dam, the river passes under another rusty bridge, followed by a constriction (called The Narrows) that causes a long series of big waves. A straightaway follows, with a large island beneath power lines, and the river turns left at some beautiful stone outcroppings on the right. When the water is high enough (and deadfall permits), a creek between these formations leads into Matthiessen State Park, winding through lovely canyons (The Dells) and under a pedestrian bridge to a 45-foot waterfall.

Downstream, after a long, straight stretch, **take out** at the Oglesby Road bridge, upstream, river-right. Pull your boat up the often muddy bank; steep steps then lead to the road, where there's room on the shoulder to park.

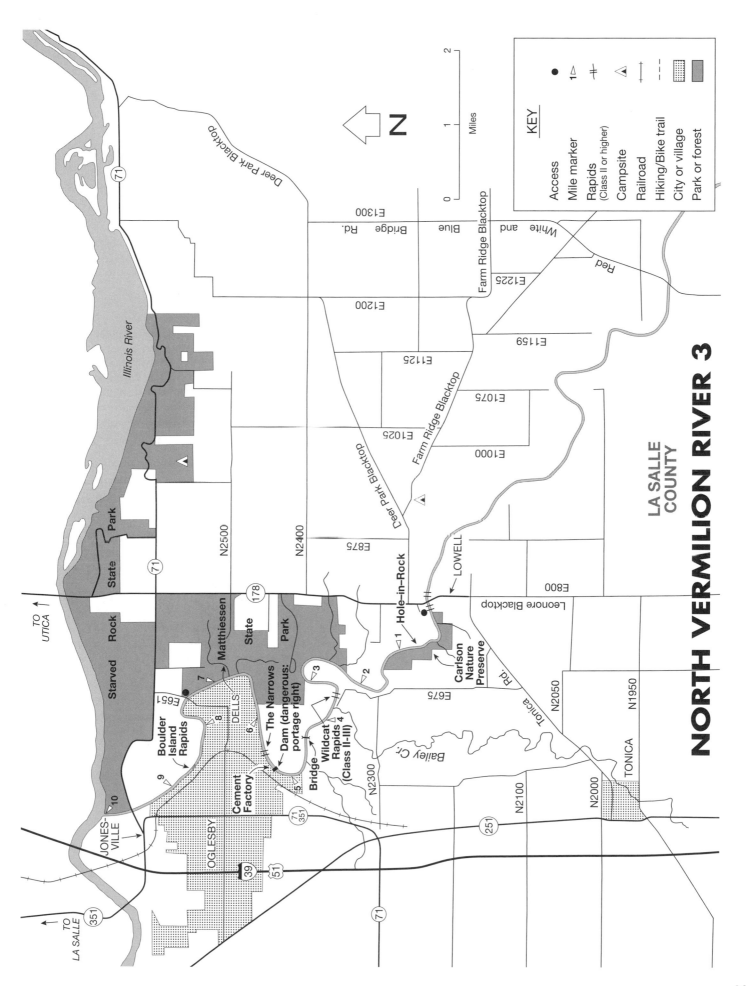

NORTH VERMILION RIVER 3

KEY

- ● Access
- ◣ Mile marker
- ╪ Rapids (Class II or higher)
- ◭ Campsite
- ╪ Railroad
- ┆ Hiking/Bike trail
- ▦ City or village
- ▨ Park or forest

N

Miles
0   1   2

LA SALLE COUNTY

Illinois River

71
TO UTICA

TO LA SALLE
351

JONES-VILLE

Starved Rock State Park

71

Matthiessen State Park

178

Deer Park Blacktop

Farm Ridge Blacktop

E1300
Bridge Rd.
Blue and White
Red
E1225
E1200
E1159
E1125
E1075
E1025
E1000
E875
E800

N2500
N2400
N2300

Deer Park Blacktop

Farm Ridge Blacktop

LOWELL

Hole-in-Rock
1
Leonore Blacktop

Carlson Nature Preserve

Bailey Cr.
E675

Tonica Rd.

N2050
N2100
N2000
N1950

TONICA

251

71

39
51

OGLESBY

Cement Factory

DELLS

E651

Boulder Island Rapids

The Narrows

Dam (dangerous: portage right)

Bridge

Wildcat Rapids 4 (Class II-III)

5
6
7
8
9
10

2
3

71
351

107

PECATONICA RIVER 1
Pecatonica to Trask Bridge Forest Preserve (11.5 Miles)

The Pecatonica isn't blessed with the rock formations, rapids, or crystalline water that draw canoeists to some other Illinois rivers, but it definitely has its own attractions. A sense of isolation is perhaps its best attribute; most of the time, the only sound is that of birds, wind, and running water, and very few houses are encountered. A low-gradient river—only 0.9 feet per mile on this stretch—it winds slowly through floodplain forests, seldom interrupted by open fields. If you check a topographical map of the Pecatonica, you'll see many places where big oxbows have detached from the main channel, forming small ponds, but the river still meanders a lot. Another big plus of the Pecatonica is outstanding accesses. The Winnebago County Forest Preserve District is exemplary in providing convenient landings and related facilities for canoeists and other outdoor enthusiasts.

Pecatonica is derived from a Sauk word meaning "muddy," and the name is appropriate. Steep earthen banks are usually 6–8 feet high and provide few places to get out of your boat when the water is at a medium level or higher, but sandbars appear at lower levels. Always be on the lookout for downed trees.

Camping opportunities are remarkable. The forest preserve district has campgrounds just south of the village of Pecatonica (Seward Bluffs), north of Shirland (Sugar River), along the river downstream from Pecatonica (Pecatonica River), and southeast of Rockton (Hononegah). Rock Cut State Park is just northeast of Rockford, while Lake Le-Aqua-Na State Park is northwest of Freeport. Camping also is allowed at the Winnebago County Fairgrounds near the put-in, with permission. A private campground (River's Edge) is located on the river at the Meridian Road bridge, and another (Sugar Shores Resort Campground) is located west of Shirland, on the Sugar River.

The **shuttle route** (11.7 miles) from the put-in goes north on Pecatonica Road, then east on Trask Bridge Road to the river.

For **water levels,** check the Freeport gauge (station #05435500) on the USGS Web site listed in the introduction.

Put in at the Sumner Park boat ramp in Pecatonica, downstream-right from the old rock dam, which once provided water power for a mill. (There is another concrete ramp upstream from the dam.) Accessed from First Street, the park has ball fields, a playground, and picnic facilities. The county fairgrounds are located nearby to the west.

Houses disappear soon after the Pecatonica Road bridge as the river heads east in a long straightaway. Farm fields can occasionally be seen through the maple trees on the banks. In the bends that follow, farm buildings are passed twice. Downstream from the second farm, the setting gets quite wild; for awhile, there is a low floodplain forest on the right, with virtually no banks. After a set of power lines, the Pecatonica River Forest Preserve appears on the left in a sharp right bend, with forest preserve signs and picnic tables. Downstream, after several tight turns, there's an excellent concrete boat landing on the left. This is a great place for a lunch stop, or for overnight canoe camping.

After the last forest preserve sign, a couple of cabins appear in a right turn, then another building atop a sheer 35-foot clay-and-sand bank filled with swallow nests. In a very long, gentle left bend the scenery is wild again, with beautiful maple, oak, and willow trees. Another home (the last of the trip) appears on top of a 20-foot bank. In the bends and straight stretches that follow, the woods gradually become less dense, with more openings for farm fields. After several curves, a final straightaway leads to Trask Bridge. **Take out** at the concrete boat ramp, upstream, river-left. The attractive 15-acre forest preserve at the bridge is tucked within the bend of a cut-off oxbow pond. Picnic facilities, toilets, drinking water, and a parking lot are provided.

Other trips. Since the previous edition of this guidebook (2004), tremendous progress has been made in providing access to the 58+ miles of river upstream from Pecatonica Village Park.

Designated the Stephenson County Water Trail, this long section is described in detail at www.paddlethepec.com. A wealth of information is provided, including recommended put-ins and take-outs, trip reports, water-level data, photos, etc. The local paddling enthusiasts and conservationists who have devoted a huge amount of time and effort to this project in recent years deserve our thanks.

The Web site breaks the stretch down into seven trips: (1) Brewster Landing (near the Wisconsin border) to West McConnell Road, 7 miles; (2) West McConnell Road to McNeil's/Damascus Landing, 7 miles; (3) McNeil's/Damascus Landing to Tutty's Crossing in Freeport, 14 miles; (4) Tutty's Crossing to Hancock Avenue Ramp, 0.5 mile; (5) Hancock Avenue Ramp To Ridott, 16 miles; (6) Ridott to North Farwell Bridge Road, 7 miles; and (7) North Farwell Bridge Road to Pecatonica Village Park, 7 miles.

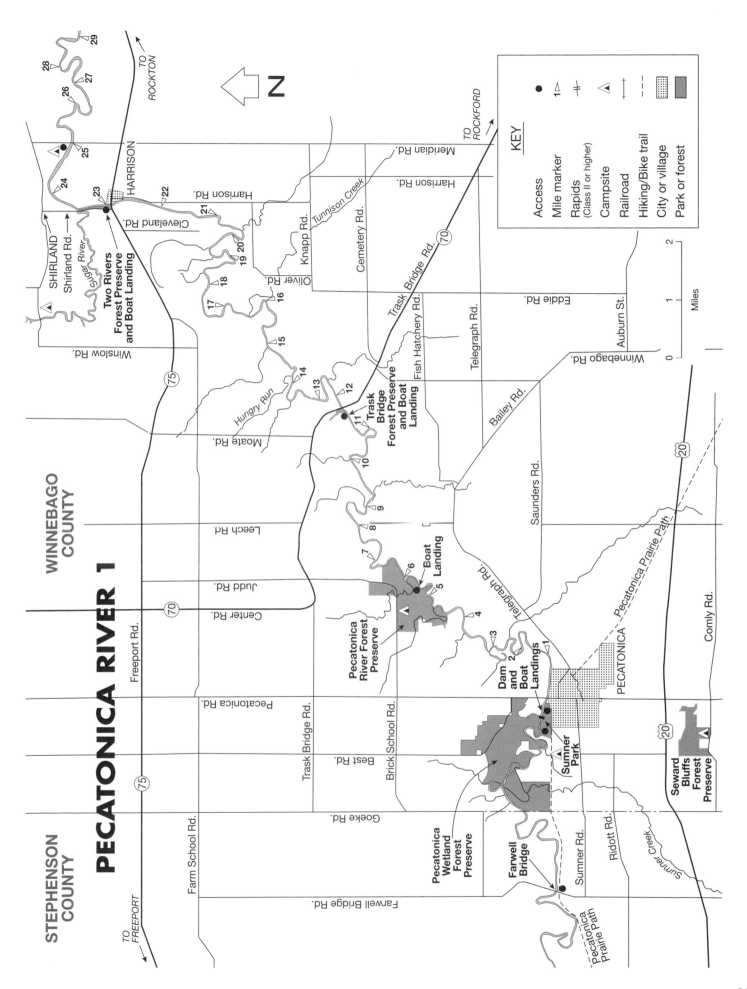

PECATONICA RIVER 1

STEPHENSON COUNTY

WINNEBAGO COUNTY

TO FREEPORT

TO ROCKTON

TO ROCKFORD

HARRISON

SHIRLAND

PECATONICA

Two Rivers Forest Preserve and Boat Landing

Trask Bridge Forest Preserve and Boat Landing

Pecatonica River Forest Preserve

Boat Landing

Dam and Boat Landings

Sumner Park

Pecatonica Wetland Forest Preserve

Farwell Bridge

Seward Bluffs Forest Preserve

Shirland Rd.
Sugar River
Winslow Rd.
Freeport Rd.
Pecatonica Rd.
Farm School Rd.
Trask Bridge Rd.
Best Rd.
Brick School Rd.
Goeke Rd.
Farwell Bridge Rd.
Center Rd.
Judd Rd.
Leech Rd.
Moate Rd.
Hungry Run
Cleveland Rd.
Harrison Rd.
Oliver Rd.
Knapp Rd.
Tunnison Creek
Cemetery Rd.
Harrison Rd.
Meridian Rd.
Trask Bridge Rd.
Fish Hatchery Rd.
Telegraph Rd.
Bailey Rd.
Saunders Rd.
Telegraph Rd.
Eddie Rd.
Winnebago Rd.
Auburn St.
Sumner Rd.
Ridott Rd.
Comly Rd.
Sumner Creek
Pecatonica Prairie Path

75
70
20

KEY

●	Access
1 △	Mile marker
╪	Rapids (Class II or higher)
▲	Campsite
┼	Railroad
╎	Hiking/Bike trail
▦	City or village
■	Park or forest

Miles
0   1   2

N

109

PECATONICA RIVER 2

Trask Bridge Forest Preserve to Two Rivers Forest Preserve (11.5 Miles)

Old Mills of Illinois

No historical landmarks are more charming or evocative than the old nineteenth-century mills that are still to be found throughout Illinois. At one time there may have been as many as 1,800 gristmills and sawmills in the state, but today there are fewer than forty. Beginning in the early 1800s, mills were erected wherever a creek or river offered enough dependable power to grind grain or saw logs. Often these structures—with their characteristic dams, millraces, and waterwheels—became the nucleus of thriving communities, only to fall into decline in the late 1800s with the advent of industrialization and the coming of the railroads.

Several of the trips in this book take you to some of the best-preserved mills in Illinois—especially the beautiful (and still operating!) Graue Mill in Hinsdale (Salt Creek of the Des Plaines River), the Baltic Mill in Belvidere (Kishwaukee River 1), the Millhurst structure (now a bed-and-breakfast) near Millbrook (Fox River 2), and the restored mill at New Salem State Park (Sangamon River 3). Other mills that are long gone still are reflected in the names of such communities as Duncan Mills (Spoon River 3). A delightful little booklet by Leslie C. Swanson, *Old Mills in the Midwest* (1985) chronicles the mills of Illinois and Iowa.

Most of the section downstream from Trask Bridge is more circuitous than the previous stretch, twisting in every possible direction. Often, as you paddle down this section, you'll find a low floodplain on one side and a high, wooded bank on the other. The feeling of isolation continues: not until the end do many houses appear. The surroundings are usually quite unspoiled and trash-free. Normally, the current is slow as a result of the slight **gradient** (0.9 feet per mile), and a number of deep pools are found, especially in bends. River-wide obstructions are uncommon, thanks to the 80- to 100-foot width, but occasional downed trees must be paddled around or portaged. The whole section flows through private property; only the put-in and take-out are on public land. Once again, the accesses are first-rate.

The river is well known for its springtime flooding (the major reason why there are so few houses). When the water goes down to safe levels, however, the banks present a spectacular display of Virginia bluebells and other wildflowers. The combination of river and dense woods provides excellent habitat for muskrat, beaver, wild turkey, owls, hawks, herons, deer, songbirds, and other wildlife. Watch for muskrat, beaver, and mink slides on the banks. Occasionally you may see fishermen in small motorboats angling for catfish, northern pike, smallmouth, crappie, and occasional walleye.

For **campgrounds** and **water levels**, see the description of Pecatonica River 1.

The **shuttle route** (7.5 miles) from the put-in goes west on Trask Bridge Road (Highway 70), north on Moate Road, east on Highway 75 (Freeport Road), and north on Shirland Road.

Put in at the concrete boat ramp at Trask Bridge Forest Preserve, in an attractive parklike setting with a parking lot, toilets, picnic facilities, drinking water, and a fishing pond (a cutoff oxbow). After a straightaway, a creek on the right precedes a very sharp left turn, at the end of which is a private boat ramp. When the river bends into a northeast straightaway, there are high, heavily wooded banks on the left—quite wild-looking. The straightaway ends with a left turn, where a shack sits on the right shore. In the following right bend, there are a couple of places between the two river-left creeks that tend to collect deadfall; you may have to do some maneuvering or even portaging here. In the straight stretch that follows, the river is beautiful; trees hang over the water on both sides. Two sharp bends lead to another straightaway and the wild surroundings continue, with many sycamores and constant birdcalls. You definitely get the impression that you're in the middle of nowhere.

Many bends follow. Along the way a couple of cabins are passed, atop 5-foot banks. After a long southeast stretch (toward Oliver Road), a farm appears at the tip of a sharp left turn; the river here flows in the shape of a boot. In the next loop (also toward Oliver Road), another farm is found in the southern tip.

After this last, sharp left turn, the river heads north into the least attractive part of the trip, coursing directly toward Harrison, with only a few little jogs here and there. Open fields begin appearing on the left, then some trailers, cabins, and homes. Eventually Harrison Road pulls alongside the river on the right. After a long straight stretch, a slight left arc leads to the Highway 75 bridge. Immediately downstream-left is the Two Rivers Forest Preserve wayside, with parking lot, picnic area, toilets, and drinking water. To **take out**, paddle another 0.3 mile downstream to the concrete boat ramp on the left. Cars can be parked on the gravelly pull-off alongside Shirland Road. The mouth of the Sugar River is only a quarter mile downstream, so this landing is also a good take-out for trips on the Sugar. After Two Rivers Forest Preserve, the Pecatonica continues for 9 miles before its confluence with the Rock River near Rockton.

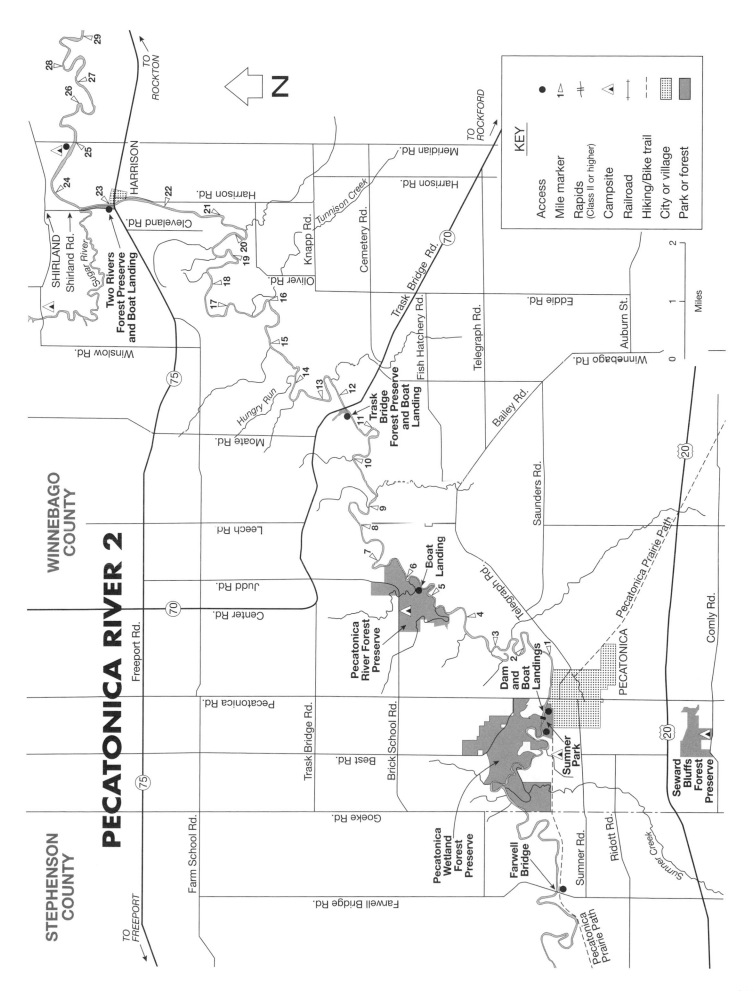

PECATONICA RIVER 2

PECATONICA RIVER 3
Two Rivers Forest Preserve to Macktown Forest Preserve (9 Miles)

The Precursor of Rockton

Originally called Pecatonic, the community of Macktown began in 1835 when the first white settler, Stephen Mack, established a trading post on the bluff overlooking the confluence of the Pecatonica and Rock Rivers. A Vermonter, Mack had been a fur trader at Grand Detour on the Rock and had married Hononegah, a Potawatomi chief's daughter. For a time, Macktown was a flourishing settlement, but it declined in the 1840s when nearby Rockton harnessed the power of the Rock and a number of mills began to thrive there. Today you can still visit the restored trading post and Mack's home. Annually, a springtime Rendezvous Living History Fair brings throngs of visitors and re-creates the atmosphere of the 1800s with craft and trade demonstrations, marksmanship competitions, pioneer-era food, Native American dwellings, and other evocations of old Macktown.

Relatively short, this final section of the river makes a leisurely float trip. Mostly wooded with occasional open areas for farm fields and pastures, it has large sandbars where you can stop to stretch your legs. Houses are infrequent, and the surroundings continue to look and feel remote. As usual on the Pecatonica, the accesses are splendid—concrete boat ramps and parklike facilities at both ends. An added bonus is the historic Macktown site at the take-out and the charming village of Rockton nearby.

For area **campgrounds** and **water levels**, see Pecatonica River 1.

The **shuttle route** (6.8 miles) from the put-in goes south on Shirland Road, east on Highway 75 (Freeport Road) to the entrance of Macktown Forest Preserve, then north on the entrance road to the boat landing.

The **gradient** is negligible (less than a foot per mile).

Put in on river-left at the concrete boat ramp 0.3 mile downstream from the Two Rivers Forest Preserve day-use area. There's room for several cars alongside Shirland Road.

Starting off straight and about 60 feet wide, the Pecatonica soon passes the mouth of the Sugar River on the left, then widens and veers off to the right. Cabins and year-round homes appear on the left as the right bend continues. A straightaway follows, ending at overhead power lines, and the Meridian Road bridge comes into view as the river arcs left. On the left, upstream of the bridge, is River's Edge Campground, where there is room along the river for tent-camping.

The banks on this section tend to be lower and sandier than on the two upper stretches, and bankside willow is common. After Meridian Road the river widens to more than 100 feet. In a series of big bends, corn-and-soybean fields are frequent, either behind the tree line or in occasional open areas along cutbanks, and sandbars begin to appear. Watch for swallow nests in the cutbanks. Often there is low, heavily wooded floodplain on one side and higher banks on the other.

For a long time the setting continues to be typical of the Pecatonica—unremarkable scenery, but peaceful, clean, and wild. Finally, in a straightaway, homes begin to appear, together with docks and pontoon boats. After a few more curves, the boundary signs of Macktown Forest Preserve begin appearing on the right.

In a right curve, the river narrows considerably to 45 feet, with crushed rock along the right shoreline. Soon the Rock River can be seen on the left—not as big as you might expect because part of it has been diverted into a canal to the east. Several small islands lie along the left shoreline immediately downstream from the confluence. You are now paddling on the Rock—but not for long. **Take out** a few hundred yards downstream at the Macktown Forest Preserve boat landing, on the right. A nearby sign indicates that this was once the site of a ferry that was established by Stephen Mack in the 1830s.

Be sure to walk a couple hundred feet up the hill to see picturesque Whitman's Trading Post, built of stone in 1846 to replace Mack's original log store at the same location. The site is very attractive and interesting, with historical markers, gardens, a Native American wigwam, and a fur trader's cabin.

Other trips. (1) One intriguing option for those who don't mind a longer trip is the possibility of doing three different rivers in a day. By putting in at Yale Bridge Road, you can paddle 7 miles on the Sugar, then 9 miles on the Pecatonica, and, finally, a few hundred yards on the Rock. For canoe campers, an even longer trip can be arranged by starting farther upstream on the Sugar and stopping at Sugar River Forest Preserve, Sugar Shores Camping Resort, or River's Edge Campground.

(2) Continuing on the Rock from Macktown, it is 3.2 river miles to the Hononegah Forest Preserve, which has a river-left boat ramp and camping, then another 5.2 miles to the Atwood Homestead Forest Preserve, which also has a boat landing. There are other landings along the river all the way to Rockford, where there's a dam south of Highway 20.

Whitman's Trading Post at Macktown

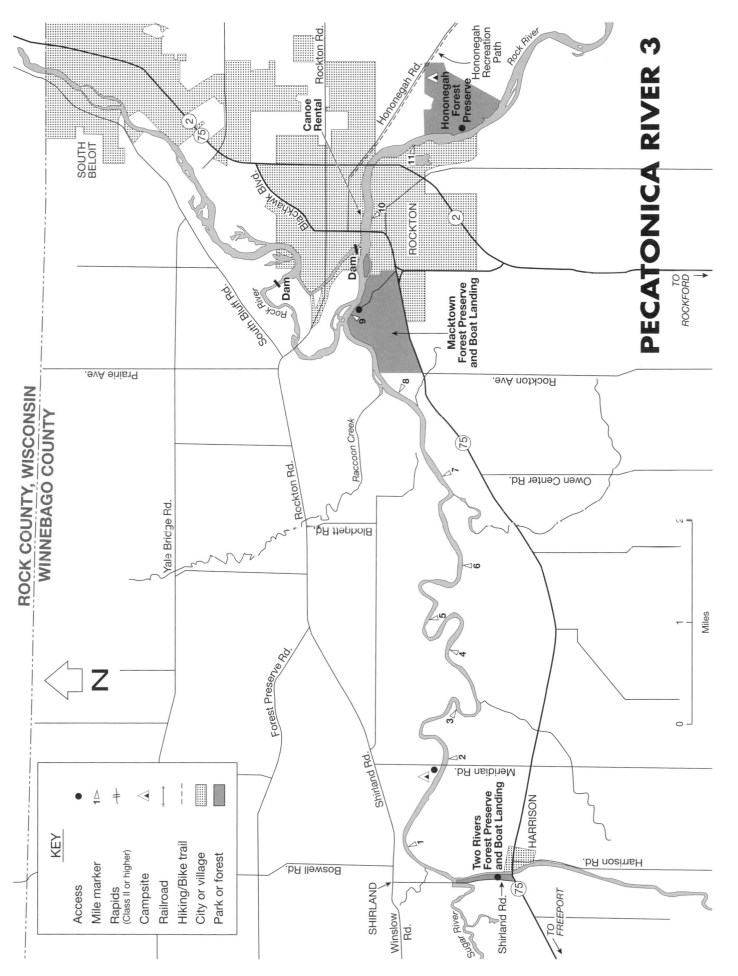

PECATONICA RIVER 3

ROCK COUNTY, WISCONSIN
WINNEBAGO COUNTY

N

KEY

●	Access
1△	Mile marker
≠	Rapids (Class II or higher)
◁	Campsite
†	Railroad
– – –	Hiking/Bike trail
▦	City or village
▨	Park or forest

SOUTH BELOIT

Canoe Rental

Hononegah Forest Preserve

Hononegah Recreation Path

Rock River

Rockton Rd.

Hononegah Rd.

Blackhawk Blvd.

11

10

ROCKTON

2

Dam

Dam

Rock River

South Bluff Rd.

Prairie Ave.

9

Macktown Forest Preserve and Boat Landing

Rockton Ave.

TO ROCKFORD

8

Raccoon Creek

Rockton Rd.

Yale Bridge Rd.

Blodgett Rd.

Owen Center Rd.

75

7

6

Forest Preserve Rd.

5

4

Shirland Rd.

3

2

Meridian Rd.

Boswell Rd.

1

SHIRLAND

Winslow Rd.

Two Rivers Forest Preserve and Boat Landing

Sugar River

Shirland Rd.

75

HARRISON

Harrison Rd.

TO FREEPORT

Miles

0   1   2

113

ROCK RIVER 1
Oregon to Grand Detour (10.6 Miles)

Lorado Taft's majestic statue looks out over the Rock River at Oregon.

Originating in Wisconsin's Horicon Marsh, the Rock River flows south and southwest for more than 300 miles before joining the Mississippi at Rock Island. For most of its 163 miles in Illinois, it passes through the Rock River hill country, which escaped the most recent (Wisconsinan) glacier and is thus generally rolling in topography. Early visitors to the region called the Rock the "Hudson of the West," partly because of its many scenic vistas and lovely outcroppings of St. Peter sandstone and dolomite. The name of the river is a literal translation of the original Algonquin name, *Sinnissippi*, which was probably based on the river's rocky bottom and outcroppings or the huge "Rock Island" at its mouth. Steamboats once plied its waters as far north as Janesville, Wisconsin, but rapids and shallowness kept the river from being developed for navigation. Seven dams slow the river in Illinois (after ten in Wisconsin), creating a number of impoundments that are popular with motorboaters. There are still many miles of good canoeing, however—especially the 46 miles from Rockford to Dixon.

The most popular canoeing stretch on the whole river is the section from Oregon to Grand Detour, thanks to the charming towns at the put-in and take-out, beautiful rock formations, forested banks, and motorboat-limiting shallow areas. Always at least 500 feet in width, the river can involve strenuous paddling when wind is out of the southwest. The Rock is suitable for beginners, but caution is always necessary: it's a big river, with deep places and sometimes tricky currents. It's considered a good fishing stream, producing catfish, walleye, northern pike, largemouth and smallmouth bass, sauger, white bass, bluegill, and bullheads. Eagles are among the frequently spotted wildlife.

Excellent public **camping** is located nearby: west of Oregon at White Pines Forest State Park, north at Lowden State Park (where Lorado Taft's famous statue, commonly known as "Black Hawk," is located), and south at Castle Rock State Park. Private campgrounds include The Stronghold north of Oregon, Lake LaDonna Campground east of the city, Hansen's Hideaway Ranch to the west, and River Road Camping to the north.

Canoe rental and shuttle service are available in Oregon at TJ's Bait, Tackle, and Canoe Rentals (815-732-4516), www.tjscanoerental.com.

The **shuttle route** (10 miles) from the put-in goes a short distance west on Highway 64 (Washington Street), then south on Highway 2 to the Grand Detour wayside.

The **gradient** is only 1 foot per mile.

For **water levels,** check the gauge upstream at Rockton (station #05437500) or downstream at Como (#05443500) on the USGS Web site listed in the introduction.

There are three **put-ins:** (1) at the private concrete boat ramp at Kevin's Bait Shop, downstream-right from the dam, off Second Street (north of Highway 64); this is a safe and convenient landing, but there's a small launching fee; (2) downstream-left from the dam at Oregon Park East (off River Road); carry boats from the parking lot to the riverbank, as far as possible downstream from the dam; at medium to high water levels, however, a big eddy can pull canoeists upstream into the very dangerous backroller of the dam; and (3) from the landing of TJ's Canoe Rentals downstream-right from the Highway 64 bridge, off First Street; canoeists with their own boats may put in here for a fee. If you use put-ins 1 or 2, be careful in negotiating your way through the piers of the Highway 64 bridge. The recommended put-ins are 1 and 3.

Big islands begin appearing immediately in the initial southerly straightaway, with buildings and cabins on the right for awhile. A huge island lies beneath an old railroad bridge. A half-mile below a set of power lines the river bends to the west; here on the left is a picturesque stone formation called Lowden Rock, topped with pines. A series of big islands follows, with a long line of cabins on the high, right shoreline.

Dwellings end where Highway 2 pulls alongside the river. Downstream, as the river gently bends left, the long stone outcropping of Castle Rock can be seen on the right, tucked between the river and Highway 2. Not far upstream is a pleasant wayside with picnic area, toilets, parking, and boat landing. This makes a convenient take-out for short trips from Oregon, or a put-in for longer trips to Lowell Park (see Rock River 2). Take the time to stop at Castle Rock; wooden stairs lead to an observation deck at the top, where the view of the river valley is gorgeous. As you approach the southern boundary of Castle Rock State Park, there is a clearing on the right for canoe-camping.

Many big islands are found in the southwest stretch that follows, and homes appear alternately on both sides. After the river heads a little to the right, then left, the guard railing of Highway 2 can be seen again on the right bank. Not far upstream from the Grand Detour wayside, which can be recognized by the attractive picnic shelters on a river-right hillside, is one last series of islands. These are private, and you should stay to the left of the islands. **Take out** 100 yards downstream from the wayside shelters at a gravel boat landing. Directly across the road from the wayside parking lot are the John Deere Historic Site and the unique village of Grand Detour.

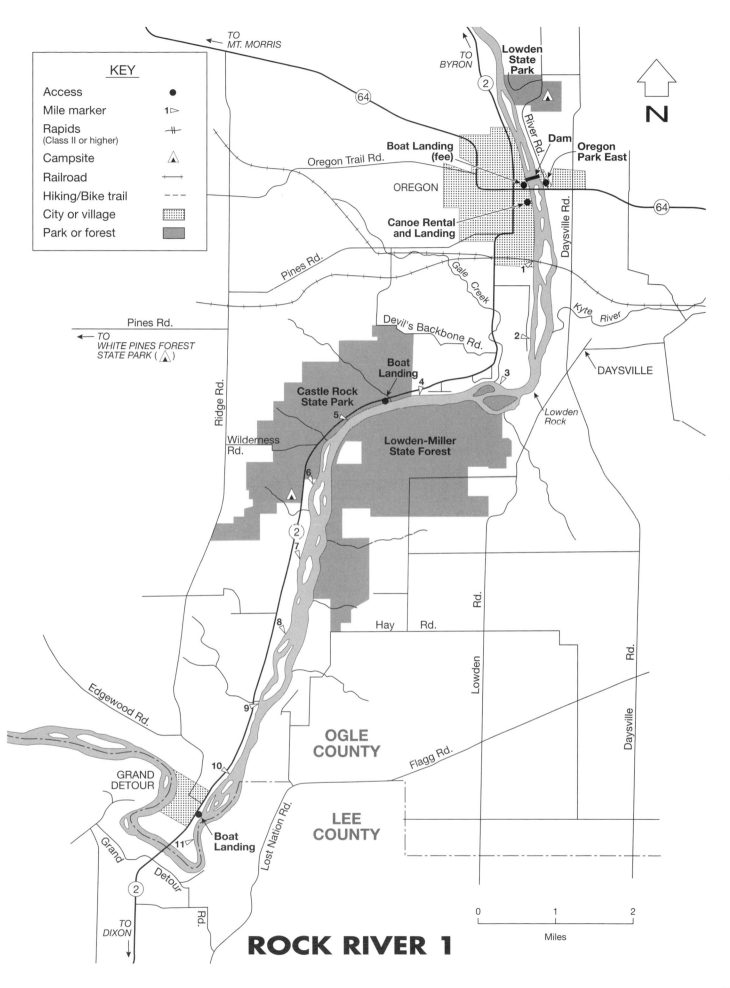

ROCK RIVER 1

ROCK RIVER 2
Grand Detour to Dixon (11 Miles)

Where the Prairie Was Tamed

One of the best things about this trip is the delightful little village at the put-in. The big river bend that begins here was named Grand Detour by the early French fur traders, and trading posts sprang up in the area. A village was laid out within the bend in 1836, and John Deere soon set up a blacksmith shop where he fashioned the famous steel plow that enabled settlers to break and turn over the rich prairie sod. Because the railroad later bypassed Grand Detour, the community stayed small and has retained its nineteenth-century atmosphere. The John Deere Historic Site—just across the highway from the put-in—is a fascinating and attractive complex of well-maintained buildings, and the village itself features lovely old homes and narrow streets.

If you were impressed by the rock formations in the previous stretch, you'll enjoy this section's outcroppings even more. They are the biggest and most beautiful cliffs on the Rock, and are complemented by the relative wildness of the surroundings. There are bankside houses, to be sure, but most of the section is undeveloped; not until the very end of the trip does the setting begin to look urban. Accesses are splendid, including an excellent intermediate landing. Big bends take you "every which way" on this low-gradient stretch (0.8 foot per mile), and a couple of large islands create narrow channels that afford relief from the otherwise wide streambed. You may have to share the river with a few motorboats, which can run from Dixon all the way to the shoals near the Grand Detour landing.

For **camping** and **water levels**, see Rock River 1.

The **shuttle route** is short (6.2 miles) and simple. From Grand Detour, go south on Highway 2 into Dixon; cross the river and go straight on Highway 52/26 (Galena Avenue) for a short distance to Fellows Street; proceed on Fellows for half a mile to the boat landing at Assembly Street.

Put in at the gravel landing just downstream-right from the Grand Detour wayside. A right bend leads to Highway 2, where small sandstone cliffs (called White Rock) appear on the left. After the bridge, the river swings sharply to the right past cabins and trailers on the right and a high cliff on the left. Known as Whirlpool Rock, this lovely, slanted formation continues for 150 yards. As the name implies, currents can be tricky and dangerous here, especially when the water

level is medium or high. In the long left bend that follows, a narrow island parallels the shoreline, forming a pleasant channel on the right. As you clear the island, more cliffs begin to appear downstream-right, locally known as First and Second Rock. The farther you go, the grander the stone formations become, culminating in the magnificent, sheer Third Rock, the scenic highlight of the trip. This last and most glorious of the cliffs occurs alongside the right channel of Big Island.

After Big Island, the right bank is open for awhile and homes are seen on the left. Eventually forest resumes on both sides, with intermittent cabins. A very long left bend finally leads to Lowell Park, where picnic tables, playground equipment, toilets, and a concrete boat ramp are seen on the right. Located 3 miles north of Dixon, Lowell Park is the largest city park in Illinois, and is an excellent place to stop for lunch or to take out. A 3.5-mile bike trail runs from the park into Dixon. As a young man growing up in Dixon, Ronald Reagan worked at Lowell Park as a lifeguard and is credited with having saved seventy-seven lives.

After the park, the right shoreline is densely wooded while cabins are seen on the left. Eventually the river begins bending to the right toward Dixon, and traffic can occasionally be seen along Grand Detour Road on the left. Except for the loud cement plant, also on the left, the environs continue to be relatively undeveloped. Finally, houses begin on both sides and a big island lies upstream from the dam and bridge; take the right channel. **Take out** within sight of the bridge and the orange warning buoys at the Fellows Street boat ramp, which appears on the right alongside several culverts, in the midst of many private docks.

Known as "Petunia City" because of the flowers that line its streets in spring and summer, Dixon is an attractive community with an interesting history. Named after John Dixon, who operated a ferry and trading post here in the 1830s, the community was the site of Fort Dixon during the Black Hawk War of 1832 (young volunteer Abe Lincoln was stationed there). Ronald Reagan's boyhood home on Hennepin Avenue has been restored and is open to visitors.

Other trips. The section from Dixon to Sterling is popular with motorboaters and is not recommended for canoeing. The following stretches are canoeable, but you're likely to see some motorboats on each: (1) Macktown Forest Preserve near Rockton to Atwood Forest Preserve north of Machesney Park (8.4 miles); (2) Blackhawk Park on the south edge of Rockford to Byron (14 miles); and (3) Byron to the Lowden Access Area northeast of Oregon (9 miles). A highlight of trip 3 is the 84-foot Lorado Taft statue that towers over the river at the take-out (see the photo on page 114). A dignified and powerful representation of a Native American, this famous sculpture was created on the site of an artists' colony called Eagle's Nest.

Third Rock, the most impressive cliff on the Rock River

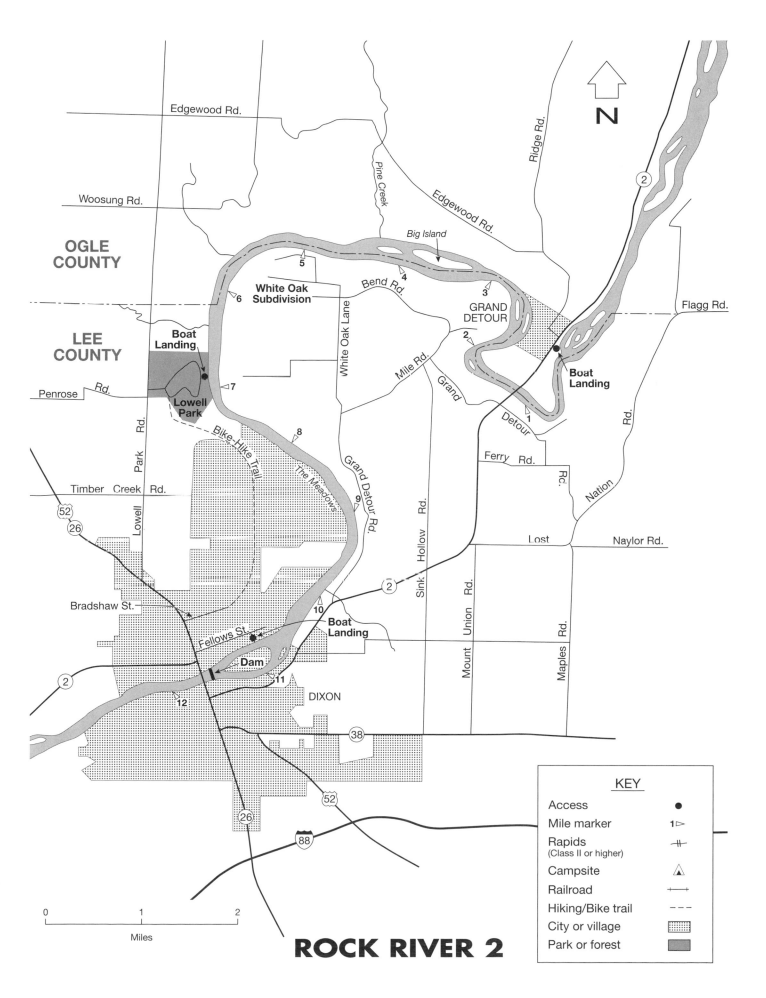

ROCK RIVER 2

KEY

Access	●
Mile marker	1▷
Rapids (Class II or higher)	—H—
Campsite	◮
Railroad	+——+
Hiking/Bike trail	- - -
City or village	▦
Park or forest	▩

SALINE RIVER
Equality to Saline Landing (14 Miles)

Several rivers and streams in Illinois are named after nearby salt deposits that were important to early inhabitants of the state. Typically, animals in search of salt licks led Native Americans to the valuable deposits that were later exploited by white settlers, especially in the early 1800s. Perhaps the most dramatic of these "salines" were those just south of the village of Equality. They gave the nearby river its name and contributed much of America's salt supply. Salt production was simple: a square well was dug and lined with logs, and brine from the well was then boiled in large kettles. At the peak of salt-making, 500 bushels a day were produced. By 1873, however, the price of salt was so low that the Saline River operations were abandoned.

The main stream of the Saline River begins near Equality where the North, Middle, and South forks converge. Upstream and immediately downstream from Equality, the river has been channelized extensively and is not recommended for canoeing. After Highway 1, however, the river winds around considerably and is densely wooded all the way to the Ohio River. A rich variety of trees covers the shoreline, including many beautiful bald cypresses in or near the water. Ranging from 80 to 200 feet in width, the river almost never has bank-to-bank obstructions. Minimal **gradient** (0.7 foot per mile) and slow current add up to a lazy float trip. Steep, muddy banks provide few places to get out of your boat, and there are no intermediate accesses. Fishing is good for catfish, largemouth and smallmouth bass, white bass, striped bass, crappies, and bluegill. You probably won't see any copperheads, rattlesnakes, or water moccasins, but they are present in the area; watch where you step.

Nearby public **campgrounds** include Pounds Hollow Recreation Area, Garden of the Gods Recreation Area, and the Saline County Fish & Wildlife Area—all located south of Equality. Even if you don't camp there, you should consider spending a couple of hours at Garden of the Gods: the rugged terrain and unique rock formations are spectacular! The Double M Campground (private) is on Thacker Hollow Road, off Highway 1, also south of Equality.

The **shuttle route** (15.8 miles) from Highway 1 to Saline Landing passes through very attractive hill country. From the put-in, go south on Highway 1, turn east onto Saline Landing Road, and drive another 3.2 miles to the landing. As soon as you turn off Highway 1, go to the left over a small bridge. While driving south to the take-out, take a look at the beautiful wooded ridges in the distance; locals call these the "foot of the Ozarks."

Water levels. There currently is no gauge on the Saline.

Put in at the Highway 1 bridge, downstream-right; a rough clay road leads down to the river, where low rock outcroppings assure a dry put-in. Cypresses appear quickly after Highway 1 as the river arcs to the right, then straightens for awhile. When a right curve begins, power lines and some old abutments precede a small island, which in turn is just upstream from Cypress Ditch. The river tends to be shallow in the vicinity of the island, where an old fishing camp can be seen on the left shoreline. Curving to the right past another beautiful stand of cypresses, the Saline heads due south, gradually widening.

After a long straightaway, the river bends sharply left where Eagle Creek enters on the right. Just below the creek are an old concrete gauging station and a ford. In the big, gentle right arc that follows, the unique Peabody Road haulage bridge appears—an old steel structure on stilt-like piers. After two creeks on the right, the river turns left again, then right, past a couple of small sandstone outcroppings. Farther downstream, in a straight stretch, an abandoned A-frame house appears high up on the right bank. Beaver Creek enters soon thereafter, then three private fishing camps appear on the left.

The first of several huge drainage culverts appears on the left (equipped with gates to prevent backflow into the nearby fields). After a final left bend, the river heads back to the right, and before long you see the cabins, trailers, and docks of Saline Landing; the Ohio River lies just around the bend. Continue past the boat docks and **take out** at the concrete boat ramp, near a towerlike pumping station. Saline Landing is a private area with permanent and seasonal residents, so you should ask permission to take out and park here.

Slavery in Illinois

To the surprise of many who think that Illinois was always a "free" state, the salines were a prime user of slave labor. The Northwest Ordinance of 1787 declared that there was to be no slavery in this region, but territorial law and the 1818 state constitution allowed an exception in Gallatin County for the specific purpose of making salt. More than 200 slaves and indentured servants were engaged in this dirty and arduous process in the 1820s, working on land leased from the state, which in turn took a healthy share of the profits. Southeast of Equality you can still see one of the old salt wells and the antebellum mansion—the "Old Slave House"—of John Crenshaw, one of the last of the slave-owning salt producers.

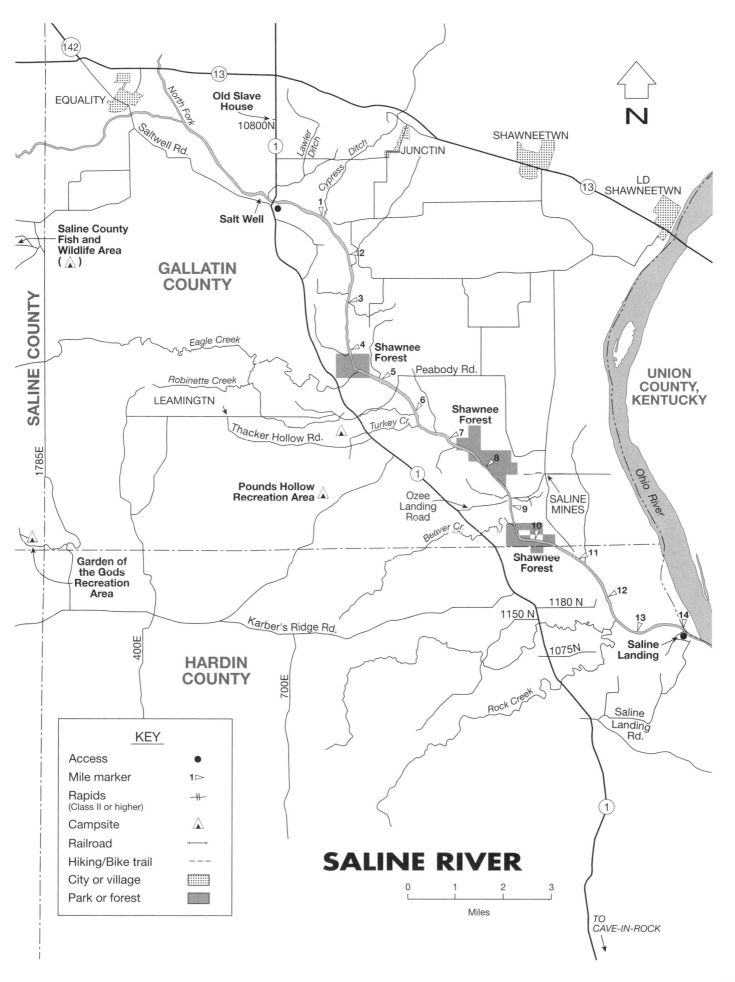

SALINE RIVER

SALT CREEK OF THE DES PLAINES RIVER

Graue Mill to Plank Road Landing (11 Miles)

Highway of the Voyageurs

When you take out at the Plank Road Meadow Forest Preserve, you aren't far from the location of the famous Chicago Portage. Until the opening of the Illinois and Michigan Canal in 1848, generations of explorers, fur traders, missionaries, and settlers traveled from Lake Michigan to the Mississippi by using this route. Paddling up the South Branch of the Chicago River and its West Branch, they then portaged their boats across several miles of wetland (Mud Lake) to the Des Plaines River where it begins its long southwestward course. Chicago Portage Woods, part of the Cook County Forest Preserves, is less than 2 miles southeast of Plank Road Meadow. Today you can still paddle part of the historic route by putting in at Stony Ford Landing (off Joliet Road on the west side of the river) and taking out at Willow Springs, Lemont, Romeoville, or Lockport (see Des Plaines River 3).

Because of its location within a highly urbanized area, Salt Creek doesn't offer high water quality as one of its recreational inducements. Arising near Palatine, it flows southward through one west suburban community after another before joining the Des Plaines River, receiving considerable urban runoff along the way. For other reasons, however, it is a very pleasant canoeing stream. Perhaps its biggest plus is the fact that forest preserves border much of the shoreline, belying the fact that you are paddling through one of the most densely populated parts of the state.

For most of this section, Salt Creek is winding, intimate, and wild. The creek changes character several times—displaying tight, tree-canopied stretches, low floodplain banks, a "braided" island area, and a brief urban setting. Because of the narrowness and heavily wooded banks, fallen limbs and trees must be avoided or portaged occasionally.

Canoe rental is available at Chicagoland Canoe Base in Chicago (773-777-1489).

The **shuttle route** (5.7 miles) is short and simple. From the Graue Mill parking lot, go south on York Road, then east on Ogden Avenue. After crossing First Avenue, turn north into the Plank Road Meadow Forest Preserve. Park along the entrance road, where there are many diagonal parking spaces near the boat landing.

The **gradient** is almost 3 feet per mile.

For **water levels**, check the Western Springs gauge (station # 05531500) on the USGS Web site listed in the introduction.

Put in alongside the Graue Mill parking lot, downstream-right from the York Road bridge. Don't miss the opportunity to visit the nearby mill, built in 1852 and still producing stone-ground grain. Located in the Du Page County Fullersburg Woods Forest Preserve, this beautiful three-story mill was once a stopping place on the Underground Railroad in the pre–Civil War era.

Only 35 feet wide at the beginning, the creek bends back and forth between low wooded banks. After a concrete bridge and some condominiums, the creek makes a quick S-turn where there's a small drop with riffles. The Interstate 294 bridges soon follow. The creek continues to be narrow and winding in the Bemis Woods Forest Preserve, often with overhanging trees. At a footbridge the creek can be accessed downstream-left from a nearby parking lot (off Wolf Road). **Be careful here**, because the piers of this low bridge tend to collect deadfall.

After the Wolf Road bridge, the forest preserve nursery can be seen on the right. Now comes an area where the creek wends its way through the narrow channels of some islands, usually requiring maneuvering around fallen limbs. At the 31st Street bridge the creek loops to the right. Later, after a sharp left turn, the creek flows alongside La Grange Road for awhile. Before the bridge, where the creek swings right, there are old abutments on the left and a small island where deadfall tends to collect—another place to **be careful**.

After La Grange Road, the creek widens somewhat and becomes quite riffly. Less than a mile downstream from the bridge, in a right bend, there's a pleasant gravel beach on the right with nearby picnic tables—a good place for a lunch stop. Power lines, a railroad bridge, and 25th Avenue soon follow. In the right turn before 17th Avenue, a major tributary enters on the left, Addison Creek. Downstream the three big openings of a large concrete flood control structure appear on the left: stay far to the right. After a few houses appear on the left on a private property, the creek loops around to 31st Street.

Paddling through the western part of the Brookfield Zoo site, you now pass under the bridges of a defunct miniature railroad. After Washington Avenue, the setting becomes progressively more urban. Just north of Brookfield Avenue, you can **take out** behing the Brookfield Village Hall. Finally, after the big modern bridge at First Avenue, Salt Creek flows into the Des Plaines. Stay to the right, because the landing is only 100 feet downstream-right from the confluence. **Take out** at the gravel access and carry boats up to the nearby drop-off road. A short distance downstream is the dangerous Hoffman Dam.

Other trips. For a description of an upstream section, see www.openlands.org/watertrails.asp.

Salt Creek: a pleasant paddle through west suburban forest preserves

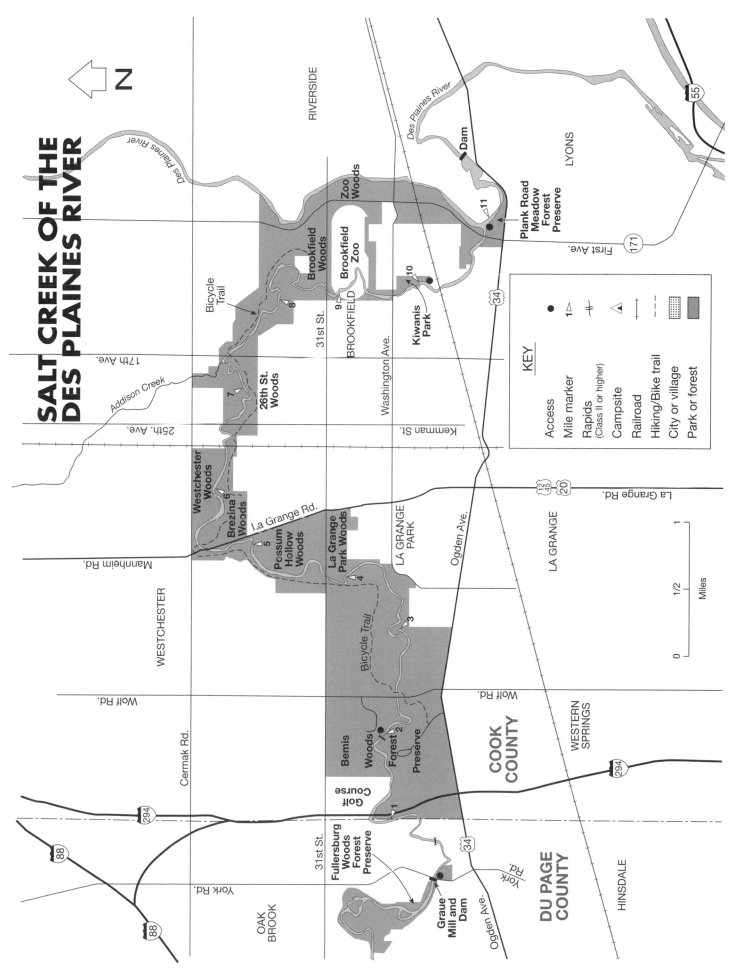

SALT CREEK OF THE DES PLAINES RIVER

N

KEY

- Access ●
- Mile marker 1△
- Rapids (Class II or higher)
- Campsite △
- Railroad
- Hiking/Bike trail
- City or village
- Park or forest

RIVERSIDE

Des Plaines River

Zoo Woods

Brookfield Woods

Brookfield Zoo

Bicycle Trail

BROOKFIELD

31st St.

Washington Ave.

9▷

8

10

Kiwanis Park

Dam

Plank Road Meadow Forest Preserve

LYONS

First Ave.

171

55

34

17th Ave.

Addison Creek

25th Ave.

26th St. Woods

7

Kemman St.

Westchester Woods

Brezina Woods

6

Possum Hollow Woods

5

La Grange Rd.

La Grange Park Woods

Manheim Rd.

WESTCHESTER

LA GRANGE PARK

Ogden Ave.

LA GRANGE

12
45
20

La Grange Rd.

4

3

Bicycle Trail

Wolf Rd.

Wolf Rd.

WESTERN SPRINGS

Cermak Rd.

294

88

Bemis Woods

Forest Preserve

Golf Course

2

1

COOK COUNTY

31st St.

York Rd.

Fullersburg Woods Forest Preserve

OAK BROOK

Graue Mill and Dam

York Rd.

Ogden Ave.

34

DU PAGE COUNTY

HINSDALE

1/2   1
Miles
0

Des Plaines River

SALT CREEK OF THE SANGAMON RIVER 1

North Fork Canoe Trail (3.7 Miles)

Originating near the small community of Saybrook, Salt Creek is a canoeable stream that eventually flows into the Sangamon north of Petersburg. Dammed early in its course to form Clinton Lake, it then gathers volume from such tributaries as Lake Fork, Kickapoo Creek, and Sugar Creek as it heads west, mostly through farmland. Occasional channelization diminishes the naturalness of some sections, but the banks are wooded and pleasant most of the time. Except for short stretches at Weldon Springs State Recreation Area and Edward R. Madigan State Park, the creek flows entirely past private property.

Landownership is not a concern on the first recommended canoe stretch, however. After Illinois Power Company constructed Clinton Lake in the 1970s to provide cooling water for a nuclear power plant, the DNR signed a 40-year lease agreement that allows the department to operate and maintain 10,000 of the company's acres (including most of the lake) for public recreational use, including fishing, hunting, hiking, and picnicking. Best of all (for paddlers) is a designated canoeing stretch on the North Fork.

There's no other canoeing area in Illinois quite like this one. No more than 3.7 miles in length—actually less than that if you wish to avoid the wide area at the south end or the brushy part to the north—the canoe trail is a good place to spend a couple of relaxing hours in your boat. Excellent for beginners, the trail is quiet, heavily wooded, gently winding, and easy to get to. You can paddle the North Fork in the traditional point-to-point fashion with a car shuttle, or (better yet) park your car(s) at the canoe landing and then paddle out and back. **Gradient** and current are usually almost nonexistent, so returning upstream is not a problem. There's always enough water to paddle. Fishing is good, too: Clinton Lake is well known for its catfish, crappie, largemouth bass, walleye, striped bass, bluegill, and bullheads.

Excellent public **camping** is located nearby: on Clinton Lake at the Mascoutin State Recreation Area south of DeWitt; north of LeRoy at Moraine View State Recreation Area; and south of Clinton at Weldon Springs State Recreation Area, which lies along Salt Creek. Situated on one of the biggest glacial ridges in the state (the Bloomington Moraine), Moraine View offers not only wonderful campsites but also an object lesson on the effects of the Wisconsin Glacier.

An out-and-back trip from the canoe landing is recommended, enabling you to paddle as far as you wish (north or south) before returning to the landing. If you prefer the **shuttle**, however, the vehicular distance from the canoe landing (off County 1200N) to the boat landing (off 900N) via 1700E is 4 miles. The bridge and parking lot at 1275N are not recommended as an access.

Put in at the excellent canoe access just south of the 1200N bridge, downstream-right. The landing and parking lot are located between 1200N and a charming, old metal-truss bridge 100 yards downstream. A hiking trail leads off to the south. Only 45 feet wide at the put-in, the creek heads south between low, wooded banks. The same setting and width continue for some time, as short straightaways and bends alternate. Farther downstream, high wooded bluffs appear, and the edges become more marshy in character. Overall, the creek is quite peaceful—with no sign of human habitation whatsoever—and resembles a small river. Be on the lookout for deer, waterfowl, hawks, osprey, and occasional eagles.

Gradually the streambed widens to several hundred feet, power lines cross overhead, and bays form on both sides. By the time you reach the boat access, downstream-left from the 900N bridge, the creek has begun to look lakelike. The advantage of a no-shuttle trip, of course, is that you can turn around and paddle back if the creek becomes too wide or windy for your taste. Incidentally, the stretch upstream from the power lines is restricted to electric motors, and the stretch downstream to the boat landing is a no-wake area for motorboaters.

If the section south of the canoe landing looks riverlike, the northern portion is definitely creeklike. The banks are higher, and the stream becomes progressively narrower as you continue north. This part of the creek twists back and forth more than the southern stretch. It is wild, often tree-canopied, a little shallow here and there, and very peaceful. By the time you get to 1275N—that is, if the deadfall allows you to get that far—the creek is only 25 feet wide.

Humongous Illinois Impoundments

Clinton Lake seems huge to canoeists, but it's certainly not Illinois's biggest impoundment. The flow of many of the significant rivers and creeks in the state has been interrupted by one or more dams—mainly to generate power, create reservoirs for drinking water, control floodwater, or provide lake-oriented recreation. Most of the impoundments thus produced are little more than long, sluggish wide spots upstream from a dam, but a few are giant lakes that have become an important part of the local economy. Fishing is the big draw, of course, but many other activities are popular as well at the four biggest artificial lakes in Illinois: (1) Carlyle Lake on the Kaskaskia (24,580 acres); (2) Rend Lake on the Big Muddy (18,900 acres); (3) Lake Shelbyville on the Kaskaskia and Okaw (11,100 acres); and (4) Clinton Lake on Salt Creek (5,000 acres).

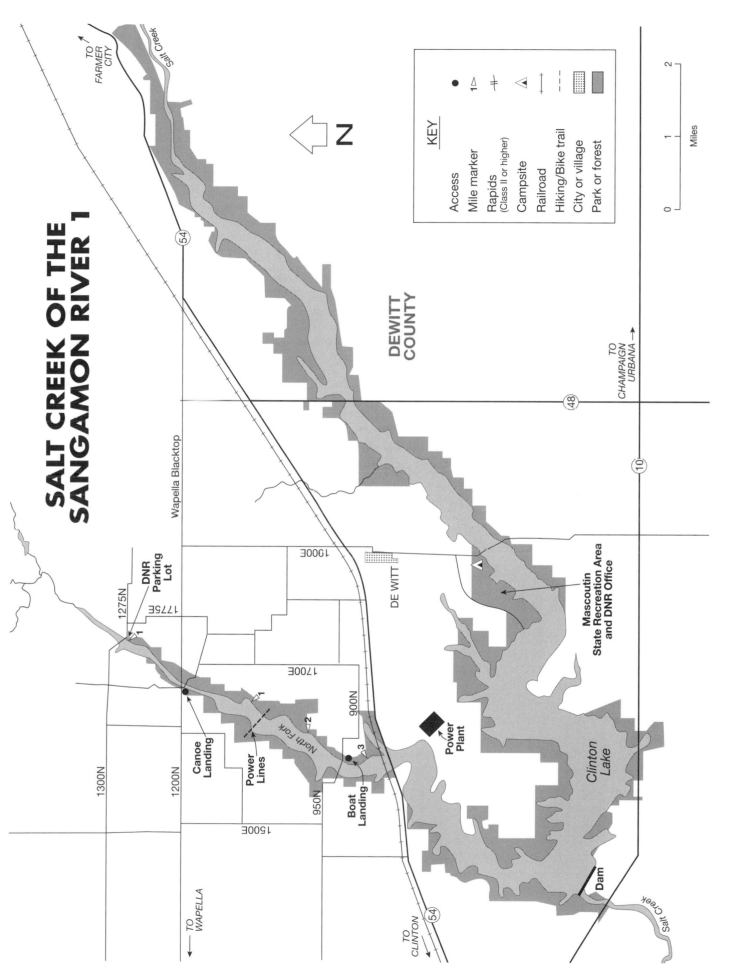

SALT CREEK OF THE SANGAMON RIVER 1

KEY

Access	●
Mile marker	1△
Rapids (Class II or higher)	⪡
Campsite	◁
Railroad	┼
Hiking/Bike trail	── ──
City or village	▦
Park or forest	▨

N

TO FARMER CITY

Salt Creek

54

Wapella Blacktop

1275N

DNR Parking Lot

1775E

1300N

1200N

TO WAPELLA

Canoe Landing

Power Lines

North Fork

1500E

950N

Boat Landing

1700E

1500E

900N

DE WITT

DEWITT COUNTY

Power Plant

Clinton Lake

Dam

Salt Creek

TO CLINTON

54

Mascoutin State Recreation Area and DNR Office

48

10

TO CHAMPAIGN URBANA →

0   1   2
Miles

SALT CREEK OF THE SANGAMON RIVER 2

Rocky Ford Bridge to Possum Hollow Bridge (6 Miles)

Paddleable all the way from the outlet of Clinton Lake to the Sangamon River, Salt Creek is most often canoed in the area downstream from Lincoln. There is a good canoe landing in Edward R. Madigan State Park just south of the city, but the most popular put-in is 4 river-miles west at Rocky Ford Bridge. From here to its mouth, the creek widens and is unlikely to present logjam problems. Always be on the lookout for deadfall, however, especially in bends. In the often-paddled 6-mile section ending at Possum Hollow Bridge, it passes over a rock-sand-and-silt bottom and through many pleasant riffles. Rocky shelves add to the attractiveness of the shoreline, and gravel bars frequently provide stopping places. There are no buildings along the way. Wildlife observations typically include herons, owls, kingfishers, hawks, swallows, waterfowl, and deer.

For **campgrounds,** see Salt Creek of the Sangamon River 1. Also in the area are Camp-A-While Holiday Park north of Lincoln (private) and Lincoln's New Salem south of Petersburg.

The **shuttle route** (5.8 miles) from Rocky Ford Bridge goes west on County 1400N, south on 450E, then west on 1300N to the Possum Hollow Bridge.

The **gradient** is 1.8 feet per mile.

For **water levels,** check the gauges upstream at Rowell (station #05578500) and downstream at Greenview (#05582000) on the USGS Web site listed in the introduction.

Put in at Rocky Ford Bridge, downstream-left, where a gravel road leads down to the creek. There is room nearby to park several cars. (To get to Rocky Ford Bridge, go west from Lincoln on County 1575N, south on 700E, and east on 1400N.)

Immediately bending right, the creek passes low, stratified rock shelves on both sides; these are most conspicuous at low water levels. After the initial right bend, the creek straightens and narrows to about 35 feet. The silt-and-sand banks are liberally sprinkled with chunks of rock and are heavily wooded. At the end of the half-mile straightaway the streambed constricts, with a small drop and riffles. This is a popular spot for bankside fishermen, who catch smallmouth bass, catfish, white bass, and occasional walleyes.

The creek now goes into a long left bend, widening to 50–60 feet. High, sandy cutbanks begin appearing, often with swallow nests, and periodic shoals provide riffles. In a couple of locations, cornfields come to the edge of the creek, with concrete riprap to retard erosion. As the creek heads to the right, a tributary enters on the left, immediately followed by a small cabin. Just downstream is a huge boulder in the streambed. As the long right bend continues, more tributaries enter on the left. Occasionally, riffles occur where rock projects out into the streambed.

Sheer cutbanks become more frequent in the outside of bends as the creek winds back and forth. Big gravel bars, often covered with mussel shells, are found opposite the cutbanks. Eventually Polecat Hill can be seen on the right, soon followed by the Possum Hollow Bridge. **Take out** on the left, upstream, at the huge gravel bar, a commonly used access area.

An additional 2.5 miles of paddling take you to the bridge north of Middletown. In this stretch, high cutbanks and big gravel bars continue, and deadfall in bends requires some maneuvering. At one point an inverted metal truss structure carries petroleum pipes over the creek. A small tributary enters on the right about 150 yards upstream from the bridge, where the take-out is downstream-right. This take-out isn't as easy as Possum Hollow. Note that all three accesses are on private property.

Other trips. Area canoeists also paddle the following sections: (1) from south of Farmer City to the Parnell boat access on the east lobe of Clinton Lake; (2) from the first bridge west of Clinton Lake to Texas Bridge (the first bridge downstream from Highway 51); (3) from Texas Bridge to Kenney; (4) from Possum Hollow Bridge to Salt Creek Bottoms Road; and (5) from Salt Creek Bottoms Road to Highway 97 (taking out on the Sangamon River). On trip 4, Salt Creek becomes much larger after the mouth of Sugar Creek. (Kickapoo Creek similarly enlarges Salt Creek just before Rocky Ford Bridge.) Some of the accesses listed above are in common use, but others require permission from landowners. Reminder: when in doubt, always ask landowner permission.

Cradle of Rivers

Incredibly, Salt Creek is one of eleven major rivers and streams that arise within a 60-mile by 50-mile area of Illinois. Other waterways that have their origin in this relatively small area near Danville, Hoopeston, Paxton, Gibson City, LeRoy, Monticello, and Champaign-Urbana are the North Fork, Middle Fork, Salt Fork, and main branch of the South Vermilion, together with the Little Vermilion, Embarras, Kaskaskia, Okaw, Sangamon, and Mackinaw Rivers. All of these waterways drain to the west, south, or east from the relatively high ground of glacial end-moraines found in this headwaters area.

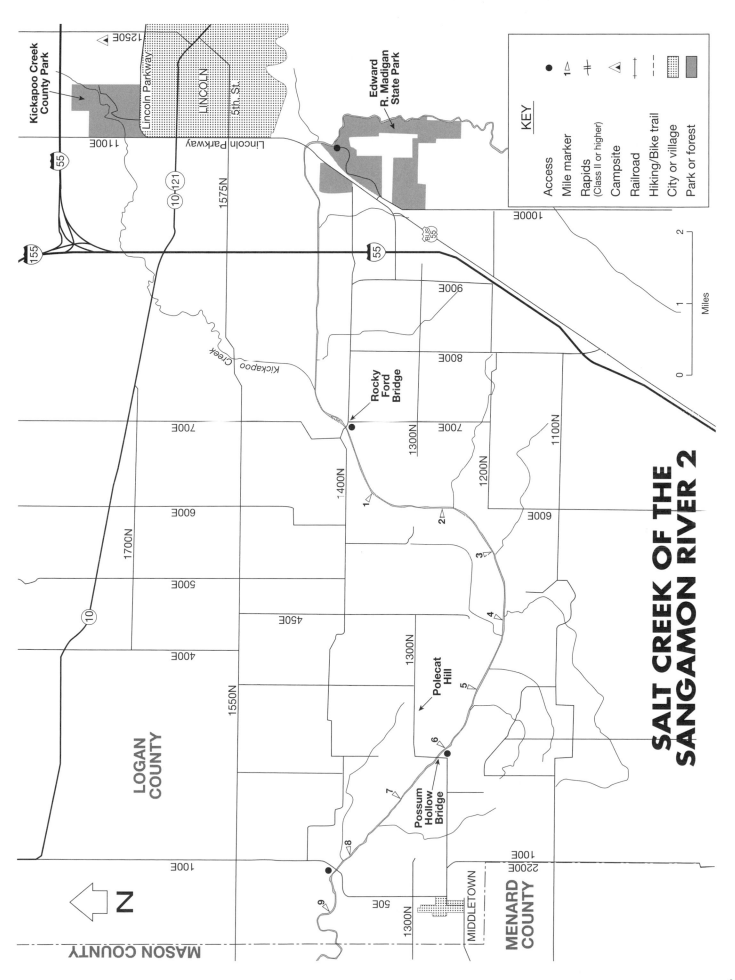

SALT CREEK OF THE SANGAMON RIVER 2

125

SALT FORK OF THE SOUTH VERMILION RIVER 1
County Line Road to Chainy Ford Bridge (13.5 Miles)

Not as well known as the nearby Middle Fork, the Salt Fork is equally beautiful. Moreover, it isn't nearly as "crowded" as its famous neighbor, and is usually still paddleable when the Middle Fork has become uncomfortably low in the summer. Originating a few miles east of Champaign-Urbana, the main stream of the river courses 44 miles to the east before meeting the Middle Fork to form the South Vermilion River; a few miles later the North Fork adds its flow to the South Vermilion, which then heads southeast to join the Wabash in Indiana. Upstream from the Champaign-Vermilion County line the Salt Fork is relatively small and subject to logjams. The 23.5-mile stretch in Vermilion County, however, is less prone to obstructions (with a couple of possible exceptions noted below), and offers experienced paddlers one of the finest canoeing streams in Illinois.

Generally isolated, the river winds through an endless succession of pleasant riffles, past many shale and sandstone outcroppings, and through a variety of wild settings. Few houses are seen, and numerous sandbars make good stopping places. The only significant downside is the scarcity of good accesses.

Excellent public **camping** is available nearby at Kickapoo State Park and the Middle Fork State Fish and Wildlife Area.

The **shuttle route** (8.9 miles) to Chainy Ford Bridge is a little circuitous. From the put-in go north on County Line Road (County 2800E), east on Lincoln Trail Road, south on 700E, and west on 1550N. Shuttling via Homer–Catlin Road, 600E, 1450N, and 630E adds a mile, but the roads are better.

The **gradient** is a riffly 3 feet per mile.

Water levels. There currently is no active gauge on the Salt Fork.

Put in about 150 feet upstream from the County Line Road bridge on the north bank, where the landowner has built a concrete ramp alongside the gravel road paralleling the river. Immediately downstream from

the bridge, pastureland is found on both sides for about half a mile. Soon, dense woods begin and the streambed narrows, creating a peaceful, tree-canopied area. After several long bends, a television tower comes into view in the distance. Riffles and a couple of houses lead to Steffy Bridge, which is preceded by some modest rock outcroppings on the right (the first of many). An old metal truss structure, the bridge is closed to traffic.

After running alongside the TV tower, the river makes three quick bends in a low-banked floodplain environment in the approach to Rutan Bridge. **Warning:** downstream from the bridge is a short, sharp S curve in which deadfall is often lodged; currents are tricky here and can carry unwary paddlers into dangerous strainers—portage if in doubt. Rock formations now begin to appear on the right, with a small seam of coal. A small drop, constriction, and riffle precede Butler Bridge. Be careful when approaching the bridge; deadfall often accumulates against the three concrete piers of this decrepit, old structure, so you must be prepared to carry your boat(s) around if necessary. There is a decent access about 100 feet downstream-right, but the tight, curving gravel road at the bridge makes it dangerous to unload and load boats here.

In the short interval to the next bridge, gravel bars and sandy beaches begin to appear, and several low cliffs add to the beauty of the setting. A creek on the right and a small wooded island precede Runyan Bridge, where the river begins to widen.

In the second half of the trip, there are no more bridges until the take-out, and the scenery keeps getting better. The streambed widens to as much as 80 feet, and forested bluffs alternate with floodplain woods. At several locations, the river is sharply deflected to one side or the other by beautiful cliffs, and riffles are often created by rock that has fallen into the river. Looping toward the east, the river passes a huge block of stone on the left, with steeply angled strata, then splits around a long island.

After another stretch to the north, the river forms a short westward loop. Back in the 1800s, water was diverted to the other (northern) side of the bend to power a mill. As you complete the bend, a big cut appears in the high rocky shoreline on the right, where the gristmill and waterwheel were once located. A log home and wooden bridge now occupy the location. Just downstream are the abutments of the old Conkeytown Covered Bridge, which burned in the 1950s. This picturesque area is definitely a highlight of the trip.

After a right bend, a tall cliff forces the river back the other way, and there's an especially impressive cliff in the left curve, ending with a beautiful, craggy outcropping. More bends and rock formations follow, and finally a large wooded island at the end of a left bend precedes the eastward swing toward Chainy Ford Bridge, a relatively new structure. **Take out** downstream on the left bank alongside a gravel road.

Poling: another way to navigate the Salt Fork

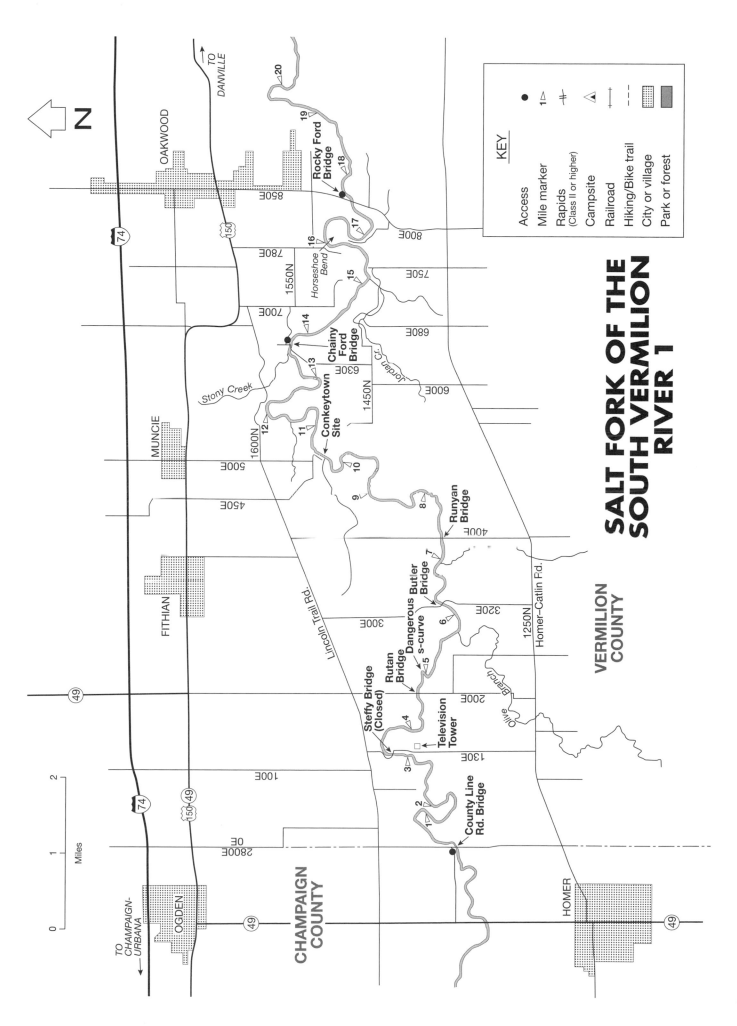

SALT FORK OF THE SOUTH VERMILION RIVER 1

KEY

●	Access
1△	Mile marker
‡	Rapids (Class II or higher)
△	Campsite
✝	Railroad
¦	Hiking/Bike trail
▦	City or village
▨	Park or forest

N

TO DANVILLE

OAKWOOD

Rocky Ford Bridge

Horseshoe Bend

Chainy Ford Bridge

Stony Creek

Jordan Ct.

Conkeytown Site

MUNCIE

Runyan Bridge

FITHIAN

Dangerous s-curve

Butler Bridge

Lincoln Trail Rd.

Rutan Bridge

Steffy Bridge (Closed)

Television Tower

Olive Branch

Homer-Catlin Rd.

VERMILION COUNTY

County Line Rd. Bridge

CHAMPAIGN COUNTY

HOMER

OGDEN

TO CHAMPAIGN-URBANA

Miles

850E
780E
1550N
700E
750E
680E
630E
1450N
600E
500E
450E
1600N
400E
300E
320E
1250N
200E
130E
100E
2800E
0E

74
150
150
49
49
49
49
74

850E

127

SALT FORK OF THE SOUTH VERMILION RIVER 2

Chainy Ford Bridge to Anderson Hill Bridge (10 Miles)

Illinois's Salt-Mining Past

To get a feel for the "salines of the Vermilion"—the salt-producing operations that were an important source of income for early settlers in the area—stop by the Salt Kettle Rest Area off I-74 east of Danville, near the Oakwood exit. The monument commemorating the salines is only a few miles from the original salt mines. Since prehistoric times, many locations in Illinois were significant sources of salt, which in the 1800s was laboriously extracted by digging brine wells, then boiling the salty water away in big kettles to obtain the then-valuable product. Most of the salt produced in Illinois came from Gallatin County in southern Illinois (see the description of the Saline River).

This trip on the Salt Fork is loaded with highlights: big gravel bars, several islands, a classic oxbow, towering cliffs, a picturesque suspension bridge, innumerable riffles, and a confluence with another river. Most of the surroundings continue to be heavily forested, and dwellings are sparse. Averaging 75 feet in width, the river in this section seldom presents problems with obstructions. After Rocky Ford Bridge, tight turns give way to big, sweeping curves. The Salt Fork puts on an impressive floral show every spring with breathtaking displays of bluebells, hepatica, redbud, spring beauties, and trillium. Because of the varied terrain (high bluffs, bottomlands, cliffs) and soil types (silt, clay, sand, sandstone, and shale), many species of trees are seen, including maple, oak, sycamore, locust, cottonwood, and cedar. The heavily vegetated environs also support sizable populations of wildlife.

For **camping** and **water levels,** see Salt Fork of the South Vermilion River 1.

The **shuttle route** (7.6 miles) heads east to County 700E, north to Highway 150, east to Batestown Road, and south on Shangri La Road to Anderson Hill Bridge.

The **gradient** is a little steeper on this section, 3.5 feet per mile.

Put in downstream-left from the Chainy Ford Bridge alongside the gravel road paralleling the river. Near the end of a long, gentle left arc toward the southeast, Jordan Creek enters on the right near a huge gravel bar—a fine place to stop, wade, and relax. Known locally as "Mouth of Jordan," this is a popular party spot. The river now goes into a long sequence of bends (left, right, then left again) that create a big, bulbous oxbow. At its narrowest point, a scant 100 feet of high bluff separates the north-flowing river from the south-flowing part. After this horseshoe bend the streambed gets narrower, rockier, and even more riffly. In the northeast approach to the next bridge, several small islands constrict the channel still further, and a house appears on the right. Rocky Ford Bridge can be accessed downstream-left; an old road leads down to the river on the upstream side, near an old pumping station.

Downstream from Rocky Ford, much of the surroundings were strip-mined years ago; fortunately, nature has recovered enough to cover up the miners' handiwork. After the bridge, the river bends right for awhile, then heads straight into a sheer, 70-foot shale cliff and veers to the left. Sheer cliffs and pleasant riffles continue for some time as the river arcs left. Then, after a wide straightaway, 90-foot cliffs tower on the right in a long, riffly left bend.

After the river heads right, a wood-and-cable suspension footbridge crosses the river at Camp Drake, a Boy Scout camp. Immediately downstream are concrete chunks from an old dam, which may need to be portaged in low water. As the river bends around the camp area, very high cliffs begin again on the right. Watch for a coal seam, with decaying mine timbers. Through most of the long left bend after the camp, the river hugs a high, wooded bluff on the right, with frequent cliffs and delightful riffles.

As the river begins to bend back to the right, traffic noise can be heard from Highway 150 and Interstate 74 to the north. (It is in this area, by the way—between the north bank of the river and the modern location of Highway 150—that the river's namesake salt springs were originally located, a significant industry in the early 1800s.) The river is about 100 feet wide here, with high, eroded banks and gravel bars. After a long left bend, the Middle Fork joins the Salt Fork on the left. Then, as soon as you turn right, the Anderson Hill Bridge can be seen downstream.

Take out 50–100 yards upstream from the bridge on the right at one of the two bare, clay landings alongside the gravel road. The easiest landing is the second, immediately upstream from Butler Branch, the creek entering on the right.

Other trips. If you continue past the Anderson Hill Bridge, 5.5 miles of canoeing take you to the mouth of the North Fork. Turn north, paddle up the North Fork for about half a mile, and take out on the left at the Ellsworth Park boat ramp. More shale cliffs, wooded bluffs, lowlands, and riffles occur in this stretch, but the last couple of miles are slow-going because of a dam downstream. A highlight is the graceful old railroad bridge known as "The Arches," not far upstream from the mouth of the North Fork. DO NOT CONTINUE on the South Vermilion past the North Fork; a short distance downstream is a low-head dam that has drowned many people over the years.

Cliffs near Anderson Hill Bridge

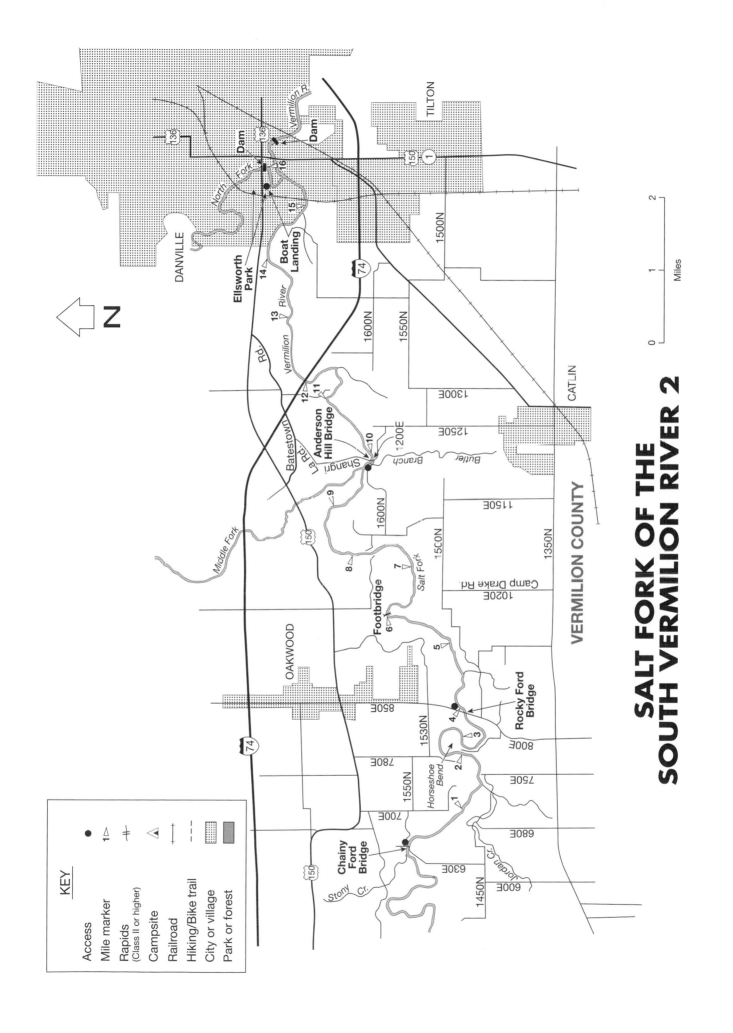

SALT FORK OF THE
SOUTH VERMILION RIVER 2

KEY

- Access ●
- Mile marker 1 △
- Rapids (Class II or higher) ⫲
- Campsite △
- Railroad ┼
- Hiking/Bike trail - - -
- City or village ▦
- Park or forest ▓

SANGAMON RIVER 1 & 2
Wheeland Park to Riverside Park (8 Miles)
Riverside Park to Irwin Bridge (16.5 Miles)

The Sangamon is a long river (241 miles), originating a few miles southeast of Bloomington, then arcing westward to the Illinois River at Beardstown. Upstream from Decatur, where a dam forms a 3,000-acre lake, the river is attractive for canoeing, but its many logjams can be frustrating. Obstructions can also be a problem in the stretch between Decatur and Springfield. North of Petersburg, the Sangamon enlarges considerably after its confluence with Salt Creek, and is channelized in its last 35 miles.

Public **camping** for the 3 stretches described here is available at Lincoln Trail Homestead State Memorial Park, Riverside Park north of Springfield, Sangchris Lake State Park southeast of Springfield, and Lincoln's New Salem south of Petersburg. There are also several private campgrounds in Springfield.

For **water levels,** check the gauge at Riverton (#05576500) on the USGS Web site listed in the introduction.

The first day-trip on which paddlers can be reasonably sure of encountering no troublesome logjams begins at Wheeland Park in Riverton and continues northwesterly for 8 river-miles to Springfield. The **shuttle route** from Wheeland Park goes west on Camp Butler Road, west on Sangamon Avenue, and north on Business 55 to Riverside Park. **Put in** at the public boat ramp in the park, some distance downstream-right from the Camp Butler Road bridge. Along the way, you'll float under 3 highway bridges and 4 railroad bridges, but the setting is generally quite natural and the **gradient** gentle. In several locations, exposed rock is visible along the river—especially when beautiful sandstone cliffs appear near the end of the trip. Houses can be seen near the banks occasionally, and sandbars are frequent. At some levels, easy rapids are found under the Business 55 bridge. **Take out** at the public boat ramp in Riverside Park, downstream-left from Business 55. For an excellent 52-page booklet on the geology, flora, and fauna of this section, see Mike Ulm's *Canoeist's Natural History Guide to the Sangamon River: From Riverton to Riverside Park* (1996).

The second section is appropriate for a long, lazy float trip. Flowing north of Springfield, it passes only a few houses and cabins. You may have to maneuver your way around a downed tree or two, but the river is generally wide enough—as much as 200 feet—to make deadfall no problem. Most of the stretch is heavily wooded

and peaceful, and there are several pleasant riffles, especially where creeks have washed rocks and gravel out into the riverbed. Gravel bars are big and plentiful and make great lunch spots.

The **shuttle route** (11.8 miles) from Riverside Park goes north on Business 55, west on Andrew Road (County 6.5N), north on 3.5W, and west on Irwin Bridge Road (7.5N).

Put in at the river-left boat ramp in Riverside Park. The setting on the right shoreline—where 2 public parks run most of the way to Highway 29—will remain quite wild for a while. Downstream, a sharp left turn follows the railroad bridge. Then, where the river heads right, the concrete intake structure of the old waterworks appears on the left. Just downstream is a constriction and an 18-inch drop, with remnants of old wood pilings. When the water is low, it's advisable to make a short and easy portage on the river-right beach.

The river now goes left, then sharply right, and suddenly an old concrete dam looms up ahead, projecting out from the right shore like a big wall. About 60 feet of it has been removed on the left, leaving a big, open channel to paddle through. On the left, a creek enters. In the tranquil stretch that follows, gravel bars continue and shale-and-sandstone outcroppings are periodically seen on the left. A very long right bend leads to the Highway 29 bridge; just downstream is a charming, old metal truss bridge.

In the series of tight turns that follow, downed trees appear on the outside of several bends, but they're usually easy to get around. There's considerable deadfall in the sharp turn after the next railroad bridge. Later, in a long northwest straightaway, several small creeks on the left carry rocks and gravel out into the river. In the following loop, the first house of the trip can be seen atop a cliff on the right; look for swallow nests in the cliff faces. Power lines cross in a long right bend, and Cantrall Creek enters on the right. In the little crook in the midst of the final right bend, there's an excellent riffle, caused by outwash boulders from another creek. Just downstream is a big island; most of the water flows to the right here.

Eventually a gravel road parallels the river on the left, with many huge boulders lying along the shoreline. After a cabin and house, a gravelly incline on the left makes a good alternate **take-out**; there's room alongside the road for several cars. At the end of the final right bend, the river turns sharply left before a couple of houses and Irwin Bridge. **Take out** at the sandy beach on the left, upstream; a short path leads to the road, where you can park a couple of cars.

Other trips. In previous printings of this book, the 9.5-mile stretch from Roby (County 725E) to Mechanicsburg Road has been recommended. Narrower and more isolated than Sangamon River 1-3, this section has in recent years developed two long and difficult-to-portage logjams. Therefore, it is no longer recommended.

The River of Lincoln

If Illinois is the Land of Lincoln, then surely the Sangamon is the River of Lincoln. Much of this storied river has direct associations with our sixteenth president and his family. In 1830, Thomas Lincoln sought a new life in Illinois by leading his family from Indiana to a site on the Sangamon about 8 miles southwest of Decatur (where the Lincoln Trail Homestead State Memorial is now located). Unfortunately, the winter of 1830–31 was one of the most severe in Illinois history and the new cabin was soon abandoned. Twenty-two-year-old Abraham canoed down the Sangamon to New Salem, where he began his rise to prominence, while his parents moved to a farm south of Charleston, near the Embarras. One of Lincoln's first jobs after moving to New Salem was to help build and float a flatboat laden with cargo all the way to New Orleans via the Sangamon, Illinois, and Mississippi Rivers. After six years in New Salem, he moved to Springfield to set up a law practice, and was never far from the Sangamon until going to Washington, D.C.

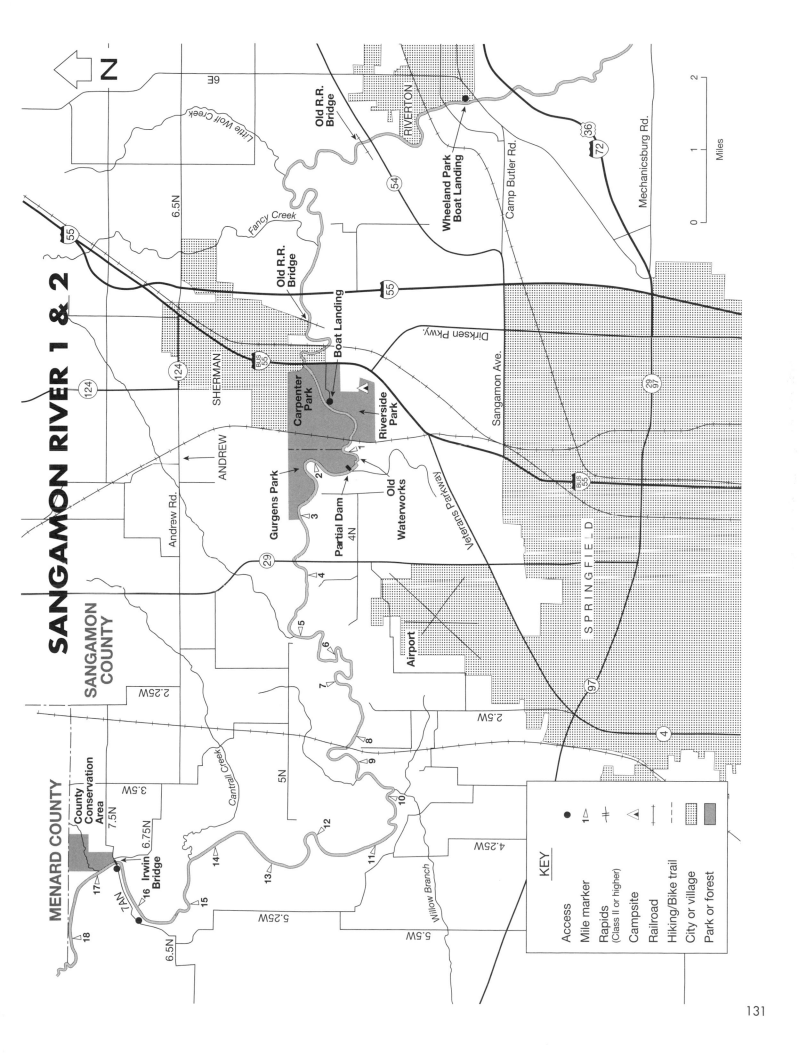

SANGAMON RIVER 3
Irwin Bridge to New Salem (10 Miles)

Historic New Salem

The village of New Salem goes back to 1828–29, when the first two settlers built a dam and gristmill on the river. Others followed—as many as twenty-five families—and soon the village was a thriving community. Young Abraham Lincoln, eager to set out on his own after his family's first trying winter in Illinois, paddled here in 1831 and spent six formative years in the village, working at a variety of jobs and eventually moving to Springfield in 1837 to practice law. Coincidentally, New Salem itself virtually ceased to exist by 1840. Its end was hastened by the realization that the Sangamon was not suitable for steamboat navigation and by the designation of nearby Petersburg as the county seat. Fortunately, twenty-three of the village's houses, shops, and stores have been faithfully restored, and Lincoln's New Salem is a marvelous place to visit. The site includes a visitor center, picnic facilities, an outdoor theater, pleasant campgrounds, and river rides on a replica of the steamboat *Talisman*.

One of the features of many of the trips in this book is a special attraction at the take-out. The charming little village of Grand Detour is a great place to end the Rock River 1 trip, for example. Other memorable take-outs include the Thompson Mill Covered Bridge on Kaskaskia River 2, Isle a la Cache on Des Plaines River 3, Macktown on Pecatonica River 3, and the city of Galena on Galena River 1. Each guarantees ending the trip on a historical and scenic high note. And so it is with the third recommended stretch on the Sangamon. Starting out where the previous trip ended, this section finishes near one of the most popular tourist destinations in the Midwest: Lincoln's New Salem. After loading up your boat(s), all you have to do is drive directly across Highway 97/123 to enter this unique recreation of life in the 1830s.

This is a good beginner's section, with big, gentle bends and a low **gradient** of 1 foot per mile. There are few houses, and the river continues to have an isolated feel to it. Cultivated fields are often close by, but generally cut off from view by the tree line. Frequent sandbars make the stretch all the more suitable for relaxing float trips.

Like most Illinois rivers, the Sangamon appeared on early maps with many different spellings: *Saguimont, Sangamo, Saukiemin,* etc. Explanations of the meaning of the name are similarly diverse, including "river of the Sauks," "river mouth," and "good earth." The most commonly accepted view is that

the name comes from a Potawatomi word meaning "where there is plenty to eat."

For **camping** and **water levels,** see Sangamon River 1.

The **shuttle route** (12.9 miles) from the put-in goes east on Irwin Bridge Road (County 7.5N), north on 3.5W into Athens, east on Little Street, north on Main Street, northwest on Athens Road, south on Highway 97/123, and east at the road opposite the entrance to Lincoln's New Salem. The road back to the landing turns right at a restaurant, then heads back to the Sangamon Picnic Area and boat landing.

Put in (1) half a mile upstream from Irwin Bridge, where a gravelly slope on the north side leads from the shoulder down to the river, or (2) at the bridge upstream on the left, where a short path leads down to a sandy beach.

Downstream from the bridge, rocks in the water create riffles. About 80 feet wide (a fairly consistent width most of the trip), the river goes into a big left bend. For a short distance, a nature preserve is located on the right, opposite farm fields on the left. A few cabins appear on the right in the big bend, which ends with a couple of quick turns. Now the river goes into a big arc to the right, with high bluffs on the left side and low wooded banks on the right. A couple of year-round homes appear on the left. Later, when the river swings left again, cabins begin appearing on the right. Two quick turns lead to the Gudgel Road bridge, which can be accessed downstream-left. Power lines cross downstream, and the river heads to the left at some bluffs on the right. In a couple of quick turns that follow, the streambed narrows to about 60 feet. The rest of the trip is dominated by several straight stretches.

Take out on river-left at the concrete boat ramp alongside the Sangamon Picnic Area. There is plenty of parking adjacent to the landing. Downstream, not far from the Athens Road bridge, is a picturesque saw and gristmill, a reconstruction of the building erected by John Camron and James Rutledge in 1829; a mill dam (which washed away long ago) stood nearby. You can visit the mill by parking at a nearby lot alongside Highway 97/123.

The stretch from New Salem to Petersburg (where a dam is located) is not recommended. If you're a fan of *Spoon River Anthology,* you might be interested in visiting the boyhood home of Edgar Lee Masters in Petersburg. Some of the character sketches in this famous book of poetry are based on Petersburg people, including Ann Rutledge, whom Lincoln is said to have loved during his New Salem years. Rutledge and Masters himself are buried here in the Oakland Cemetery. Incidentally, Masters also authored an interesting book on the Sangamon for the American Rivers series.

The *Talisman,* a reminder of the steamboat era on the Sangamon

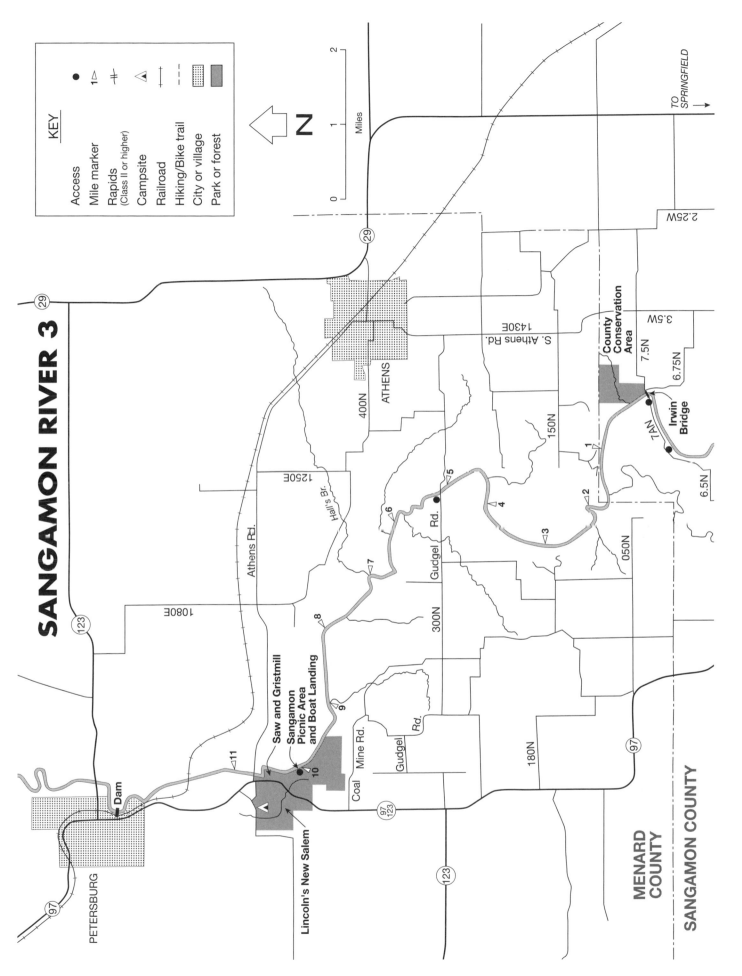

SANGAMON RIVER 3

KEY

- Access
- 1 Mile marker
- Rapids (Class II or higher)
- Campsite
- Railroad
- Hiking/Bike trail
- City or village
- Park or forest

N

Miles
0   1   2

PETERSBURG

Dam

Lincoln's New Salem

Saw and Gristmill
Sangamon Picnic Area and Boat Landing

Athens Rd.

Hall's Br.

ATHENS

S. Athens Rd.

Gudgel Rd.

Coal Mine Rd.

Gudgel Rd.

1080E

1250E

1430E

400N

150N

300N

050N

180N

County Conservation Area

Irwin Bridge

TO SPRINGFIELD

2.25W

3.5W

7.5N

6.75N

7.4N

6.5N

MENARD COUNTY

SANGAMON COUNTY

29

29

123

123

97

97

97
123

133

SPOON RIVER 1
Dahinda to Maquon (14.5 Miles)

West-central Illinois's best paddling stream is the legendary Spoon River, which is canoeable over most of its 142 miles. Originating southeast of Kewanee, it parallels the Illinois River for about 100 miles before veering eastward to join the Illinois at Havana. A geologically mature river, it has had time to meander a great deal and to cut a deep streambed over most of its course, creating the high, steep banks that are associated with the Spoon. One of the least channelized rivers in Illinois (only 21 miles have been altered), the Spoon also is unfettered by dams except for one dangerous low-head at Bernadotte. The entire watershed is lightly populated and rural, and the picturesque countryside consists mostly of gently rolling hills. Fulton, Knox, and Stark counties capitalize on the beauty of the Spoon River valley by sponsoring popular fall-color tours the first two weeks of October.

Until it approaches the Illinois, where it widens to 125 feet, the river is never very wide, averaging about 80 feet. Total obstructions are infrequent; when they do occur, however, they can be very trying (**and sometimes dangerous**) because of the steep banks. The environs of the river are completely undeveloped, and usually forested with maple, cottonwood, oak, hickory, and pine. Much of the area is planted with corn and soybeans, and fields often are cultivated to the river's edge, aggravating the river's erosion problems. Usually muddy-colored, the Spoon pours more silt into the Illinois than any other tributary. Not surprisingly, it has a long-standing reputation as an excellent catfish river, but smallmouth bass, bluegill, sunfish, bullhead, carp, and drum are also taken.

An unfortunate impediment to canoeing on the Spoon River is a shortage of good accesses. On the whole river there are only two designated landings: one in the middle at London Mills and another near the mouth. All the other accesses range from adequate to very difficult. In the first recommended section, none of the three accesses is easy.

Public **camping** is available at Rice Lake State Fish and Wildlife Area on the Illinois River east of Canton, Anderson Lake State Fish and Wildlife Area on the Illinois River east of Astoria, Fulton County Conservation Area near St. David, Riverside Park in London Mills, and Jubilee College State Park northwest of Peoria. Private campgrounds include Webb's Valley View Campground near Lewistown, Galesburg East Holiday Travel Park Campground near Knoxville, and Timberview Lakes Campground near Bushnell.

The **shuttle route** (10 miles) for the trip to Maquon goes south from Dahinda on County 1725E, east on Highway 150, south on 1800E, and west on 650N. The trip length can be shortened by using 1200N (Fort Wallace Bridge) as an access.

The **gradient** is 1.5 feet per mile.

For **water levels**, check the London Mills gauge (station #05569500) on the USGS Web site listed in the introduction.

Put in at the bridge on the east side of Dahinda, downstream-left. A rough access road leads to an often muddy landing used by fishermen. This far upstream, the river is still relatively narrow—about 45 feet—and is intimately canopied with trees. A road hugs the right shoreline for awhile before the river bends left into a long southeastward straightaway. After passing under Highway 150, the river bends right into a series of sharp turns that end at the Fort Wallace Bridge.

This bridge can be used as an alternate put-in, downstream-right. There's a small parking area near the bridge, but the steep bank requires care and physical fitness if you plan to use it as an access. A few hundred yards downstream the river flows under the Interstate 74 bridges, then goes into a couple of big, gentle bends. After sharply turning right alongside County 980N, where the channel constricts and forms riffles, the river heads back to the left. Immediately downstream from a conspicuous coal seam in the right bank is the historic Wolf Covered Bridge, recently reconstructed after the original was burned by vandals. Watch out for rocks in the river underneath the bridge.

Very small outcroppings of shale and sandstone now appear occasionally. After a couple of bends, the bridge at 900N appears. In the right bend after the bridge, several old auto chassis on the left momentarily detract from the aesthetics; fortunately, such intrusions are rare on the Spoon. Periodic riffles continue in the big bends that follow, and the river setting is quiet and isolated. Then, in a series of sharp turns, the river passes sheer 15-foot cutbanks, several gravel bars, and a small stone cliff. Cemetery Bridge—a little northeast of Maquon—comes at the end of a big left bend where power lines cross the river. **Take out** downstream-left.

For brief descriptions of several additional sections, see "Other Trips" in Spoon River 2.

River of the Squash/Pumpkin

The name of the village of Maquon has the same origin as the original name of the river. In early maps, the river is variously designated as the *Emicouen, DemiQuian, Mequen, Amequon,* etc., generally interpreted as meaning "mussel shell." For a long time, amateur linguists theorized that Native Americans used mussel shells as spoons, and that the river later came to be known by this application. In a 1998 issue of *The Living Museum,* however, Duane Esarey of Dickson Mounds Museum makes a good case for *Emiquon* being an Illiniwek word meaning "squash/pumpkin" (thus, Emiquonsippi = "river of the squash/pumpkin"); later the Potawatomi used the Illiniwek word for the river, but mistook it for their soundalike word *emikwan,* which means "spoon."

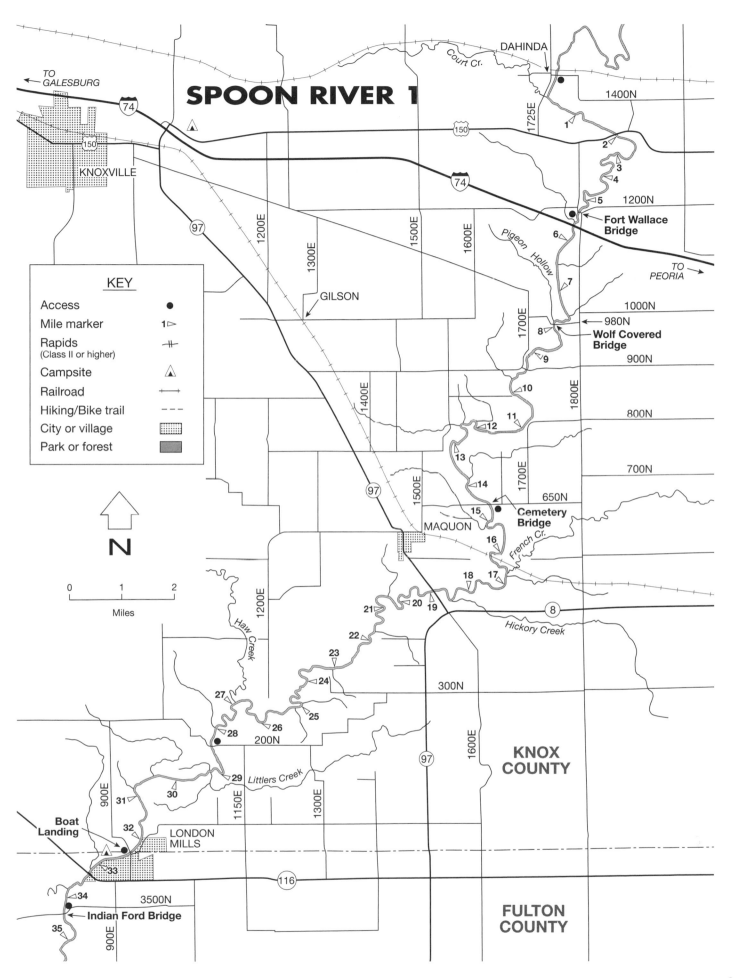

SPOON RIVER 1

SPOON RIVER 2
Blyton to Seville (11 Miles)

The Spoon is perfect for lazy float trips.

If you paddled the upper part of the river described in Spoon River 1, you can sample the middle portion on this stretch. As usual on the Spoon, you're likely to get muddy at the put-in and take-out, but both accesses are adequate. Mud is less prevalent in the summer and fall, of course, when numerous gravel bars appear, creating pleasant stopping places for lolling or fishing. The environs are peaceful and isolated, lending themselves to lazy float trips. As usual, most of the river corridor is wooded, with occasional farm fields along the steep banks. Throughout most of this section, the river flows between tall cutbanks, often populated by swirling colonies of swallows. Not until the end do you see any houses. Log-jams are infrequent, but are occasionally a problem: **be careful.**

For **camping,** see Spoon River 1.

The **shuttle route** (9 miles) from the put-in goes east on County 2500N, south on Smithfield Road, west on Highway 95 across the bridge, and south a short distance on Seville Road. If you're paddling the longer trip (described below), continue on Seville Road until just past the railroad tracks; there's room to park several cars in the grassy area alongside the tracks, downstream-right from the bridge.

The **gradient** is negligible (less than 1 foot per mile).

For **water levels,** check the Seville gauge (station #05570000) on the USGS Web site listed in the introduction.

Put in a mile downstream from the Highway 9 bridge, at the end of 2500N. This narrow gravel road runs all the way to the river, where you can easily launch your boat(s) from a gently sloping shoreline. A ferry was located here in the 1840s. Don't block farm field turn-ins while unloading boats. Curving to the right, the river begins about 55 feet wide. At one point, a 60-foot bluff rises on the left—the only one of the trip. Gradually the streambed widens. After many bends, the County 2350N bridge appears. Downstream, the first big tributary—Put Creek—enters on the left in a big right bend. Fifteen-foot cutbanks are common as the river curves back and forth, and sandbars are frequent when the river is at medium to low levels. Until the end, the only signs of human habitation are bridges, fields, and occasional fishing boats tied to the banks.

After another large tributary on the right—Shaw Creek—the river passes under Highway 95, then constricts and quickly bends left. For a shorter trip, you can **take out** at the bare bank on river-right just before the left turn, only a few hundred yards downstream from Highway 95. Carry boats up to the shoulder of the nearby road.

The 2-mile loop downstream from Highway 95 is well worth paddling; it's very narrow, intimate, and woodsy. Soon a charming old steel-truss bridge appears, often with johnboats moored nearby. Then the river heads right, at one point passing a lovely sandstone outcropping that projects over the water from the left shoreline. Finally, there are several cabins on the right just before the next bridge. **Take out** just downstream-right from the bridge. If you wish to take out here, be sure to ask permission in advance from the bankside homeowner. A nearby sign identifies the site as "VAN-OPOLIS. Paper-town of Isaac Seville. Early railroad town. Waubonsee Trail passed here, a river crossing of the Indian trail to the Mississippi." A gristmill and ferry were located here in the 1800s. Incidentally, Seville is pronounced "SAY-ville" locally.

Other trips. (1) For a good exposure to the creeklike headwaters area, try the 6.5-mile stretch from County 1175E north of Modena to Grain Bin Road (County 800N) north of Wyoming. (2) A very pleasant 13-mile float runs westward from the bridge on the northeast side of Elmore to Dahinda; the river here is relatively small. The bridge at County 2100E provides a decent intermediate access. (3) In the past, the section from Cemetery Bridge near Maquon to London Mills was the site of an annual 17-mile canoe race. This is a long canoe trip, but it has the advantage of an excellent concrete boat ramp and Riverside Park at London Mills. (See the map for Spoon River 1.) To shorten the trip by 3 miles, you can take out at County 200N northeast of London Mills. (4) A pleasant 5-mile trip puts in at 200N northeast of London Mills and takes out at the first bridge downstream from Highway 116 (Indian Ford). (See the map for Spoon River 1.) There are no decent accesses downstream from Indian Ford until the Blyton area, where Spoon River 2 begins. (5) Although sometimes paddled, the 9-mile section from Seville to Bernadotte is not recommended because of the lethal low-head dam at the take-out; the dam is difficult to see from upstream, and many people have drowned there over the years. The dam was built originally for a gristmill in the 1840s. (6) Below Bernadotte (put in well below the dam!), 13 miles of paddling take you to Duncan Mills, with a rough intermediate access at County 100E (a former bridge location). Duncan Mills is not a good access (high, steep banks), but determined, fit paddlers can seek permission to take out or put in just upstream from the riverside park.

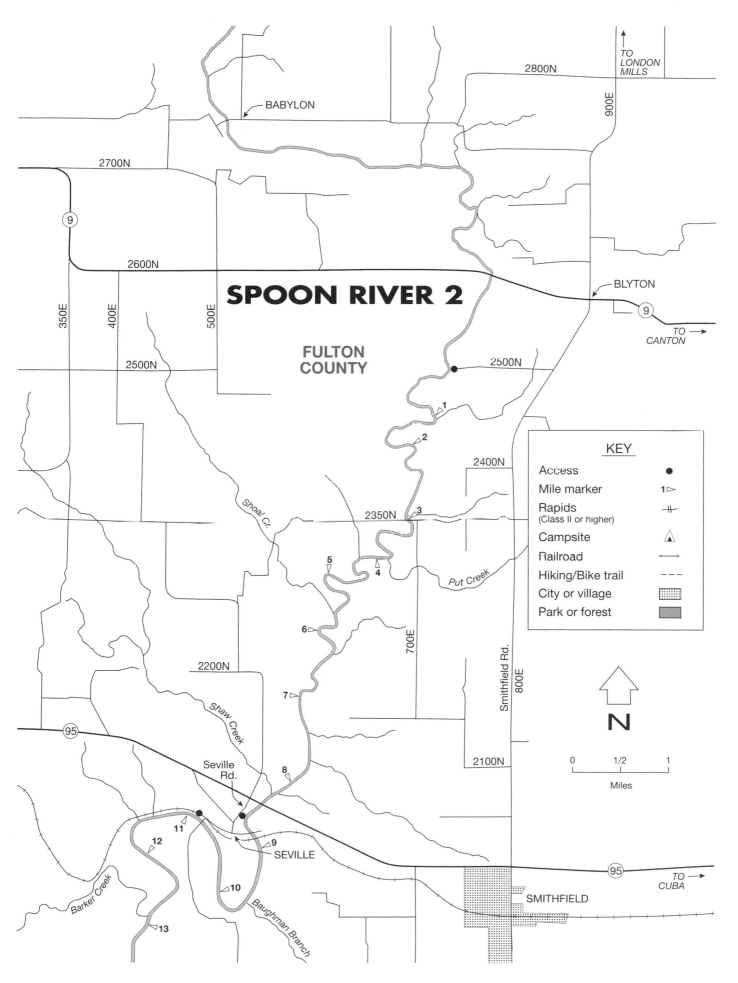

SPOON RIVER 2

FULTON
COUNTY

BABYLON

TO
LONDON
MILLS

2800N

BLYTON

TO
CANTON

Shoal Cr.

Put Creek

Shaw Creek

Seville
Rd.

SEVILLE

Barker Creek

Baughman Branch

SMITHFIELD

TO
CUBA

KEY	
Access	●
Mile marker	1▷
Rapids (Class II or higher)	╫
Campsite	△
Railroad	┼
Hiking/Bike trail	- - -
City or village	▦
Park or forest	▨

N

0   1/2   1

Miles

SPOON RIVER 3
Duncan Mills to Emiquon Landing (10.5 Miles)

In its final leg, the Spoon flows through a broad valley before joining the Illinois River near the city of Havana. Most of the way, high, steep banks enclose the streambed, which increases in width to 125 feet. Most of the stretch is wooded, but there are more open fields along the shoreline than there are in upstream sections. Over the full length of the river, the average **gradient** of the Spoon is 1.5 feet per mile, but here it dwindles to less than half a foot. Sandbars are frequent in the big, gentle bends that characterize this stretch. The two accesses contrast strongly: after starting out at a very difficult put-in, the section ends at an easy and convenient boat ramp 1.5 miles upstream from the mouth. Highlighting the trip are two nearby attractions: a huge wildlife refuge and one of the country's major archaeological museums.

For **camping** and **water levels,** see Spoon River 1.

The **shuttle route** (7.1 miles) from Duncan Mills goes east on County 1045N, east on Highway 136, and north on Highway 78/97.

Put in at the tiny community of Duncan Mills, upstream from the small village park, on the south bank. Alongside the park, the bank is too high and steep for an access, but a little farther upstream, near a small reproduction of the covered bridge that used to stand here, the bank is less steep and boats can be lowered down to the river carefully. This is on private property, so you must ask permission of the nearby homeowner. **Be careful: this is a very tough put-in, and you could easily take a tumble. Please note: paddlers who are not in excellent condition should not put in here.** Before heading downriver, look just upstream at the tight riffly turn where an old mill once stood. Immediately downstream from the put-in are the stone abutments that supported a covered bridge.

After passing under the Highway 24/100 bridge, the river bends left into a straightaway where attractive masses of broken shale and sandstone are found on the right. On the left are the 12- to

15-foot sheer banks that are typical of the Spoon River. A thin band of trees lines the edge as the river goes into a series of big bends, straightening out a little in between curves. Soon 1045N pulls alongside the right bank for awhile before the river heads back to the left, where a house and a low stone outcropping appear on the right.

In the bends that follow, deadfall is sometimes found on the outside, but the width usually makes getting around it easy. Trees grow sparser, the river gradually widens, and johnboats are occasionally tied up along the steep banks. As you continue downstream, the current gradually diminishes and the banks become lower. Eventually the smokestacks of the power plant near Havana come into view.

As the river curves back and forth toward the southeast, traffic noise from Highway 136 begins to be heard and trees get thicker on both sides. In the final left bend, the river flows under an old metal truss bridge (no longer used), with a house downstream-right. Finally, a right bend takes you to the Highway 78/97 bridge. **Take out** downstream-right at the excellent concrete ramp of Emiquon Landing, adjacent to a parking lot.

Those who love wildlife and natural places will be pleased by what they see near the take-out. In 1993 the U.S. Fish and Wildlife Service established the 1,600-acre Emiquon National Wildlife Refuge at the confluence of the Spoon and Illinois Rivers, eventually to be expanded to 11,000 acres. Trails lead along the river and the wetland to observation decks where you can see egrets, herons, geese, and a multitude of other wading birds, waterfowl, and shorebirds. The refuge will have a significant impact on preserving wildlife, providing recreational opportunities, and giving floodwater a place to go.

Only a few miles from the take-out (between Havana and Lewistown) is an extraordinary museum. Native Americans inhabited the area near the mouth of the Spoon River for 12,000 years, and Dickson Mounds Museum chronicles the Ice Age hunters, Mound Builders, and other cultures that have lived here. Artifacts, murals, photos, and hands-on exhibits make the museum a lively and informative place to visit. Originally a privately excavated burial mound that annually drew thousands of visitors, the site was sold to the state in 1945 and became part of the Illinois State Museum. In the 1990s, controversy swirled around the display of Native American remains, and the burial exhibit was closed.

Troubled Tales of Spoon River Country

Many rivers of the world have been celebrated in music and poetry, but few have achieved the literary fame of the Spoon River. Back in 1915, the Chicago lawyer and writer Edgar Lee Masters made the river internationally known in his *Spoon River Anthology*, translated into many foreign languages and published in thirty editions. Masters spent his boyhood years in Petersburg (on the Sangamon) and Lewistown (near the Spoon), and later turned his memories of small-town life into a book of short monologues. Speaking from the grave in free-verse epitaphs, the lawyers, housewives, doctors, priests, and other citizens tell us their fascinating stories of personal aspiration, sexual repression, official corruption, religious hypocrisy, and other triumphs and tragedies (mostly the latter). The book's realistic treatment of the lives of everyday people made it immensely popular, and it's still a "good read."

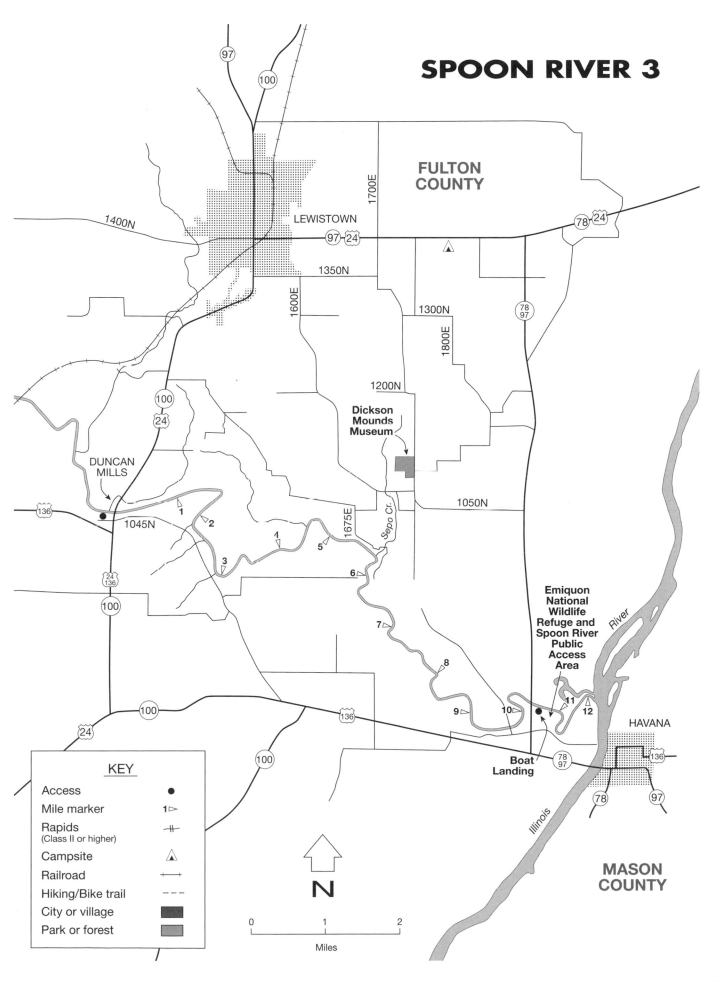

SPOON RIVER 3

SUGAR RIVER

Colored Sands Forest Preserve to Two Rivers Forest Preserve (8.2 Miles)

One of the wildest and most isolated rivers in Illinois, the Sugar runs through a low floodplain where there are almost no houses. Like the nearby Pecatonica, it lies in an ancient lake bed left by the last glacier. Unlike the muddy Pecatonica, however, the Sugar flows through a sandy basin; consequently, the water tends to be clearer. Banks are usually low—sometimes almost nonexistent—with sandy bluffs, sandbars, and small sloughs off the main channel. Dense bottomland forest is found along the banks—mostly maples—and downed trees require maneuvering and sometimes portaging.

As you might expect in such an environment, wildlife is diverse and plentiful. Fishermen catch smallmouth bass, catfish, crappies, bluegill, and carp. When the weather is warm and windless, mosquitoes can be a nuisance, so bring repellent. Much of the shoreline lies in several Winnebago County forest preserves. This stretch also gives you the "added value" of paddling two different rivers in a day: the trip ends with a brief upriver stint on the Pecatonica. A couple of riverside campgrounds make overnight canoe-camping trips possible. The name of the river comes from an Algonquin word meaning "sweet water"—perhaps (some say) because of the Native Americans' use of sugar maples to make syrup, perhaps (say others) because of the sand in the water.

Camping is available on the river at the Sugar River Forest Preserve downstream from Yale Bridge Road (public) and Sugar Shores Resort Campground at Winslow Road (private). For other campgrounds in the area, see Pecatonica River 1.

The **shuttle route** (5.8 miles) from the put-in goes east on Haas Road, south on Hauley Road, east on Winslow Road, and south on Shirland Road.

The **gradient** is only 1 foot per mile.

Water levels. The nearest gauge is upstream at Brodhead, Wisconsin; check station #05436500 on the USGS Web site listed in the introduction.

Put in at the north end of the Colored Sands Forest Preserve, off Haas Road. Near the unique Sand Bluff Bird Banding Station, a path leads from the parking lot down through the woods to a designated canoe landing.

Almost from the outset, where the river is 65 feet wide, there's deadfall along the edges, but it's usually easy to get around. In the right bend that soon begins, a high, steep sand bluff appears with a split-rail fence along the top. A big left bend flows past two creeks on the right, widens to 90 feet, and finally leads to Yale Bridge Road, where a concrete/asphalt landing is located upstream on the left, with nearby parking lot and toilets.

After the bridge the river arcs gently to the left. The forest preserve environment continues to be extremely peaceful, with constant birdcalls. In an S curve, an open, grassy area with picnic tables and pine trees appears on the left atop a 4-foot cutbank, followed by another high sand bluff and more pines. Just after a creek mouth on the right, a very attractive picnic area appears on the left, with a good place to land canoes. The banks now become quite low at times, and the surroundings are completely wild and unspoiled as the river bends back and forth, widening to more than 100 feet. The Sugar Shores Campground follows the Winslow Road bridge, on the left.

From Winslow Road to the mouth there are no more bridges or forest preserves but many bends. Still over 100 feet wide, the river twice passes farm buildings. In its final, eastward course, it narrows and becomes quite twisty. Banks get lower and lower in the tight bends, and all you can see on both sides are swampy wetlands. Finally, in the approach to Shirland Road, the river straightens out and widens. Just before the final turn to the Shirland Road bridge, there's a private landing on the right. Immediately after the bridge, the Sugar flows into the Pecatonica. Turn right and paddle a quarter mile upstream to **take out** at the Two Rivers Forest Preserve landing on river-left (i.e., on your right as you paddle upstream). There is room to park a number of cars in the gravelly pull-off area alongside Shirland Road.

Other trips. (1) If you want to lengthen your trip by 6 miles, you can head north into Wisconsin and put in at the gravel landing off Nelson Road (about 150 yards downstream-right from the bridge, in Sugar River Park). Four miles farther upstream, there's an access downstream-left from the bridge on Beloit-Newark Road just west of the tiny community of Avon. There is usually a great deal of deadfall in the river between Beloit-Newark Road and the state line. (2) Another way to lengthen your trip is to continue 9 miles downstream on the Pecatonica to Macktown Forest Preserve. There's another campground at Meridian Road for two-day trips.

Counties that Promote Wilderness

Winnebago County is one of several counties in Illinois that have done an outstanding job of protecting riverside land for public use. Large tracts along the Sugar, Pecatonica, Kishwaukee, and Rock rivers have been secured and turned into forest preserves that include campgrounds, biking/hiking trails, picnic areas, and canoe landings that are a boon to paddlers. Other "green-thinking" counties to which the paddling community owes gratitude are Lake, Cook, McHenry, Kane, Du Page, Will, and Boone.

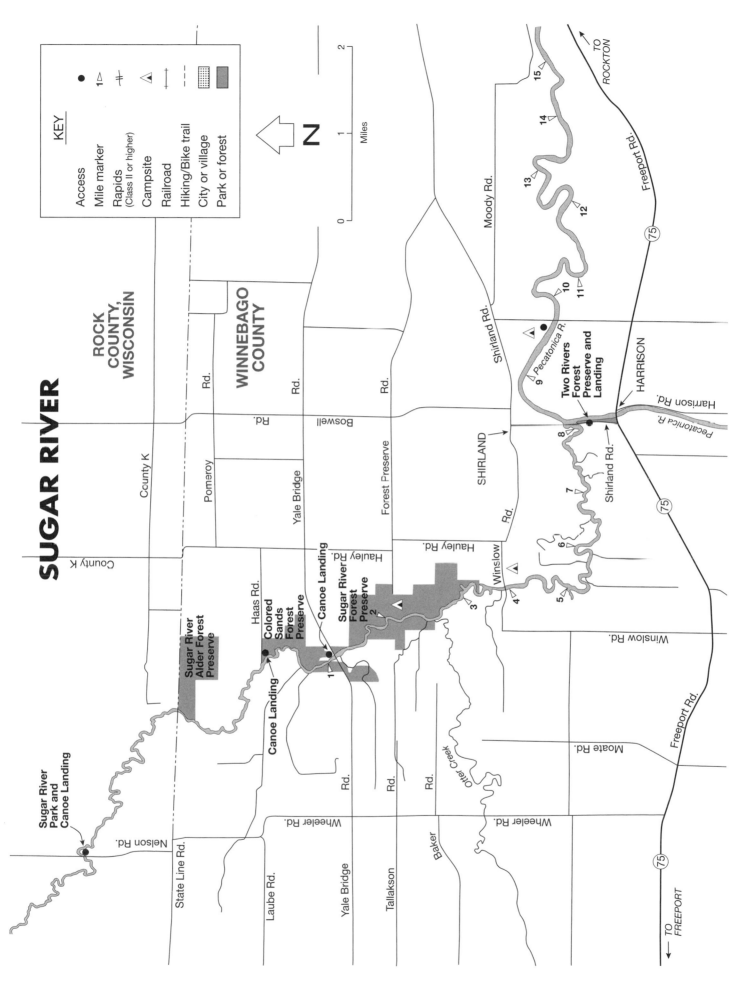

SUGAR RIVER

KEY

Access
Mile marker
Rapids (Class II or higher)
Campsite
Railroad
Hiking/Bike trail
City or village
Park or forest

N

Miles
0   1   2

ROCK COUNTY, WISCONSIN

WINNEBAGO COUNTY

County K

State Line Rd.

Nelson Rd.

Sugar River Park and Canoe Landing

Laube Rd.

Haas Rd.

Sugar River Alder Forest Preserve

Colored Sands Forest Preserve

Canoe Landing

Canoe Landing

Sugar River Forest Preserve

Wheeler Rd.

Yale Bridge

Tallakson

Baker

Otter Creek

Moate Rd.

Freeport Rd.

Wheeler Rd.

Winslow Rd.

Hauley Rd.

Hauley Rd.

Winslow Rd.

Forest Preserve

SHIRLAND

Shirland Rd.

Boswell

Pomeroy

Yale Bridge

County K

Rd.

Moody Rd.

Pecatonica R.

Two Rivers Forest Preserve and Landing

HARRISON

Harrison Rd.

Pecatonica R.

Shirland Rd.

75

TO ROCKTON

Freeport Rd.

TO FREEPORT

75

1
2
3
4
5
6
7
8
9
10
11
12
13
14
15

141

APPENDIX I

PADDLING SECTIONS GROUPED BY SKILL LEVEL

Under normal circumstances (i.e., low to medium water levels and warm air and water temperatures), the sections described in this book are generally suitable for properly equipped paddlers of the following skill levels. Please note that even beginning-level stretches can present unexpected situations that require caution, maneuvering, and good judgment (e.g., a recently fallen tree, or bridge repair work that has left broken concrete in the streambed). When the water is high, no river or creek is appropriate for beginners. A couple of sections could possibly be categorized either as Beginner or Experienced/Intermediate; each of these has been placed in the latter group.

BEGINNER
Apple River 2
Big Muddy River
Cache River 1, 2
Des Plaines River 1, 2, 3
Embarras River 1, 2
Fox River 1, 2, 3
Galena River 2
Hennepin Canal 1, 2, 3
Illinois and Michigan Canal 1, 2
Iroquois River 1, 2
Kankakee River 1, 2, 3
Kaskaskia River 1, 2
Kishwaukee River 2
Little Wabash River
Mackinaw River 1, 2, 3
North Vermilion River 1, 2
Pecatonica River 1, 2, 3
Rock River 1, 2
Saline River
Salt Creek of the Sangamon River 1, 2
Sangamon River 1, 2, 3
Spoon River 2, 3

A pleasant west suburban paddle on Salt Creek

EXPERIENCED/INTERMEDIATE
Apple River 1
Big Bureau Creek
Chicago River–North Branch
Du Page River 1, 2
Galena River 1
Kishwaukee River 1
Little Vermilion River 1
Lusk Creek
Mazon River
Middle Fork of the South Vermilion River
Nippersink Creek
Salt Creek of the Des Plaines River
Salt Fork of the South Vermilion River 1, 2
Spoon River 1
Sugar River

ADVANCED/EXPERT
Little Vermilion River 2
North Vermilion River 3

Nice waves and exposed bluffs on Big Bureau Creek

APPENDIX 2

HIGHLY RECOMMENDED READING

Several hundred printed sources were consulted in the preparation of this book—ranging from works that are outdated and only minimally or tangentially of interest to paddlers, to works that are extremely valuable to anyone who loves paddlesports. The following is a highly selective listing of a few outstanding publications that are particularly recommended to serious Illinois canoeists and kayakers. Other works are mentioned elsewhere in the book.

Akerlund, Nels, and Ted Landphair. *Our Rock River.* Washington, D.C.: Chelsea Publishing, 1995. This stunningly illustrated book traces the Rock from its origin in Horicon Marsh in Wisconsin to its union with the Mississippi, with a wealth of interesting historical detail.

Buisseret, David. *Historic Illinois from the Air.* Chicago: University of Chicago Press, 1990. A beautiful book that tells the story of Illinois with aerial photos, thematic maps, satellite images, historic photos, and text—much of which is directly related to the waterways covered in *Paddling Illinois.*

Illinois Department of Natural Resources (Springfield, 1997-2002): Assessments of numerous Illinois watersheds (Big Rivers Area, Big Muddy River Area, Cache River Area, Calumet River Area, Chicago River/Lake Shore, Du Page River Area, Driftless Area, Embarras River Area, Fox River Area, Headwaters Area, Illinois River Bluffs Area, Kankakee River Area, Kaskaskia River Area, Kinkaid Area, Kishwaukee River Area, La Moine River Basin, Lower Des Plaines River Area, Lower Rock River Area, Lower Sangamon River Area, Mackinaw River Area, Prairie Parklands, Rock River Area, Sinkhole Plain Area, Spoon River Area, Sugar/Pecatonica River Area, Thorn Creek Area, Upper Des Plaines River Area, Upper Rock River Area, Upper Sangamon River Area, Vermilion River of the Illinois River Basin, Vermilion River of the Wabash River Basin).

An outgrowth of the DNR's Critical Trends Assessment Program, these detailed reports exhaustively review the physical, natural, and human resources of the above-listed watersheds, together with early historical accounts. Reports for other watersheds will be published in the future. In conjunction with each of the multivolume reports, the DNR publishes a slick 22-page *Inventory of the Region's Resources* that summarizes the report, including excellent photos, charts, and maps. The reports and inventories are an invaluable contribution to the systematic study and improvement of the state's rivers and streams.

Michael R. Jeffords, Susan L. Post, and Kenneth R. Robertson. *Illinois Wilds.* Urbana: Phoenix Publishing, 1995. A gorgeously illustrated survey of wild places in Illinois, with 165 color photos of animals, plants, and habitats. The photos and text depict what the state was like before settlement, and show the best of Illinois's remaining natural heritage. There is excellent material on such rivers as the Apple and Cache.

McCollum, Dannell A., and James O. Smith. *A Guide to the Big Vermilion River System.* Champaign: Shakerag Publishing, 1982. In this somewhat dated but still useful little book, the authors meticulously describe forty-three short sections of the Salt Fork, Middle Fork, North Fork, and South Vermilion Rivers, with many interesting historical details. Hand-drawn maps and thirty-two photos are included.

Edward Ranney, Emily Harris, and Tony Hiss. *Prairie Passage: The Illinois and Michigan Canal Corridor.* Urbana: University of Illinois Press, 1998. A book that celebrates the 150th anniversary of the opening of the I&M Canal, *Prairie Passage* recounts the construction of the waterway, the growth (and sometimes decline) of the communities along it, and the recent development of the cultural and recreational potential of the corridor. The text is complemented by 250 marvelous photographs.

Solzman, David M. *The Chicago River: An Illustrated History and Guide to the River and Its Waterways.* Chicago: Loyola Press, 1998. One of the best books ever written about an American river, Solzman's book not only traces the history of the Chicago River and its environs but also constitutes a practical guidebook for anyone who wants to explore the river firsthand. Excellent photos and maps are included.

Tyler, Bob C. *Canoeing Adventures in Northern Illinois: Apple River to Zuma Creek.* iUniverse, 2004. Descriptions of numerous canoe-trips on streams in the northern one-third of Illinois, including many out-of-the-way, seldom-paddled waterways. Contains no maps, but descriptions are cross-referenced to pages in the De Lorme Gazetteer.

Vierling, Philip E. *Illinois Country Landings No.2: Kishwaukee River.* Chicago, 1990. This extremely detailed and well-researched publication maps the Kishwaukee and its branches and tributaries. The author provides a wealth of information on landings, geology, parks, forest preserves, mills, fishing prospects, river-distances, and gradients. Some details need to be updated, but the book is still admirable in its thoroughness. Also valuable is Vierling's 1989 *Illinois Country Landings No. 1: Du Page River.*

Vogel, Virgil J. *Indian Place Names in Illinois.* Springfield: Illinois State Historical Library, 1963. Illinois paddlers continually encounter place-names of Native American origin. This classic book is scholarly but very readable, and provides insight into the background of many names that we tend to take for granted.

Wiggers, Raymond. *Geology Underfoot in Illinois.* Missoula, Mont.: Mountain Press Publishing, 1997. A fascinating guide to thirty-seven readily accessible locations in Illinois—each illustrating an aspect of the state's geological history. Many Illinois rivers and streams are included in Wiggers's wonderfully readable book.

Excellent books on the flora and fauna of Illinois include Donald Hoffmeister's *Mammals of Illinois* (Urbana: University of Illinois Press, 1989), Robert Mohlenbrock's *Forest Trees of Illinois* (Springfield: Illinois DNR, 1996), Sylvan Runkel and Alvin Bull's *Wildflowers of Illinois Woodlands* (Ames: Iowa State University Press, 1994), and Mary Kay Judd Murphy and John W. Mellen's *Illinois Wildlife and Nature Viewing Guide* (Springfield: Illinois DNR, 1997).

Several charming, older books still make good reading, sometimes with an antiquarian flavor: Reuben Gold Thwaites's *Down Historic Waterways: Six Hundred Miles of Canoeing upon Illinois and Wisconsin Rivers* (Chicago: A. C. McClurg, 1902), Edgar Lee Masters's *The Sangamon* (New York: Farrar & Rinehart, 1942), Harry Hansen's *The Chicago* (New York: Farrar & Rinehart, 1942), and James Gray's *The Illinois* (New York: Farrar & Rinehart, 1940).

Enjoying the many riffles of the Mazon

APPENDIX 3

CANOEING AND KAYAKING WEB SITES

The World Wide Web is an increasingly rich source of information that is directly and indirectly valuable to paddlers. In addition to the information available at a given Web site, "links" often point to a multitude of other sites. A number of paddling clubs also have excellent Web sites (see Appendix 6). For Web sites of canoe-and-kayak rental companies, see Appendix 9.

American Canoe Association: www.americancanoe.org
American Rivers (organization): www.amrivers.org
American Whitewater: www.americanwhitewater.org
Bear Paw Outdoor Adventure Resort: www.bearpawoutdoors.com
Canoe & Kayak magazine: www.canoekayak.com
Canoeing, kayaking, and rafting information: www.paddling.net
Chicago Area Paddling & Fishing Pages: www.chicagopaddling.com
Chicagoland Canoe Base: www.chicagolandcanoebase.com
Cook County Forest Preserve District: www.fpdcc.com
County plat maps: www.rockfordmap.com
Du Page County Forest Preserve District: www.dupageforest.com
Friends of the Chicago River: www.chicagoriver.org
Great Outdoor Recreation Pages: www.gorp.com
Illinois Community Profiles: www.villageprofile.com/states/il.html
Illinois Department of Natural Resources: http://dnr.state.il.us
Illinois Department of Transportation: www.dot.state.il.us
Illinois Paddling Council: www.illinoispaddling.org
Illinois State Parks: http://dnr.state.il.us/lands/landmgt/parks
Illinois State Water Survey: www.sws.uiuc.edu
Illinois Water Quality (EPA): www.epa.state.il.us/water/water-quality
Lake County Forest Preserve District: www.lcfpd.org
Mackinaw Canoe Club: www.rivers-end.org/mcc/mcc.html
Northwest Passage: www.nwpassage.com
Offshore: www.offshore-chicago.com
Openlands Project: www.openlands.org
Pecatonica River (Stephenson County): www.paddlethepec.com
Prairie Rivers Network: www.prairierivers.org
Real-time Water Data: http://waterdata.usgs.gov/il/nwis/current/?type=flow
Rivers, Trails, & Conservation Program: www.nps.gov/ncrc/programs/rtca/nri/states/il.html
Rutabaga Paddlesport Shop (Madison WI): www.rutabaga.com
Salt Creek Watershed Network: www.saltcreekwatershed.org
Sierra Club: www.sierraclub.org/il
Silent Sports Magazine: www.silentsports.net
State of Illinois: www.state.il.us
Topographical maps: www.topozone.com
United States Canoe Association: www.uscanoe.com
Vermilion River: www.rivers-end.org/vermilion/index.html or http://wpr.pair.com/vermilion
Water Trails of Northeastern Illinois: www.openlands.org/watertrails.asp
Yellow Creek Watershed Partnership: www.ycwp.org

APPENDIX 4

PADDLING INSTRUCTION FOR ILLINOIS CANOEISTS AND KAYAKERS

The best way to learn how to canoe or kayak is to enroll in a class or clinic offered by a college, paddling group, park or forest preserve district, or outdoor store. Such instruction in conjunction with canoe trips in the company of experienced paddlers will get you off to a good start. The following are some of the instructional resources available. Many of the organizations also offer scheduled trips.

American Canoe Association Midwest Division: www.americancanoe.org/divisions/midwest.lasso

American Safari Company, Normal IL, 309-451-9955: canoeing and kayaking classes.

Atwood Outdoor Education Center, Rockford, 815-874-7576: canoeing class.

Bear Paw Outdoor Adventure Resort, White Lake, WI, 715-882-3502 or www.bearpawoutdoors.com: full range of canoe and kayak classes.

Blackwell Forest Preserve, Warrenville, 630-933-7200: canoeing class.

Chicago Area Sea Kayaking Association, www.caska.org: sea kayak classes.

Chicago River Canoe & Kayak, Chicago and Skokie, www.chicagoriverpaddle.com: paddling classes.

Chicago Whitewater Association, www.chicagowhitewater.org: beginning whitewater instruction.

College of DuPage, Glen Ellyn, www.cod.edu/academic/field/field_Int.htm: canoe trips with instruction.

Emily Oaks Nature Center, Skokie, 847-677-7001 or www.skokieparkdistrict.org: canoe program for children, basic family instruction.

Evanston Environmental Association, 847-864-5181 or www.laddarboretum.org/eea.htm: canoe trips with instruction.

Friends of the Chicago River, www.chicagoriver.org: paddling lessons.

Geneva Kayak Center, Geneva IL, 630-232-0320 or www.genevakayak.com: full range of kayak instruction.

Heller Nature Center, Highland Park, 847-433-6901 or www.hellernaturecenter.org: canoe trips with basic instruction.

Kayak Chicago, www.kayakchicago.com: sea kayaking lessons.

Lake County Forest Preserve District, Van Patten Woods, 847-948-7750: canoeing classes on Sterling Lake.

Lincoln Park Boat Club, www.lpbc.net: sea kayak lessons.

Northbrook Park District, Northbrook IL, 847-291-2995, ext.125: summer canoeing instruction.

Northwest Passage, Wilmette, IL, www.nwpassage.com: sea kayak classes.

Offshore, Vernon Hills, IL, www.offshore-chicago.com: kayak lessons.

Prairie Coast Paddlers, www.prairiecoastpaddlers.org: sea kayak instruction.

Prairie State Canoeists, www.prairiestatecanoeists.org: variety of classes.

Rutabaga Outdoor Programs, Madison, WI, www.rutabaga.com: canoe and kayak classes.

Watertrail Adventures, Madison, WI, 608-255-2958 or www.watertrailadventures.com: canoe and kayak classes.

BOOKS AND VIDEOS TO IMPROVE PADDLING SKILLS

BOOKS

American Canoe Association, *Introduction to Paddling: Canoeing Basics for Lakes and Rivers*. Menasha Ridge Press, 1996.

Bechdel, Les. *River Rescue*. Appalachian Mountain Club Books, 1997.

Bennett, Jeff. *The Essential Whitewater Kayaker: A Complete Course*. International Marine Publishing, 1999.

Gordon, I. Herbert. *The Complete Book of Canoeing*. Globe Pequot, 2001.

Grant, Gordon. *Canoeing: A Trailside Guide*. W.W. Norton, 1997.

Gullion, Laurie. *Canoeing: A Woman's Guide*. International Marine Publishing, 1999.

Jackson, Eric. *Whitewater Paddling: Strokes and Concepts*. Stackpole Books, 1999.

Jacobson, Cliff. *Basic Essentials Canoeing*. Globe Pequot, 1999.

Johnson, Shelly. *Sit-on-top Kayaking*. Globe Pequot, 2000.

Landry, Paul, and Matty McNair. *The Outward Bound Canoeing Handbook*. Lyons & Burford, 1992.

Lessels, Bruce. *Paddling with Kids: AMC Essential Handbook for Fun and Safe Paddling*. Appalachian Mountain Club Books, 2002.

Mattos, Bill. *The Practical Guide to Kayaking and Canoeing*. Lorenz Books, 2002.

Nealy, William. *Kayak: A Manual of Technique*. Menasha Ridge Press, 1986.

Ray, Slim. *The Canoe Handbook: Techniques for Mastering the Sport of Canoeing*. Stackpole Books, 1992.

Swenson, Allen. *L. L. Bean Canoeing Handbook*. Lyons Press, 2000.

Wortham Webre, Anne, and Janet Zeller. *Canoeing & Kayaking for Persons with Physical Disabilities*. American Canoe Association, 1990.

VIDEOS

Heads Up! River Rescue for River Runners (29 mins.)
Grace Under Pressure: Learning the Kayak Roll (47 mins.)
From Here to There: Canoe Basics (50 mins.)
Essential Boat Control (58 mins.)
The Kayaker's Edge (58 mins.)
Complete Guide to Canoe Trips and Camping (45 mins.)
River Rescue: The Video (55 mins.)
Kayaking 101: Mastering the Basics (45 mins.)
Whitewater Self Defense (65 mins.)

The channelized headwaters of the Mackinaw on a late winter day

APPENDIX 6

CANOE AND KAYAK CLUBS AND ORGANIZATIONS IN ILLINOIS

Paddling with other boating enthusiasts adds immeasurably to the enjoyment and safety of canoeing and kayaking. For beginners, clubs are a great introduction to the sport and an excellent way to meet other paddlers. Illinois canoeing clubs are quite varied, ranging from small, loosely organized groups with only a few trips a year to organizations with several hundred members and a multitude of scheduled trips. Because club officers change from time to time, it is difficult to maintain an up-to-date listing of contact persons for all clubs. For current information, check the Web site of the Illinois Paddling Council: www.illinoispaddling.org.

Abbott Labs Canoe Club (a corporate Chicago-area club open to employees of Abbott Laboratories and their families).

American Canoe Association Midwest Division: www.americancanoe.org/divisions/midwest.lasso

Central Illinois Whitewater Club (group of whitewater paddlers whose main focus is on the North Vermilion and Little Vermilion Rivers).

Chicago Area Sea Kayaking Association: www.caska.org

Chicago Whitewater Association: www.chicagowhitewater.org

Illini Downstreamers Club (Chicago area).

Illinois Dragon Boat Association (promotes dragon boat racing): www.illinoisdragonboat.org

Illinois Paddling Council: www.illinoispaddling.org

Lincoln Park Boat Club (Chicago-area rowers, sea kayakers, sprint kayakers, and downriver canoeists): www.lpbc.net

Mackinaw Canoe Club (primarily central Illinois): www.rivers-end.org/mcc/mcc.html

Morris Marathon Canoe Club (Morris-area group specializing in marathon canoe racing and promotion of paddling on the Illinois and Michigan Canal).

Prairie Coast Paddlers (Chicago-area sea kayakers on lakes and flatwater rivers): www.prairiecoastpaddlers.org

Prairie State Canoeists (statewide but primarily northeastern Illinois; one of the largest clubs in the country): www.prairiestatecanoeists.org

Saukenuk Paddlers (Quad Cities-area group that paddles both flatwater and whitewater): www.rivers-end.org/saukenuk

Southern Illinois University Canoe and Kayak Club (student whitewater organization): www.siu.edu/~kayak/main.htm

Southwest Brigade (Chicago-area group that paddles voyageur canoes, participates in historical reenactments, and paddles recreationally).

St. Charles Canoe Club (flatwater canoeists, with emphasis on competitive racing).

Tippee Canoe Club (a Decatur-based group).

One of several excellent boat landings on the Embarras

APPENDIX 7

DNR LIST OF PUBLIC BODIES OF WATER

The Rivers, Lakes, and Streams Act requires the Illinois Department of Natural Resources to "make a list by counties of all the waters of Illinois, showing the waters, both navigable and non-navigable." This list is to be found in 17 Illinois Administrative Code, Chapter I, Section 3704, Appendix A. Because of its importance to the issue of paddling access, it is quoted below verbatim.

PUBLIC BODIES OF WATER

The following public bodies of water were navigable in their natural condition or were improved for navigation and opened to public use. The entire length and surface area in Illinois, including all backwater lakes and sloughs open to the main channel or body of water at normal flows or stage, are open to the public unless limited to a head of navigation as stated. Head of navigation descriptions use the U.S. rectangular survey system and these abbreviations: T=township; R=range; PM=principle meridian; Sec.=section; 1/4=quarter section; N=north; E=east; S=south; W=west; USGS=U.S. Geological Survey.

1. Lake Michigan;
2. Chicago River: Main Branch;
3. Chicago River: North Branch to North Shore Channel;
4. Chicago River: South Branch;
5. Chicago River: South Fork of South Branch;
6. Chicago River: East and West Arms of South Fork of South Branch;
7. Chicago River: West Fork of South Branch to Chicago Sanitary and Ship Canal;
8. Calumet River;
9. Lake Calumet and entrance channel to Calumet River;
10. Grand Calumet River;
11. Little Calumet River;
12. Wolf Lake (Cook County);
13. Mississippi River (including all backwater lakes such as Frentress Lake in Jo Daviess County, Boston Bay in Mercer County and Quincy Bay in Adams County);
14. Sinsiniwa River to North Line of Sec. 9, T28N, R1W, 4th PM in Jo Daviess County, which is located approximately two-thirds mile downstream from the U.S. Highway 20 bridge; this area is shown on the Galena, Ill.-Iowa, 7.5 minute USGS quadrangle map;
15. Galena River to East Line of Sec. 6, T28N, R1E, 4th PM in Jo Daviess County, which is located approximately one-half mile upstream from the County Highway 67 bridge; this area is shown on the Galena, Ill.-Iowa, 7.5 minute USGS quadrangle map;
16. Apple River to North Line of Sec. 35, T26N, R2E, 4th PM in Jo Daviess County;
17. Plum River to North Line, T24N, R3E, 4th PM in Carroll County, which is located approximately one and one-half miles upstream from the U.S. Highway 52 bridge; this area is shown on the Savanna, Ill., 15 minute USGS quadrangle map;
18. Rock River;
19. Pecatonica River;
20. Sugar River (Winnebago County);
21. Stillman Creek to South Line, T25N, R11E, 4th PM in Ogle County, which is located approximately one-third mile downstream from the Illinois Highway 72 bridge; this area is shown on the Stillman Valley, 7.5 minute USGS quadrangle map;
22. Henderson Creek (new channel) to East Line, SW 1/4, Sec. 6, T10N, R5W, 4th PM in Henderson County; the river has been relocated and the old channel abandoned;
23. The Sny in Adams, Pike, and Calhoun Counties; the area has been drained with levees and ditches and it is uncertain that any descendent body of water exists;
24. Bay Creek to West Line, Sec. 29, T8S, R3W, 4th PM in Calhoun County; the head of navigation is the limit of meanders on the official plat of survey; but it is uncertain that any descendent body of water exists;
25. Illinois River (including all backwater lakes such as Peoria Lake in Peoria, Tazewell, and Woodford Counties; Matanzas Bay in Mason County; and Meredosia Lake in Cass and Morgan Counties);
26. Des Plaines River to Hoffman Dam in Cook County, which is located one-half mile downstream from the junction with Salt Creek; this area is shown on the Berwyn, 7.5 minute USGS quadrangle map;
27. Kankakee River;

28. Iroquois River to South Line, SW 1/4, Sec. 30, T27N, R12W, 2nd PM in Iroquois County, which is located approximately one mile downstream from the junction with Sugar Creek; this area is shown on the Gilman, l5 minute USGS quadrangle;

29. Fox River (Illinois River Basin);

30. Griswold Lake (McHenry County);

31. Fox Chain-o-Lakes (Lake and McHenry Counties): Bluff Lake, Lake Catherine, Channel Lake, Fox Lake, Grass Lake, Lake Marie, Nippersink Lake, Dunns Lake, Pistakee Lake, Lake Jerilyn, Lac Louette, Redhead Lake;

32. Vermilion River (Illinois River Basin) to approximately one-half mile above the mouth near Oglesby in La Salle County;

33. Spring Lake (Tazewell County);

34. Spoon River to North Line, Sec. 24, T6N, R1E, 4th PM in Fulton County, which is located approximately one-half mile upstream from the Illinois Highway 95 bridge; this area is shown on the Smithfield, 7.5 minute USGS quadrangle map;

35. Sangamon River to South Line, NE 1/4, Sec. 1, T15N, R4W, 3rd PM in Sangamon County, which is located approximately one mile south of the Mechanicsburg Road bridge; this area is shown on the Mechanicsburg, 7.5 minute USGS quadrangle map;

36. Sangamon River: South Fork to South Line, Sec. 33, T16N, R4W, 3rd PM in Sangamon County, which is located approximately two miles upstream from the mouth; this area is shown on the Springfield-East, 7.5 minute USGS quadrangle map;

37. Macoupin Creek to East Line, Sec. 25, T9N, R13W, 3rd PM in Green and Jersey Counties, which is located approximately one mile downstream from the junction with Boyer Creek; this area is shown on the Boyer Creek, 7.5 minute USGS quadrangle map;

38. Otter Creek to East Line of Sec. 3, T7N, R13W, 3rd PM in Jersey County, which is located approximately two miles east of the Illinois Highway 100 bridge; this area is shown on the Nutwood, 7.5 minute USGS quadrangle map;

39. Kaskaskia River to East Line, SW 1/4, Sec. 31, T8N, R2E, 3rd PM, which is located nine miles south and two miles west of Herrick; this area is shown on the Vera, 7.5 minute USGS quadrangle map;

40. Big Muddy River to East Line, T8S, R2W, 3rd PM in Jackson County, which is located approximately one mile northwest of the Southern Illinois Airport; this area is shown on the Murphysboro, 7.5 minute USGS quadrangle map;

41. Ohio River;

42. Wabash River;

43. Vermilion River (Wabash River Basin) to West Line, T19N, R11W, 2nd PM in Vermilion County, which is located approximately one mile upstream from the junction with the North Fork; this area is shown on the Danville, SW, 7.5 minute USGS quadrangle map;

44. Little Wabash River to the Illinois Highway 1 bridge in Carmi in White County;

45. Saline River to junction of North Fork and South Fork;

46. Saline River: North Fork to North Line, Sec. 5, T8S, R8E, 3rd PM in Gallatin County, which is located approximately three miles south of the junction of Illinois Highway 141 and U.S. Highway 45; this area is shown on the Ridgway, 7.5 minute USGS quadrangle map;

47. Saline River: South Fork to West Line, T9S, R8E, 3rd PM in Gallatin County, which is located at the Gallatin-Saline County line; this area is shown on the Equality, 7.5 minute USGS quadrangle map;

48. Horseshoe Lake (Alexander County).

The following public bodies of water are primarily artificial navigable waters that were opened to public use.

1. Illinois and Michigan Canal;

2. Illinois and Mississippi (Hennepin) Canal and Canal Feeder;

3. North Shore Channel (Cook County);

4. North Branch Canal of North Branch Chicago River (Cook County);

5. Relocated South Branch Chicago River (Cook County);

6. Chicago Sanitary and Ship Canal;

7. Calumet Sag Channel;

8. Marseilles Canal (La Salle County);

9. Chain of Rocks Canal (Madison County);

10. Relocated Kaskaskia River.

APPENDIX 8

RECURRING CANOE-RELATED EVENTS IN ILLINOIS

The following list contains many regularly scheduled events that are of potential interest to canoeists and kayakers. Exact dates vary from year to year. Names of contact persons are not included because these change fairly often as different individuals assume responsibility for coordinating events. The best single source of up-to-date information on such activities is the Illinois Paddling Council, which publishes a canoe calendar every spring in its quarterly newsletter. For information about the IPC and names of current contacts, see the organization's Web site: <www.illinoispaddling.org>. Information about regularly scheduled events also can be obtained from Illinois paddling clubs and organizations (see Appendix 6) and from local chambers of commerce.

MARCH
Canoecopia, Madison, Wisconsin: a big, annual canoe and kayak exposition with equipment, exhibits, and lectures; attended by many Illinois boaters.

APRIL
Vermilion River Race, near Pontiac.
Illinois Paddling Council's Annual Spring Kickoff canoe trip.

MAY
Des Plaines Canoe Marathon, Libertyville: 19.5-mile race starting at Oak Spring Road.
Current Buster Canoe Race, St. Charles: sponsored by the St. Charles Canoe Club; 6- and 10-mile races.

JUNE
Mid-American Canoe Race, Aurora: sponsored by the Fox Valley Park District; 15-mile race.
Voyageur Landing Race, Elgin.
Illinois Rivers Appreciation Month: a couple of dozen river-related events coordinated by the Illinois DNR.
Rock River Canoe Rally, Oregon: sponsored by the Oregon Lions Club; 4- to 18-mile trips.
Middle Fork Appreciation Day: an annual paddling event.
Montreal Canoe Weekend, Starved Rock State Park, Utica: rides in voyageur canoes.
Vermilion River Canoe Race, Pontiac.

JULY
Founder's Day Canoe Race, on the Fox River, Algonquin.
Lyndon to Prophetstown Canoe Race, Rock River.
The Great River Rumble: 147-mile paddle on the Mississippi from Quincy to St. Louis.

AUGUST
Sauk Valley Canoe Race: 10-mile race on the Rock River in the Rock Falls area.

SEPTEMBER
Chicago River Flatwater Classic: 7.5-mile canoe/kayak race and "friendly float."
I&M Canal and Du Page River Race, Channahon.
Vic Hopp Memorial Canoe Race, Wheeling.
Yorkville Riverfront Festival, Yorkville Riverfront Park: includes canoe races.

OCTOBER
Gathering at the Confluence: annual trip that includes the Du Page, Des Plaines, Grant Creek, Kankakee, Illinois, and the Illinois and Michigan Canal.

APPENDIX 9

CANOE AND KAYAK RENTALS FOR ILLINOIS PADDLERS

There is a surprisingly large number of companies that rent canoes, kayaks, and inflatables for paddling on the rivers, streams, and lakes of the state. In addition to boat rentals, many operations also provide shuttles to and from the body of water being paddled. Moreover, such businesses are also a good source of information on water conditions.

Many are praiseworthy for their careful stewardship of the rivers and streams on which they rent boats, and are consistently safety-conscious (not launching boats, for example, when water-levels are dangerously high).

Because of the nature of the business, it is rather difficult to maintain a completely up-to-date listing of current rental companies. In recent years, for example, liveries on the Embarras, Pecatonica, Sugar, Des Plaines, and Cache have gone out of business, but new companies have started up on the Kishwaukee, Chicago, Galena, Fox, Middle Fork, Salt Fork, and North Fork Rivers.

The following list of liveries provides the most recent compilation at the time of this printing of *Paddling Illinois* (2007), and is obviously subject to change. Because the book is limited to paddling trips on moving water (i.e., rivers and streams), boat rentals for lakes are not included here.

This information has been prepared for informational purposes only, and is not intended to provide an endorsement for any business.

For other listings, see (a) www.chicagopaddling.org, (b) www.prairierivers.org, (c) www.propaddle.com, and (d) www.rivers-end.org/mcc/mcc.html (see "links").

1. Ayers Landing, 3494 E. 2089th Road, Wedron IL 60557 (Fox River): 815-434-2233 or 800-540-2394 or www.ayerslandingcanoerental.com
2. Bayou Bluffs Recreational Park, RR1, Cornell IL 61319 (Rooks Creek and North Vermilion River): 815-358-2537
3. C & M Canoe Rental, PO Box 178, 3401 E. 2062nd Road, Wedron IL 60557 (Fox River): 815-434-6690 or www.cmcanoerental.com
4. Canoe Shack, 42W612 Steeple Chase Court, St. Charles IL 60174 (Fox and Du Page Rivers): 630-584-8017 or www.canoeshack.com
5. Canoe the Kish at Larsen's Landing, New Milford IL (Kishwaukee River): 815-544-1823 or www.canoethekish.com
6. Canoe the Vermilion, RR 4, 1903 E. 1251 Road, Streator Road, Streator IL 61634 (North Vermilion, Illinois, and Fox Rivers, and the I&M Canal): 815-673-3218 or www.canoethevermilion.com
7. Chicagoland Canoe Base, 4019 N. Narragansett Avenue, Chicago IL 60634-1512 (southern Wisconsin and northern Illinois rivers and streams): 773-777-1489 or www.chicagolandcanoebase.com
8. Chicago River Canoe & Kayak, Chicago and Skokie IL (Chicago River): 773-704-2663 (Chicago) or 847-414-5883 (Skokie) or www.chicagoriverpaddle.com
9. Discovery Center, 2940 N. Lincoln Avenue, Chicago (North Vermilion rafting): 773-348-8120 or www.discoverycenter.cc
10. Du Page County Forest District (Du Page River): 630-933-7248 or www.dupageforest.com/recreation/boating.html
11. Fever River Outfitters, 525 S. Main Street, Galena IL 61036 (Galena River): 815-776-9425 or www.feverriveroutfitters.com
12. Freeman's Sports, 129 E. Hydraulic, Yorkville IL 60560 (Fox River): 630-553-0515 or 630-553-7151
13. Geneva Kayak Center, 34 N. Bennett, Geneva IL (Fox River): 630-232-0320 or www.genevakayak.com
14. Geneseo Campground, Geneseo IL (Hennepin Canal): 309-944-6465
15. Grafton Canoe & Kayak, PO Box 142, Grafton IL (Lower Kaskaskia River): 618-786-2192 or www.graftonoutdooractivities.com
16. Kaskaskia River Bait & Campground, East Rt. 16, Shelbyville IL 62565 (Kaskaskia River): 217-774-4721
17. Kickapoo Landing (Middle Fork River): 217-446-8399
18. Lundeen's Landing, 21119 Barstown Rd., East Moline IL 61244 (Rock River): 309-781-9766
19. Northbrook Park District, 545 Academy Drive, Northbrook IL 60062: 847-291-2960, ext. 181 or www.nbparks.org
20. North Park Rental Service, Machesney Park IL (Rock River): 815-633-9234
21. Offshore, 701 N. Milwaukee Avenue, Suite 348, Vernon Hills IL 60061 (Des Plaines River): 847-362-4880 or 800-346-4141 or www.offshore-chicago.com

22. Potawatomi Park Canoe & Pedal Boat Rentals, 8 North Avenue, St. Charles, IL 60174 (Fox River): 630-584-1028
23. Reed's Canoe Trips, 907 N. Indiana Avenue, Kankakee IL 60901-2194 (Kankakee River): 815-932-2663 or 815-939-3119 or www.reedscanoetrips.com
24. River Adventures, 3215 E. 1969th Road, Ottawa IL (Fox River): 815-434-2142 or www.canoethefox.com
25. Rutabaga Paddlesport Shop, 220 W. Broadway, Madison WI 53716 (Southern Wisconsin and Northern Illinois rivers): 608-223-9300 or 800-472-3353 or www.rutabaga.com
26. Schmidt's Canoeing Service, 1232 Ridgeway Drive, Elgin IL 60123 (Fox River): 847-697-1678 or www.canoetrips.net
27. Slow Canoe Rentals, 462 S. Main, Wood River IL 62095 (Lower Illinois and Mississippi Rivers): 618-254-6966
28. The Paddlin' Shop, 202 S. Dickinson St., Madison WI 53703 (southern Wisconsin and northern Illinois rivers): 608-284-0300 or 800-386-1299 or www.paddlin.com
29. TipACanoe Canoe Rentals, Burlington WI (Nippersink Creek and Upper Fox River): 262-537-3227 or www.tipacanoellc.com
30. T.J.'s Bait, Tackle, and Canoe Rental, 305 S. 1st Street, Oregon IL 61061 (Rock River): 815-732-4516 or www.tjscanoerental.com
31. Vermilion River Rafting, 781 N. 2249 Road, Oglesby IL 61348 (North Vermilion River): 815-667-5242

RENTAL COMPANIES LISTED BY RIVER OR STREAM

Three companies (7, 25, and 28) offer canoe and kayak rental without shuttle for many of the waterways described in this book, especially in northern Illinois. Others limit their service to certain rivers, as listed below:

Chicago River: 8
Des Plaines River: 21
Du Page River: 4, 10
Fox River: 1, 3, 4, 6, 12, 22, 24, 26
Galena River: 11
Hennepin Canal: 14
Illinois & Michigan Canal: 6
Kankakee River: 23
Kaskaskia River: 15, 16
Kishwaukee River: 5
Middle Fork River: 17
Nippersink Creek: 29
North Vermilion River: 2, 6, 9, 31
Rock River: 18, 20, 30

MORE GREAT TITLES FROM TRAILS BOOKS

ACTIVITY GUIDES

Biking Illinois: 60 Great Road and Trail Rides, *David Johnsen*

Biking Iowa: 50 Great Road and Trail Rides, *Bob Morgan*

Biking Wisconsin: 50 Great Road and Trail Rides, *Steve Johnson*

Great Iowa Walks: 50 Strolls, Rambles, Hikes and Treks, *Lynn L. Walters*

Great Minnesota Walks: 49 Strolls, Rambles, Hikes, and Treks, *Wm. Chad McGrath*

Great Wisconsin Walks: 45 Strolls, Rambles, Hikes, and Treks, *Wm. Chad McGrath*

Paddling Illinois: 64 Great Trips by Canoe and Kayak, *Mike Svob*

Paddling Iowa: 96 Great Trips by Canoe and Kayak, *Nate Hoogeveen*

Paddling Northern Minnesota: 86 Great Trips by Canoe and Kayak, *Lynne Smith Diebel*

Paddling Northern Wisconsin: 82 Great Trips by Canoe and Kayak, *Mike Svob*

Paddling Southern Minnesota: 85 Great Trips by Canoe and Kayak, *Lynne and Robert Diebel*

Paddling Southern Wisconsin: 82 Great Trips by Canoe and Kayak, *Mike Svob*

Walking Tours of Wisconsin's Historic Towns, *Lucy Rhodes, Elizabeth McBride, Anita Matcha*

Wisconsin's Outdoor Treasures: A Guide to 150 Natural Destinations, *Tim Bewer*

Wisconsin Underground, *Doris Green*

TRAVEL GUIDES

Classic Wisconsin Weekends, *Michael Bie*

Great Indiana Weekend Adventures, *Sally McKinney*

Great Iowa Weekend Adventures, *Mike Whye*

Great Midwest Country Escapes, *Nina Gadomski*

Great Minnesota Taverns, *David K. Wright & Monica G. Wright*

Great Minnesota Weekend Adventures, *Beth Gauper*

Great Weekend Adventures, *the Editors of Wisconsin Trails*

Great Wisconsin Taverns: 101 Distinctive Badger Bars, *Dennis Boyer*

Great Wisconsin Winter Weekends, *Candice Gaukel Andrews*

Minnesota Waterfalls, *Steve Johnson and Ken Belanger*

Tastes of Minnesota: A Food Lover's Tour, *Donna Tabbert Long*

The Great Indiana Touring Book: 20 Spectacular Auto Trips, *Thomas Huhti*

The Great Iowa Touring Book: 27 Spectacular Auto Trips, *Mike Whye*

The Great Minnesota Touring Book: 30 Spectacular Auto Trips, *Thomas Huhti*

The Great Wisconsin Touring Book: 30 Spectacular Auto Tours, *Gary Knowles*

Twin Cities Restaurant Guide, *Carla Waldemar*

Wisconsin Family Weekends: 20 Fun Trips for You and the Kids, *Susan Lampert Smith*

Wisconsin Lighthouses: A Photographic and Historical Guide, *Ken and Barb Wardius*

Wisconsin's Hometown Flavors, *Terese Allen*

Wisconsin Waterfalls, *Patrick Lisi*

For a free catalog, phone, write, or visit us online.

TRAILS BOOKS

A Division of Big Earth Publishing

923 Williamson Street, Madison, WI 53703

800.258.5830 · www.trailsbooks.com